The Regulated La

The Regulated Landscape

Lessons on State Land Use Planning from Oregon

Gerrit Knaap, Ph.D.
Associate Professor of Urban and Regional Planning
University of Illinois at Urbana–Champaign

and

Arthur C. Nelson, Ph.D., AICP
Professor of City Planning, Public Policy, and International Affairs
Georgia Institute of Technology

LINCOLN INSTITUTE OF LAND POLICY
Cambridge, Massachusetts

The Lincoln Institute of Land Policy is a nonprofit and tax-exempt school organized in 1974, with a specialized mission to study and teach about land policy, including land economics and land taxation. The major goal of the institute is to integrate theory and practice in understanding the impact of land and land-related tax policy on the lives and livelihood of all people.

The Lincoln Institute is supported by the Lincoln Foundation, established in 1947 by John C. Lincoln, a Cleveland industrialist. Mr. Lincoln drew inspiration from the ideas of Henry George, the nineteenth-century American political economist and social philosopher.

The Lincoln Institute assembles experts with different points of view to study, reflect, exchange insights, and work toward consensus in creating a more complete and systematic understanding of land policy. The Lincoln Institute itself has no institutional point of view.

Publication of a manuscript by the Lincoln Institute signifies that it is thought to be worthy of public consideration but does not imply endorsement of conclusions, recommendations, or organizations that supported the research.

The Lincoln Institute is an equal opportunity institution in employment and admissions.

Library of Congress Catalog Card Number: 92-54330

International Standard Book Number: 1-55844-120-4

Printed in the U.S.A. on acid-free text stock.

Lincoln Institute of Land Policy
Cambridge, Massachusetts

Second Printing, 1993

Dedication of Gerrit-Jan Knaap

To Mrs. Leonie E. Knaap,
My mother, my teacher, my friend

Dedication of Arthur Christian Nelson

To Monika and Emily,
Wife and daughter, fellow travelers and companions from Oregon

Knute, Lori, Meryl, and Eric,
Parents, sister, and brother, who've been through it all

Victor G. Atiyeh,
The unsung hero of the Oregon Planning Act

Nohad A. Toulan, Kenneth Dueker, and James G. Strathman,
My mentors

Contents

5
Protecting Oregon's Farmland 125

Figures

Tables

Preface

THE SEEDS OF THIS BOOK were planted during the sixties, when we, as residents of Oregon, became captivated by the state's progressive approach to social and environmental issues. We learned then that Oregon was different. We saw it during family vacations south to California and north to Puget Sound; we heard it from neighbors who had recently migrated from the East and Midwest. We observed it in other ways too—in the passion of Governor Tom McCall, in the creativity of Ken Kesey, and in the determination of Steve Prefontaine. Oregon was a state to cherish—not only when camping at Gleneden Beach, skiing on Mount Hood, hiking the Skyline Trail, or rafting the McKenzie River—but every day in our Willamette Valley homes.

The seventies was a period of growth and development, both for us and for Oregon's land use and environmental policies. As undergraduates, at Willamette University and Portland State University, we gained new perspectives on the issues of our time and place. Our student projects traced the development of pioneering legislation that placed deposits on all beverage containers, protected the beaches from private development, and banned billboards from enclosing highways. We lobbied against field burning; we marched for equal rights; and we witnessed firsthand the passage of Senate Bill 100—Oregon's Land Use Act. Indeed, we had a hand in writing it.

As graduate students we sharpened our analytical skills and probed more deeply into the politics and economics of statewide land use planning. For a Ph.D. in economics from the University of Oregon, Knaap examined the influence of urban growth boundaries on land values; for a Ph.D. in urban studies from Portland State University, Nelson studied the interaction between urban and prime agricultural land in the Willamette Valley. Then, with degrees in hand, we and 65,000 others left the state, exiled by the severity of the 1981 recession. But, convinced that there was much more to learn about statewide land use planning, we continued our research into the causes and effects of Oregon's innovative land use program.

At the University of Wisconsin-Green Bay, Knaap explored the politics of state land use planning and examined the influence of planning on Oregon's economy. At Kansas State University, then the University of New Orleans, Nelson examined the effectiveness of farmland preservation and infrastructure planning and finance. Now, with Knaap at the University of Illinois and Nelson at Georgia Institute of Technology, we attempt in this book to pull together what we have learned from our own research and from the research of others. It is impossible to identify the influence of colleagues and the environments they provided at the various institutions where we have worked. It is clear, however, that they have been influential.

This book represents a collaborative effort, although the chapters clearly reflect our distinct areas of expertise, and in some cases our personally held opinions. In spite of some differences, however, we share a common bias, which we hasten to make clear at the start: We believe in planning. We believe that urban development, housing, farming, infrastructure provision, and economic development—especially in the United States at the close of the twentieth century—are better served by public and private participation. Further, we believe that both the public and private sectors perform more efficiently when critical decisions are made with foresight and with attention to many, often competing, goals. Such decision making, we feel, is what planning is all about.

Furthermore, as we argue throughout the book, we feel that the level of government at which land use plans are made and implemented makes a difference. Our review of statewide land use planning in Oregon suggests that the difference is not easily measurable and not always positive. But we are convinced, and with this book hope to convince others, that the Oregon experience offers considerable insights into what kind of difference state land use planning can make—for Oregon and for other states as well.

We owe a great debt, of course, to others who made this book possible. To the past and present Oregon pioneers, we owe for the subject matter that comprises this book. To our mentors, we owe for the analytical tools that we bring to bear on the subject. Special mention is due Ken Dueker, Jim Strathman, Nohad Toulan at Portland State University, and Ed Whitelaw at the University of Oregon. To our colleagues, family—

especially our wives, Jody and Marika,—and friends, we owe for the tangible and intangible support that made this book possible.

To many people dedicated to the practice of statewide land use planning, we owe for resources and material support. These people include many staff members of the Oregon Department of Land Conservation and Development, 1000 Friends of Oregon, and The Metropolitan Service of Portland, Oregon, as well as Ray Bartlett of ECO Northwest and Russ Beaton of Willamette University. Finally, to many individuals who provided us with extremely helpful comments on one or more chapters, we express thanks. These people include Ronald Eber, Robert Einsweiler, Lewis Hopkins, Paul Ketchem, Henry Markus, Mike Murphy, Mitch Rohse, Ethan Seltzer, and especially, William Fischel, who provided detailed comments on every chapter. Last and furthest from least, we thank Mary Beth Martin and Ben Chinitz—Mary Beth for helping us communicate our ideas more effectively and Ben for believing our ideas have merit.

Introduction

OREGON—A LAND USE LABORATORY

The 1980s was a decade of decline for most forms of regulation. Deregulation began during the administration of President Carter, continued through both terms of President Reagan, and shows no signs of slowing in the administration of President Bush. No new federal regulatory agencies have been created since 1980, and regulation has been reduced in the trucking, air travel, finance, and communication industries. There is a market, however, in which regulation has not been reduced and perhaps has even grown: the market for land. The forms of land use regulation have changed over time—planned unit developments evolved from Euclidian zoning, comprehensive plans unfolded out of tax-lot maps, and regional planning agencies now oversee the city planner's office. But in few places, if any, are land markets less regulated today than during the regulatory decade of the 1970s.

Nowhere are these generalizations more true than in Oregon. Since the late 1960s, land in Oregon has become among the most extensively planned and regulated land in the U.S. In Oregon, every local government must prepare a comprehensive plan for all land within its jurisdiction; every comprehensive plan must be *acknowledged* [1] by the state government; and every local government must use its regulatory powers to implement its comprehensive plan. Following acknowledgment of the 278th and final comprehensive plan in 1985, every acre of Oregon land is zoned, every zone is planned, and every plan is state-approved. As a result, the state is nationally recognized as a leader in land use controls and offers a unique laboratory for examining the effects of statewide land use planning and regulation.

1

Oregon's statewide land use program has probably received more analysis than the program of any other state. No other state planning program has been the topic of a major book; two have been written about planning in Oregon. No other state planning effort has been accorded more than one article in a major American planning journal; many have been written about planning in Oregon. Research on the effects of Oregon's land use program has been published in a variety of government documents, professional journals, and academic reviews, yet there has been no previous attempt to combine all these works into a comprehensive, critical review. This book offers such a review.

There are many good reasons for examining land use planning and regulation in Oregon. First, the Oregon countryside is highly diverse and offers a micromodel of the national landscape. The coastal region represents the heart of the U.S. Pacific coast. The Willamette Valley resembles the farmland of the upper Midwest, middle Atlantic, and, to some degree, California's central valley. The Cascade mountain range stands in stature between the Rocky and Appalachian mountains. And, eastern Oregon stretches without interruption much like the Great Plains.

Second, the diversity of the Oregon countryside brings forth a variety of regulatory participants and instruments. Participants in the Oregon land use program include city and county planning departments, special service districts, a state land use commission and department, federal agencies which control 52 percent of Oregon lands, land use "watchdog" groups, and more. Oregon's land use instruments are large in number and in detail but include such unusual instruments as urban growth boundaries, exclusive farm and forest use zoning, open-space tax deferrals, and solar-access easements. The combination of intergovernmental structure and innovative land use instruments enhances both the appeal and complexity of analyzing land use policy in Oregon.

Finally, Oregon is recognized as a first-generation planning state. Oregon, with Hawaii, Vermont, Florida, and California, led what became known as the "quiet revolution," in which the power to regulate land returned in whole or in part to state government. Today, as a second generation of states—including Connecticut, Georgia, New Jersey, Maine, Rhode Island, and Washington—joins the quiet revolution, policy makers look to Oregon for lessons on statewide land use planning and regulation.

This book of course is not the first view of Oregon as a land use laboratory. The Oregon land use program was discussed in the seminal work by Bosselman and Callies, whose title first proclaimed *The Quiet*

Revolution. But perhaps the first to realize the national significance of the Oregon program was Charles Little, who documented the 1973 passage of the Oregon land use statutes in *The New Oregon Trail.* Subsequently, the Oregon experience provided material for national reviews on land use reform, including Heally and Rosenberg's *Land Use and the States,* Rosenbaum's *Land Use and the Legislatures,* Pelham's *State Land Use Planning and Regulation,* and DeGrove's *Land, Growth, and Politics.* Recently, entire books on the Oregon land use program have been written by Leonard, *Managing Oregon's Growth,* and by Rohse, *Land Use Planning in Oregon.* These books have enhanced national awareness and interest in Oregon's land use program. But, with exception, these books provide primarily descriptive information for the general public. This book does not.

ABOUT THIS BOOK

This book reviews the now substantial literature on the Oregon land use program. The purpose of the review is twofold. For the academician, the book reviews research on one of the great land reform experiments of the 1970s. For the practitioner and policy maker, the book offers insights on planning from the diverse fields of economics, geography, law, planning, political science, sociology, public administration, and environmental science. The book is organized as follows. The opening chapter offers a brief description of the Oregon land use program and places the program in historical context. The following six chapters address specific features of the program, which include urban growth management, state housing policy, public service planning and management, farmland protection, economic development, and state land use politics. The final chapter summarizes the findings and offers policy lessons from Oregon.

Chapter 1 introduces the Oregon land use program by describing the historical-political context in which the program was conceived. The progressive McCall administration faced a host of socioeconomic problems: the timber industry was in decline; water and air sheds were degraded; population in the Willamette Valley was exploding; and cities were marching over the cherished Oregon countryside. When conceived, Oregon's land use program constituted little more than statements of legislative intent and planning procedure. Only as planning began did the substance of the program—the goals, the administrative rules, the judicial interpretations, and the implementing ordinances—begin to take shape. But the shape of the program was not permanently cast; instead the program adapted to the changing fortunes of Oregon's highly cyclical economy. As a national leader in social and environmental policy, Oregon offers an evolutionary model of land use policy change.

Chapter 2 focuses on a key feature of the Oregon land use program: urban growth boundaries (UGBs). According to economic theory, UGBs can influence land markets in different ways: as though they were ordinary zoning restrictions, as instruments controlling the timing of zoning restrictions, or as multidimensional instruments affecting land values in various ways. The available evidence is consistent with theory: land values inside UGBs are higher than land values outside them, and the influence varies by location. But residential patterns—both inside and outside UGBs—raise important questions about using them as long-term policy instruments.

Chapter 3 addresses a most sensitive aspect of the Oregon land use program: the effects of the program on housing costs. A major goal of the program is to provide reasonably priced housing for all segments of society. According to microeconomic theory, exclusionary zoning by local governments can escalate housing prices and contribute to urban sprawl. Through state review of local land use plans, however, Oregon was able to remove regulatory barriers to affordable housing and compact urban growth—without escalating housing prices above those in neighboring states. But because statewide planning does not alter fundamental economic conditions, it offers only a partial solution to problems of housing affordability and urban sprawl.

Chapter 4 addresses an issue closely tied to urban growth management and housing: planning and management of urban public services. Critical issues in public service planning and management include intergovernmental coordination, economies of scale, economies of scope, and public service finance. Oregon's land use program addresses these issues by requiring local governments to prepare detailed public facility plans. Research focusing on the performance of a regional sewer agency suggests that regional service providers offer cost savings, which are passed on to residents in the form of lower service fees and improved land values. Thus statewide planning can help establish institutions that offer improved public service planning, management, and finance.

Chapter 5 addresses Oregon's nationally acclaimed farmland preservation program—a program that seeks not only to protect farmland but also to enhance farm productivity. To arrest declines in farmland and farm productivity, which are being experienced both nationally and regionally, Oregon's farmland preservation program combines urban growth boundaries, exclusive farm use zoning, minimum lot requirements, and tax deferrals. Since the program was established, Oregon's farmland base has stablized and farm productivity has risen—especially in the relatively small farm-size classifications. These trends reflect favorably on Oregon's efforts to protect farmland and create new challenges for preserving productivity on small farms.

Chapter 6 addresses perhaps the most difficult and least researched aspect of the Oregon land use program. Oregon remains widely viewed as the no-growth state, a reputation earned in the 1970s and reflected in its land use program. Attitudes toward economic growth changed, however, following the 1981 recession, leaving the land use program as a scapegoat for the state's economic malaise. The evidence available, though scarce, offers little to suggest that statewide planning harmed the Oregon economy. Instead the evidence suggests that statewide planning, by increasing certainty in the regulatory environment and by preserving environmental amenities, may actually foster economic growth. Statewide planning, therefore, can serve as a positive—though perhaps minor—instrument for economic development.

Chapter 7 begins the unification of the previous chapters by examining state land use politics. Repeated initiative petitions and referenda to repeal statewide planning offer evidence of strongly divided popular support but little evidence that support is divided by social class. Although divisions in the general population remained relatively constant over the life of the program, perhaps the most interesting feature of Oregon's land use politics is the changing posture of interest groups. The development industry, once strongly opposed to statewide planning, joined with 1000 Friends of Oregon as one of statewide planning's strongest supporters. As a result, statewide planning and regulation became highly popular with the regulated industry.

Chapter 8 reviews the Oregon experience in a search for general lessons on statewide land use planning. Based on experience in Oregon, statewide land use programs that focus on resource conservation and urban growth arise in states that experience rapid urban growth, environmental degradation, and spatially concentrated political power. Once in place, statewide land use programs continue to be shaped by the state legislature, the state executive, and the state judiciary. While state participation in the planning process can influence the content of local comprehensive plans, the influence of comprehensive plans on land use and development depends to a great extent on which policy instruments are used, how forcefully they are applied, and how suitable they are for dealing with the task at hand.

Note

1. Terms related to the Oregon planning program are italicized in the
   text and explained in the Glossary on page 7.

Glossary of Oregon Planning Terms

Acknowledgment. Official approval by the LCDC of a local government's comprehensive plan and implementing ordinances. The complete phrase is "acknowledgment of compliance with statewide planning goals."

Agricultural land. West of the Cascades, land comprised predominantly of U.S. Soil Conservation Service soils classifications I, II, III and IV. East of the Cascades, class I to VI soils. The term also includes other lands that are suitable for farming, which are discretionary.

Buildable lands. Lands in urban and urbanized areas that are suitable, available, and necessary for urban development.

Built or committed. Rural land that is physically built on or that is committed to nonfarm use because of subdivision, improvements, or development in the area.

Commercial agricultural enterprise. A farm operation that will contribute in a substantial way to an area's agricultural economy and help maintain the agricultural infrastructure.

Committed lands. Identifies lands where it is "impracticable" to carry out farming, forest, or other open-space activities since they are "irrevocably committed" to nonfarm and nonforest uses. The commitment must result from factors that prevent resource management. This term evolved through efforts by rural local governments to accommodate such situations.

Consistency review. First, a process by which development permits issued by state agencies are checked for consistency with statewide planning goals and acknowledged local comprehensive plans. Second, a process by which specific types of development proposals in coastal zones are checked for consistency with federally approved coastal zone management plans.

Continuance. An order issued by LCDC declaring that parts of a local government's proposed plan are inconsistent with statewide planning goals.

7

It specifies a period of time within which the inconsistencies must be corrected. Continuances are typically issued for 150 days.

Enforcement order. An order issued by the LCDC to compel a local government to make specific progress toward complying with one or more of the statewide planning goals. Enforcement orders are a last resort and are preceded by continuances. In practice, enforcement orders place a moratorium on all land partitionings and all building permits until the problem is resolved. The moratorium may apply to the entire local government jurisdiction or to specific areas, such as agricultural lands.

Exception. In land use planning, the abatement of applying a statewide planning goal to a parcel or an area, as in abating the application of Goal 3 (Agricultural Lands) to a developed subdivision outside a UGB. In general, exceptions are extended to: (1) land that is already physically developed and simply cannot revert to resource uses, (2) land that is irrevocably committed to nonresource uses because of existing development patterns and commitments to development, and (3) land in certain situations where for other reasons the state policy embodied in the applicable goals should not apply.

Exclusive farm use (EFU) zoning. A special kind of zoning that protects agricultural lands. The statutes define farm use, list the uses allowed outright, specify conditional uses, create procedures for land partitionings, and identify the conditions under which nonfarm dwellings may be built.

Farm dwelling. A dwelling on a farm that is occupied by the owner or manager or operators of the farm or by a relative (defined as a grandparent, grandchild, parent, child, brother, or sister of the farm operator or the farm operator's spouse), whose assistance in managing the farm is or will be required by the farm operator. Residential dwelling units permitted for EFU districts that do not meet these criteria but meet exception criteria are called nonfarm dwellings.

Farm use. The current employment of land primarily for the purpose of generating income by harvesting and selling crops, or by raising livestock and marketing their products.

Fasano **procedures.** Derived from a landmark court case in which decisions on land uses were required to follow certain procedures to assure constitutional due process.

Findings. Statements of the standards, facts, and conclusions supporting a land use decision, including: (1) the criteria applied to the decision, (2) a description of the facts justifying the decision, and (3) an explanation of the "justification for the decision based on the criteria, standards and facts set forth."

Goals. "Mandatory statewide planning standards adopted by the [Land Conservation and Development Commission]."

Guidelines. Suggested approaches to the preparation, adoption and implementation of comprehensive plans in compliance with statewide goals to aid state agencies and special districts in the preparation, adoption and implementation of plans, programs, and regulations; guidelines are advisory.

Growth management agreement. An agreement between a county and its constituent cities specifying how unincorporated land inside the UGB will be managed until it is developed or annexed.

Key facilities. "Basic facilities that are primarily planned for by local government but which also may be provided by private enterprise and are essential to the support of more intensive development, including public schools, transportation, water supply, sewage and solid waste disposal."

Land use decision. A decision by a local government or a special district that is required to be consistent with statewide planning goals (in the absence of an acknowledged plan) or consistent with an acknowledged comprehensive plan. Legally defined as a final decision or determination that concerns the adoption, amendment, or application of the statewide goals, a provision in a comprehensive plan, a land use regulation, or a new land use regulation.

Marginal lands. Farmlands or forest lands exempted from Goals 3 (Agricultural Lands) and 4 (Forest Lands) because of their low productivity.

Market factor. An allowance in the size of a UGB. Goal 14 (Urbanization) requires that UGBs include enough buildable land to meet projected urban development needs to some target date, usually the year 2000. Some urban areas then add 10 to 25 percent more buildable land to the UGB as a market factor, arguing that surplus land is needed to assure reasonable variety in development opportunities, to reduce monopolistic pricing behavior by land owners, and to provide a hedge against faster-than-expected growth. The counter argument is that UGBs are not inflexible and can be adjusted over time to accommodate new needs. But providing more land than needed induced urban sprawl. Therefore, LCDC consistently rejected market factors. Only major urban areas, such as Portland and Salem, successfully defended the use of market factors; Portland, by arguing its unique complexities (three counties and over 20 cities inside the regional UGB), and Salem, principally because its UGB preceded implementation of statewide planning goals.

Need. First, an element that must be assessed in local comprehensive plans; specifically plans must identify how much land is needed for recreational facilities, commercial activities, industry, and residential use. Second, a quality that must be documented for some kinds of quasi-judicial proposals, such as a zone change to allow a specific development proposal. These can be approved only after a developer demonstrates a public need for the proposal. In practice, this policy has been extended to mean that where a need has been shown for housing within a UGB at particular price ranges and rent levels, housing types determined to meet that need will be permitted if there is sufficient buildable land to satisfy that need. The policy is not construed as an infringement on a community's prerogative to set approval standards under which a particular housing type is permitted outright, to impose special conditions upon approval of a specific development proposal, or to establish approval procedure. However, approval standards, special conditions, and procedures must be clear and objective and must not have the effect, either of themselves or cumulatively, of discouraging, such as through unreasonable cost or delay, the needed housing type.

Needed housing.   Housing types determined to meet the need shown within an urban growth boundary at particular price ranges and rent levels.

Periodic review.   First, the regularly scheduled review by DLCD of acknowledged comprehensive plans and implementing ordinances. If necessary, cities and counties must revise plans to bring them back into compliance with statewide planning goals. Second, the review of an acknowledged comprehensive plan and regulations by a local government in accordance with a schedule for review and revision adopted during acknowledgment. Reviews take place at least every two years, although local governments make major plan revisions more frequently.

Postacknowledgment.   The phase of the Oregon program that began after all local comprehensive plans had been acknowledged.

Quasi-judicial action.   A decision involving specific people or properties, such as a request for a conditional use permit or a rezoning. Contrast to "legislative actions," which involve new policies or local law applied to everyone, for example, a series of plan amendments occasioned by updated population forecasts, and to "ministerial actions," which involve routine decisions guided by clear and objective requirements, for example, the siting of a mobile home in a residential district. Sometimes it is not clear whether a decision is quasi-judicial or legislative. Normally, variances, conditional use permits, and rezonings of single, small parcels are considered quasi-judicial, while changes to the text or map of a plan affecting several individual parcels are considered legislative. A plan amendment or rezoning involving several contiguous parcels or a single large tract that may influence community development patterns could be either.

Redivision plan.   Also known as a "concept plat." This is a plan for an individual parcel suggesting how it can be subdivided into small lots in the future. Redivision plans are usually required as a condition of approval for homes built on large lots in urbanizable areas outside the reach of urban services. When urban services extend to the parcel, the redivision is relied on to guide future subdivision decisions. The principal objective of redivision plans is to locate homes in such a manner as to allow efficient subdivision in the future.

Resource land.   First, an informal description of areas outside UGBs that are agricultural or forest lands as defined in Goals 3 or 4. Second, a formal designation for farmland, forest land, estuarine resource lands, coastal shorelands, beaches, and dunes.

Rural facilities and services.   Facilities and services appropriate for the needs of rural use. Formally, excludes wastewater systems and includes telephones and electrical service. Water systems may be included if they predate the planning goals or if they serve a prescribed area that has received an exception.

Rural lands.   Lands outside a UGB.

Urban facilities and services.   Defined as police protection; fire protection; sanitary facilities; storm drainage facilities; planning, zoning, and subdivision control; health services; recreation facilities and services; energy and communication services; community government services; public schools; transportation; water supply; sewage and solid waste disposal. Some of these systems may also serve rural development.

Urban growth area.   Land that is inside a UGB but outside the city limits or the service area of water and sewer systems.

Urban growth boundary (UGB).   A line on a map showing the outermost limit of urban development within the planning horizon While not explicitly defined in the goals, the LCDC imposed the concept on all cities and counties. All UGBs are designed to accommodate urban development needs to the year 2000. In theory, only after 2000, and only if a UGB is fully developed, would the boundary be extended outward to accommodate new growth. In practice, it is likely to be very difficult to move UGBs outward even when the UGB is built out.

Urbanizable lands.   Lands within a UGB that are identified and deemed necessary as future urban areas. Only these lands may be served by urban services and facilities.

Urban lands.   Lands in incorporated cities and lands adjacent to and outside cities that comprise concentrations of people who generally reside and work in the area and that have supporting public facilities and services.

Milestones in Oregon Planning

1919 Legislature enables cities to plan and zone

1947 Legislature enables counties to plan and zone

1969 Legislature adopts Senate Bill 10

1970 Senate Bill 10 survives initiative petition ballot measure

1971 Legislature adopts Oregon Coastal Zone Management Act and creates Oregon Coastal Conservation and Development Commission

1973 Legislature adopts Senate Bill 100 and creates Land Conservation and Development Commission (LCDC)

1974 Senate Bill 100 survives first initiative petition ballot measure

1975 Legislature transfers coastal zone management responsibilities to LCDC

1978 Senate Bill 100 survives second initiative petition ballot measure

1981 Legislature makes first round of major changes to LCDC plan review procedures and creates postacknowledgment procedures

1982 Senate Bill 100 survives third initiative petition ballot measure and Governor's Task Force recommends changes in LCDC review procedures

1983 Legislature makes second round of major changes to LCDC review procedures

1986 LCDC acknowledges last local comprehensive plan

1

The Oregon Land Use Program

T HE STATE OF OREGON is widely recognized as a leader in land use planning and regulation—and for good reason. In the late 1960s and early 1970s, a "quiet revolution" took hold in land use control. During that period, state governments retracted from local governments some or all powers to control land use (Bosselman and Callies 1971). Oregon played a leading role in this revolution. It was one of the first states: to require local governments to plan and zone, to establish binding statewide land use *goals* and *guidelines,* and to establish areas of statewide concern (Rosenbaum 1976). What is more, Oregon has nurtured and enhanced its land use program for nearly 20 years. Today, a second wave of states joins the quiet revolution, and these states look to Oregon for lessons on statewide land use planning and regulation.

Not all state land use programs are the same, however—even among states leading the quiet revolution. State programs differ in land use objectives, administrative structure, planning procedure, and implementation tools. Extracting policy lessons from Oregon, therefore, requires an understanding of the state's land use issues, its administrative structure, and the instruments used there to plan and regulate land use. With such an understanding, policy makers in other states can identify land use issues of concern to them, examine how Oregon addressed the issues, and derive lessons provided by the Oregon experience. This chapter, therefore, reviews the evolution of Oregon's land use program and describes its fundamental features. The chapter concludes by interpreting the history of the program and laying out a strategy for analyzing its effects.

HISTORICAL ANTECEDENTS

In 1919, the Oregon legislature enabled cities to plan and regulate land use. For the next 50 years cities adopted zoning ordinances that were supervised by planning commissions or city councils. Some of those ordinances were guided by comprehensive plans, but most were not. Local planning commissions reviewed subdivision and other development proposals, requests for zone changes, variances, conditional use permits, and other routine zoning decisions. Some planning commissions also planned. But by 1963, only 24 of the state's 60 cities with populations greater than 2,500 had comprehensive plans, while all but one had zoning ordinances (BGRS 1984).

Under the 1919 enabling act, cities could not control land use in unincorporated areas. As a result, unplanned urban development frequently spilled over municipal boundaries. It also stemmed from special service districts for water and sewer in the unincorporated areas and from cities that extended urban services without annexation. Oregon's annexation laws, which made annexation extremely difficult, imposed further obstacles to effective control of urban growth.[1] Uncontrolled development in unincorporated areas subsequently strained the capacity of urban services and undermined city planning.

In 1947, planning and zoning authority was extended to counties, although county zoning was limited to unincorporated urban areas. By 1963, 28 of the state's 36 counties had planning commissions and 16 counties, primarily the highly populated counties of the Willamette Valley, had zoning ordinances. Only eight counties, however, had land use plans for all or part of the county (BGRS 1984).

In drafting land use plans and in adopting zoning ordinances to implement plans, cities and counties sought to prevent land use conflicts, protect public safety, and minimize the costs of infrastructure. More comprehensive objectives, such as resource conservation, economic development, affordable housing, and open space protection, generally exceeded the scope of local planning and zoning. Local governments also lacked interest in coordinating plans between and among cities and counties—or, if they were interested, they lacked the ability to do so. Without comprehensive and coordinated land use plans, Oregon's city and county governments were ill-prepared to handle the rapid urban and suburban development of the 1960s and 1970s.

RAPID SOCIAL CHANGE

Rapid urban and suburban growth in Oregon during the 1960s and 1970s reflected national trends. During the 1960s, America's urban population increased by about 20 million people, four-fifths of whom settled in the urban fringe. Urban sprawl, the term popularly used to describe low-density, leap-frog, and radial development around urban areas, consumed land at a rapid pace. While total U.S. urban population increased by 21 percent, the consumption of land for urban uses increased by 36 percent. Between 1960 and 1970, the number of acres in urban use increased by nearly 9,000 square miles (Nelson 1984).

Local manifestations of national urban and suburban trends profoundly influenced Oregon's political climate. Before World War II, Oregon was a sparsely populated state, highly dependent upon agriculture and forest products for its economic base. Cities had grown at transshipment points between interior locations of natural resources and exterior access points to markets, but dispersion rather than concentration characterized the spatial structure of the population.

The postwar period, however, brought dramatic and rapid social change to Oregon. The base of the state's economy began its transition from agriculture and forest products to trade, services, and light manufacturing. At the same time western population migration spilled over the California border, largely into the cities of Oregon's interior valleys (see table 1). By the late 1960s, rapid population growth had put pressure on the carrying capacity of the environment, on the fiscal capacity of city governments, and on the state's tolerance of new residents. Characteristic of the political climate in Oregon was the sign at the California border that read, "Welcome to Oregon, Enjoy Your Visit" (to which then–Governor Tom McCall would add, "but don't stay"). These economic, social, and environmental conditions fostered and shaped a pioneering system of land use controls.[2]

Unlike many southern and midwestern states, Oregon does not have an abundance of land easily developed to accommodate rapid social change. State and federal governments own 54 percent of the state's 96,000 square miles. Mountains, sensitive landscapes, and deserts render much of the remaining private land difficult to develop. Only one region in the state offers substantial amounts of land easy to develop with interstate access by river, rail, and freeway—the Willamette River Valley.

Table 1.   Oregon Population by Region, 1900 to 1990

Year	Population	Change in population	Percentage in urban areas	Percentage in valleys[a]
1900	413,536	n.a.	32.2	56.4
1910	672,765	259,229	45.6	61.9
1920	783,389	110,624	49.6	63.4
1930	953,786	170,397	51.4	64.0
1940	1,089,684	135,898	48.8	63.4
1950	1,520,341	430,657	53.8	65.3
1960	1,768,687	248,346	62.2	66.1
1970	2,091,385	322,698	67.1	69.2
1980	2,633,105	541,720	67.9	67.9
1990	2,842,321	209,216	70.5	69.1

[a]Includes Benton, Clackamas, Lane, Linn, Marion, Multnomah, Polk, Washington, and Yamhill Counties.

SOURCES: U.S. Dept. of Commerce 1983; U.S. Dept. of Commerce 1991a

The Willamette Valley extends about 120 miles north to south from the Columbia River to the city of Eugene. The valley measures 20 to 50 miles in width (see figure 1). It comprises just an eighth of Oregon's land area but is home to more than three-quarters of the state's three million residents. While it accounts for just 10 percent of the state's available farmland, the valley produces about half of the state's agricultural products, which have traditionally been the state's economic strength. Much of the interest in planning in Oregon centers on balancing the demand for urban development against the need to sustain agriculture in the Willamette Valley.[3]

Oregon leaders were quick to recognize the sensitivity of the state's environment to the urbanization trends of the 1960s and 1970s. During this period, Oregon's population, which grew at a rate roughly twice the national average, concentrated in the Willamette Valley. Concerned about growth, then–Governor Tom McCall commissioned Lawrence Halprin to report on the valley's urbanizing trends and future prospects. Halprin and Associates (1972) estimated that, without government intervention, the amount of urban land in the valley would increase by 75 percent, or by about 340,000 acres, between 1966 and 2020. In the state, then, more than 770,000 acres would become developed for urban use. Almost all of this development would displace high-quality agricultural land, resulting in

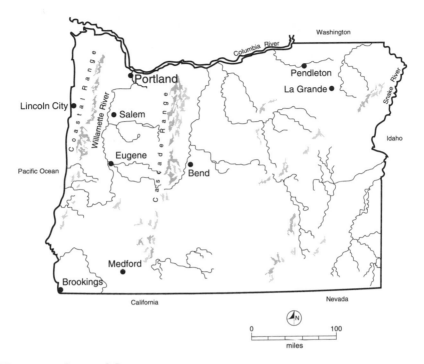

Figure 1.   State of Oregon

nearly a quarter of the valley's prime farmland being taken for urban use by the year 2020. Perhaps more important, however, rapid urbanization of the Willamette Valley invoked images of southern California, familiar images many Oregonians sought to avoid.

Concerns about uncontrolled development were not limited to the Willamette Valley. Rapid subdivision and sale of farmland, often without adequate plans for roads or public services, caused problems in eastern Oregon as well. The problems were epitomized by the 82,000-acre Christmas Lake subdivision in remote southeastern Oregon. The subdivision lacked basic services, such as water and sewer, but buyers—typically from outside the state—were led to believe that they were forthcoming. A study by the Oregon Department of Revenue in 1972 showed that about 160,000 acres of eastern Oregon rangelands had been subdivided into nearly 43,000 lots (DeGrove 1984). Thus, increasing speculation and development on Oregon's wheatlands and rangelands sparked land use conflicts in the eastern portion of the state.

Uncontrolled development along the coast during the 1960s presented additional problems. The 20-mile stretch extending south along the coast from Lincoln City, locally billed as the "twenty miracle miles," was once called the "twenty miserable miles" by then–Governor (later U.S. Senator) Mark Hatfield. Increasingly, residents from recreation and retirement homes along the coast congested streets, parks, and tourist facilities. Battles raged between visitors and property owners over access to ocean beaches. Municipal and septic systems dumped undertreated, and sometimes untreated, sewage into rivers, estuaries, and the Pacific Ocean. In 1965, 39 of the 60 water systems in Lincoln County failed to meet potability standards and demand (BGRS 1984). By the late 1960s, Oregon's land use problems were serious, widespread, and worsening. Planning and zoning at the option of cities and counties seemed unlikely to resolve those problems. As a result, a political consensus developed that something equally serious and widespread must be done to address them.

PIONEERING LAND USE STATUTES

Oregon's land use program was born in an era of land use reform. In 1961 Hawaii established control over all land in the state; in 1965 California required all local governments to plan; in 1966 Wisconsin began state regulation of its shoreline; and in 1963 the American Law Institute began work on its Model Land Development Code (Rosenbaum 1976). Reformers in Oregon were naturally influenced by concurrent reforms in nearby states; but by enacting three successive land use statutes, Oregon established a unique and revolutionary program.

Senate Bill 10

Oregon's program began in earnest in 1969 with the passage of Senate Bill 10, the state's first mandate for land use planning.[4] Senate Bill 10 required all cities and counties to prepare comprehensive land use plans. The bill also directed the governor to prescribe and administer comprehensive plans and zoning ordinances for land not included in city or county plans. Senate Bill 10 required plans to address nine issues.

1. Air and water resources
2. Open space, and natural scenic resources
3. Recreation

4. Farmland conservation
5. Floods, landslides, and other natural disasters
6. Transportation
7. Public facilities
8. The economy, and
9. Physical limitations of the land

The bill did not, however, contain provisions ensuring that local plans achieved—or furthered—statewide goals.

Ultimately, Senate Bill 10 failed to resolve the problems it was designed to address. Many local governments did not wish to commit resources to preparing comprehensive plans, and the state did not provide resources for such planning. Although then–Governor Tom McCall threatened to exercise his power to preempt local land use control, he never did. Thus there was general agreement that Senate Bill 10 did not provide local governments adequate guidance, resources, or incentives to carry out the mandate (DeGrove and Stroud 1980). Although the Oregon electorate defeated a ballot measure to abolish Senate Bill 10 in 1970 by a margin of three to two, 30,000 acres of Willamette Valley farmland (roughly 2 percent) were urbanized in 1973 alone (Leonard 1983).

The Oregon Coastal Zone Management Act

The state became further involved in land use planning with the passage of the Oregon Coastal Zone Management Act (OCZMA) in 1971. Passed in part as a response to federal coastal zone legislation, the OCZMA created the Oregon Coastal Conservation and Development Commission (OCC&DC), whose members were mainly city, county, and port officials. The commission was charged with preparing "a comprehensive plan for preserving and developing the resources of the coastal zone." In its report to the legislature in 1975, the OCC&DC provided inventories of economic and natural resources and recommended several resource management policies (BGRS 1984).

The OCZMA set several precedents for a new approach to planning. Unlike Senate Bill 10, which was vague in assigning plan review responsibilities, the OCZMA established a state-level commission—appointed by the governor and approved by the senate—to prepare a plan for coastal areas which would supersede local plans. The commission also received state funding to support its planning efforts. Its chief limitation, however, was its inability to enlist the support of local governments, which was essential to implement the plan. Moreover, the OCC&DC lacked the staff needed to administer such an ambitious plan. Thus in 1976, the OCC&DC became absorbed into the larger statewide planning program, which had been created in 1973.

Senate Bill 100

In 1973, the Oregon legislature passed Senate Bill 100—the Oregon Land Use Act.[5] Senate Bill 100 created the Land Conservation and Development Commission (LCDC), a seven-member commission appointed by the governor and approved by the senate. The act also created the Department of Land Conservation and Development (DLCD) as the LCDC's administrative arm. Senate Bill 100 goes beyond requiring local governments to plan and beyond state planning for areas of statewide concern; it establishes a significant role for state government in planning and regulating land use throughout the state.

The journey of Senate Bill 100 through the legislature provides an interesting and well-documented case study of state land use politics.[6] In its original formulation, Senate Bill 100 identified eight areas and seven activities of critical concern, over which the state would have exercised exclusive land use control. The original bill would also have created 14 regional councils of government (COGs), responsible for coordinating local plans at the regional level. After considerable compromise, however, the provision for coordination by regional COGs was removed, and provisions for establishing activities of statewide concern were weakened and never exercised. As a result, Senate Bill 100 leaves land use control as the joint responsibility of state and local governments in all areas of the state, including areas of statewide concern.

ELEMENTS OF STATEWIDE PLANNING IN OREGON

Senate Bill 100, though somewhat compromised, dramatically changed the process in which land use plans are formulated and implemented in Oregon. The new process includes mandatory local comprehensive planning, state review of local plans, plan enforcement, and an appeals process.

Mandatory Local Comprehensive Planning

At the heart of Senate Bill 100 is the requirement that all cities, counties, regional agencies with planning authority, and other state and local agencies that affect land use prepare coordinated, comprehensive land use plans consistent with state goals. The Oregon legislature defines comprehensive plans as follows:

> "Comprehensive plan" means a generalized, coordinated land use map and policy statement of the governing body of a state agency, city, county or special district that integrates all functional and natural systems and activities relating to the use of lands, including but not limited to sewer and water systems, recreational facilities, and natural resources and air and water quality management programs. "Comprehensive" means all-inclusive, both in terms of geographic area covered and functional and natural activities and systems occurring in the area covered by the plan. "General nature" means a summary of policies and proposals in broad categories and does not necessarily indicate specific locations of any area, activity or use. A plan is "coordinated" when the needs of all levels of governments, semipublic agencies and the citizens of Oregon have been considered and accommodated as much as possible. "Land" includes water, both surface and subsurface, and the air. (ORS 197.015(5))

To assure public accountability, comprehensive plans had to be adopted by locally elected governing bodies (city councils, boards of county commissioners, or county courts). These bodies also had to adopt functional plans for transportation, recreation, economic development, and public facilities. Finally, elected bodies were required to adopt implementing ordinances to assure that land use activities would be consistent with local comprehensive plans and functional plans. Locally appointed planning commissions often participated in plan formulation and implementation; however, state law limited their authority to an advisory role (BGRS 1984).

Acknowledgment Review

Although local governments were charged with preparing comprehensive land use plans and coordinating their plans with other local governments and state agencies, Senate Bill 100 charged LCDC with determining whether locally prepared plans were consistent with statewide planning goals through an acknowledgment process. The acknowledgment process began when a local government sent its plan materials to DLCD. The department then reviewed the plan, invited comments from interested parties, and submitted a report to the commission. At a public hearing, the commission reviewed the report, heard testimony, and decided if the plan complied with all relevant statewide goals and guidelines.

Until a local plan was acknowledged by LCDC, the state officially retained authority over all local land use actions.[7] In exchange for achieving acknowledgment status, the state re-delegated land use control to local governments. Incomplete plans or plans that were inconsistent with state-

wide land use goals were remanded to local governments with specific
instructions on how to improve them.[8]

Plan Enforcement

Unlike Senate Bill 10, Senate Bill 100 included strong provisions for enforcement. Under Senate Bill 100, LCDC could prepare and enforce its
own land use plan and land use regulations in cities and counties that did
not prepare plans or did not receive acknowledgment by January 1, 1976.
LCDC could impose development moratoria in local governments that
refused to plan and could grant building permits if local governments
imposed their own development moratoria. Further, LCDC could charge
the city or county for enforcement costs and withhold state grants or
shared revenues to recover its costs.

Appeals Process

Senate Bill 100 also contained provisions for appealing *land use decisions* at
the state and local levels. At the local level, appeals could be heard by
planning commissions or hearings officers established by most local governments. The decisions of those tribunals could then be appealed to the local
governing body. At the state level, land use appeals could be heard by
LCDC and the relevant circuit court. When the circuit court and LCDC
heard the same case, the circuit court judge generally deferred jurisdiction
to LCDC. Appeals from LCDC or the circuit court could be made to the
court of appeals and the supreme court.

MAKING PLANNING WORK

Senate Bill 100 established bold new procedures for preparing and implementing land use plans, but left many questions to be worked out. What
would be the goals of state land use planning? How would such goals be
interpreted? What would be the legal standing of local zoning and comprehensive plans? What would happen after all plans had been acknowledged?
These questions were not addressed until well after Senate Bill 100 was
passed, and LCDC and local governments were forced to make the process
work.

Statewide Land Use Goals

In 1974, following a series of public hearings throughout the state, LCDC adopted 14 goals and guidelines for statewide planning, which encompassed the following (Oregon LCDC 1975):

1. Citizen Involvement
2. Land Use Planning Processes
3. Agricultural Lands
4. Forest Lands
5. Open Spaces, Scenic and Historic Areas, and Natural Resources
6. Air, Water, and Land Resources Quality
7. Natural Hazards and Disasters
8. Recreation
9. Economic Development
10. Housing
11. Public Facilities and Services
12. Transportation
13. Energy Conservation
14. Urbanization—chiefly the containment of urban growth

Within two years, LCDC adopted five more goals:

15. Willamette River Greenway
16. Estuarine Resources
17. Coastal Shorelands
18. Beaches and Dunes
19. Ocean Resources

In 1975, LCDC adopted Goal 15, creating the Willamette River Greenway, from the city of Eugene to the confluence of the Willamette River and the Columbia River in the city of St. Helens, about 30 miles north of Portland. In 1976, the goals of the OCC&DC were transferred to the LCDC, adding the four final goals (see box insert).

Although somewhat vague and contradictory, the statewide planning goals served as a framework for guiding the planning process; they were a type of planning "constitution." As such, the goals were used for three purposes. Prior to acknowledgment of comprehensive plans, the goals were the basis for legal challenges to local land use decisions. That is, prior to acknowledgment, land use decisions by local governments could be

State Land Use Goals and Guidelines

Goal 1: Citizen Involvement To develop a citizen involvement program that insures the opportunity for citizens to be involved in all phases of the planning process.

Goal 2: Land Use Planning To establish a land use planning process and policy framework as a basis for all decisions and actions related to use of land and to assure an adequate factual base for such decisions and actions.

Goal 3: Agricultural Land To preserve and maintain agricultural lands.

Goal 4: Forest Lands To conserve forest lands by maintaining the forest land base and to protect the state's forest economy by making possible economically efficient forest practices that assure the continuous growing and harvesting of forest tree species as the leading use on forest land consistent with sound management of soil, air, water, and fish and wildlife resources and to provide for recreational opportunities and agriculture.

Goal 5: Open Spaces, Scenic and Historic Areas, and Natural Resources To conserve open space and protect natural and scenic resources.

Goal 6: Air, Water, and Land Resources Quality To maintain and improve the quality of the air, water, and land resources of the state.

Goal 7: Areas Subject to Natural Disasters and Hazards To protect life and property from natural disasters and hazards.

Goal 8: Recreational Needs To satisfy the recreational needs of the citizens of the state and visitors and, where appropriate, to provide for the siting of necessary recreational facilities including destination resorts.

Goal 9: Economic Development To provide adequate opportunities throughout the state for a variety of economic activities vital to the health, welfare, and prosperity of Oregon's citizens.

Goal 10: Housing To provide for the housing needs of citizens of the state.

Goal 11: Public Facilities and Services To plan and develop a timely, orderly, and efficient arrangement of public facilities and services to serve as a framework for urban and rural development.

Goal 12: Transportation To provide and encourage a safe, convenient, and economic transportation system.

Goal 13: Energy Conservation To conserve energy.

Goal 14: Urbanization To provide for an orderly and efficient transition from rural to urban land use.

Goal 15: Willamette River Greenway To protect, conserve, enhance, and maintain the natural, scenic, historical, agricultural, economic, and recreational qualities of lands along the Willamette River as the Willamette River Greenway.

Goal 16: Estuarine Resources To recognize and protect the unique environmental, economic, and social values of each estuary and associated wetlands; and to protect, maintain, where appropriate develop, and where appropriate restore the long-term environmental, economic, and social values, diversity and benefits of Oregon's estuaries.

Goal 17: Coastal Shorelands To conserve, protect, where appropriate develop, and where appropriate restore the resources and benefits of all coastal shorelands, recognizing their value for protection and maintenance of water quality, fish and wildlife habitat, water-dependent uses, economic resources, and recreation and aesthetics. The management of these shoreland areas shall be compatible with the characteristics of the adjacent coastal waters. Also, to reduce the hazard to human life and property and the adverse effects upon water quality and fish and wildlife habitat resulting from the use and enjoyment of Oregon's coastal shorelands.

Goal 18: Beaches and Dunes To conserve, protect, where appropriate develop, and where appropriate restore the resources and benefits of coastal beach and dune areas; and to reduce the hazard to human life and property from natural or man-induced actions associated with these areas.

Goal 19: Ocean Resources To conserve the long-term values, benefits, and natural resources of the nearshore ocean and the continental shelf. All local, state, and federal plans, policies, projects, and activities which affect the territorial sea shall be developed, managed, and conducted to maintain, and where appropriate, enhance and restore, the long-term benefits derived from the nearshore oceanic resources of Oregon. Since renewable ocean resources and uses, such as food production, water quality, navigation, recreation, and aesthetic enjoyment, will provide greater long-term benefits than will nonrenewable resources, such plans and activities shall give clear priority to the proper management and protection of renewable resources.

(Oregon LCDC 1990)

challenged in court on the grounds that they violated state land use goals. During the acknowledgment process, the goals were a checklist for determining whether local plans furthered state land use objectives. After acknowledgment, the goals were a basis for reviewing amendments to local land use plans.

Administrative Rules

After the goals were adopted, the acknowledgment process began. Unfortunately, the goals provided little detail on what local comprehensive plans needed to include before they could receive acknowledgment. In one of the first meetings of the newly constituted LCDC in 1974, then–chairman John Mosser told a local government official, "We don't know what acknowledgment is, but we'll know it when we see it."

Because the goals were unspecific, the requirements for acknowledgment were established during the acknowledgment process. As LCDC reviewed comprehensive plans, it set precedents concerning what would and would not be permitted in such plans. Many precedents established during the acknowledgment process were subsequently codified into administrative rules. Over time, the administrative rules became greater in number and increasingly specific.

LCDC's actions related to housing illustrate how plan requirements became increasingly specific through the adoption of administrative rules. Goal 10 as adopted in 1974 stated that comprehensive plans "shall encourage the availability of adequate numbers of housing units at price ranges and rent levels which are commensurate with the financial capabilities of Oregon households" (OAR 660-15-000). In 1981, the LCDC adopted the Metropolitan Housing Rule, which required that "Multnomah County and the cities of Portland, Gresham, Beaverton, Hillsboro, Lake Oswego, and Tigard, must provide for an overall density of ten or more dwelling units per net buildable acre" (OAR 660-07-035).

Judicial Interpretations

As the legislature and the LCDC established land use laws and regulations, the Oregon courts were active interpreting them. In a landmark decision, the Oregon Supreme Court interpreted local zoning decision making as a *quasi-judicial* process (*Fasano v. Washington County Board of Commissioners*). When local boards and governing bodies apply general policy to identifiable persons or property, the Supreme Court ruled, they must accord affected parties with procedural safeguards, such as notice, an opportunity to participate in a hearing, and the opportunity to present and rebut evidence. The *Fasano decision* significantly changed the rules of land use decision making—increasing the burden of those who want a zone change and reducing the burden of those who do not (Rohse 1987).

The Oregon courts have established several other key principles fundamental to the Oregon program. Soon after *Fasano,* the Oregon Supreme Court ruled that zoning decisions must conform to comprehensive plans (*Baker v. City of Milwaukie*). In the *Baker* decision, the Supreme Court established comprehensive plans as the controlling instruments governing land use. In *Peterson v. Klamath Falls,* the supreme court held that annexation is a planning responsibility because of its "significant impact on present and future land uses" (*Peterson v. Klamath Falls*). Ever since *Peterson,* the "significant impact" test has been used to determine if a local government action is a land use decision. The *Peterson* decision expanded significantly the scope of decisions subject to land use laws and regulations. Finally, in *Meyer v. Lord,* the supreme court answered some fundamental questions in favor of the land use program, including its constitutionality (*Meyer v. Lord*). (See box insert for a summary of important court cases.)

The consequence of these and other landmark decisions was that local comprehensive plans became legally binding blueprints for all land use decisions. In turn, local plans had to conform to statewide planning goals. If local conditions changed such that the plans were no longer consistent with state planning goals, then the plans had to be revised and brought back into consistency.

Enforcement Orders

Although Senate Bill 100 authorized LCDC to prepare and administer comprehensive plans for cities and counties that did not meet LCDC's acknowledgment guidelines by 1976, such authority was never used, and it was not considered a credible threat. The 1977 legislature therefore repealed LCDC's preemptory authority and replaced it with authority to issue *enforcement orders.*

When the LCDC adopts an enforcement order it must specify the nature of the local noncompliance and the corrective action local governments must take. If such an order is continued after granting a hearing and, perhaps, an appeal, LCDC may limit or prohibit specific land use actions—including subdivision approvals and the issuance of building

Key Oregon Court Cases

This is a summary of key court cases in Oregon that guide or are based on Oregon's statewide land use planning program. Many are now cited in legal texts and in court cases of other states.

Fasano v. Washington County Board of Commissioners 240 OR 574; 507 P2d 23 (1973). This case established the difference between quasi-judicial and legislative land use matters. Quasi-judicial zoning hearings must afford the parties enhanced due process, including the right to be heard and rebut evidence. The case also established critical decision making criteria, including: (1) the decision must be consistent with the comprehensive plan, (2) there must be a public need for the change requested, and (3) the need must be best served by changing the classification of the particular property.

Baker v. City of Milwaukie 271 OR 500; 533 P2d 772 (1975). This case established that zone changes and amendments must be consistent with the comprehensive plan. The case involved a zone change to a higher density than reflected in the city land use map.

Green v. Hayward 275 OR 693; 552 P2d 815 (1976). Established that the record built during a quasi-judicial hearing on a land use matter must be sufficiently based on state planning goals and guidelines to be justified.

Peterson v. City of Klamath Falls 279 OR 249; 566 P2d 1193 (1977). Furthered the requirement that planning and zoning decisions be consistent with statewide planning goals. The case also implied that certain goals, such as agricultural land preservation, were more important outside urban areas than were other goals, such as housing and urbanization.

Seaman et al. v. City of Durham LCDC 77-025 (1977). An administrative ruling by the LCDC, which found that the city of Durham's downzoning of residential density was in violation of the state's housing goal (Goal 10) in that it decreased housing diversity and did not result in the city providing its regional fair share of low-income housing.

Still v. Board of Commissioners of Marion County 600 P2d 433 (1979) and *Jurgenson v. County Court for Union County* 600 P2d 1241 (1979). Established that, in the absence of LCDC approval of a local comprehensive plan, subdivision approval within an area zoned for the density proposed for the subdivision must itself be consistent with statewide planning goals.

Columbia Hills Development Company v. Land Conservation and Development Commission 624 P2d 157 (1981). Established that, in subdivisions approved before enactment of the state planning goals and in the absence of a local plan approved by the LCDC, the first issuance of building permits, which is normally a ministerial function, must instead be reviewed in a quasi-judicial hearing for consistency of the subdivision with the statewide planning goals.

Dickas v. City of Beaverton 757 P2d 451 (1988). Established that one consideration in allowing a change to local plans or land use regulations must be consistency with the statewide planning goals. The case also established that the capacity of public facilities and services may be considered in changes to plans or land use regulations.

Smith v. Clackamas County 797 P2d 1058 (1990). Established that nonfarm dwellings cannot be physically constructed on prime agricultural farmland even if the nonfarm dwelling otherwise meets all other criteria for construction

permits. LCDC may also withhold grants and state aids and seek enforcement through court action.

Periodic Review

Because Senate Bill 100 was silent on the role of LCDC after plans were acknowledged, the legislature amended the Oregon Land Use Act in 1981 and again in 1983 to extend the act into this new era. The amended act did not require local governments to submit to LCDC all plan amendments, but did require local governments to notify the LCDC if a proposed amendment might affect one of the statewide goals. The amended act required LCDC to review all acknowledged plans at three- to five-year intervals, to identify potential problem areas, and to see that local governments adjusted their plans accordingly.[9] The LCDC retains the power to issue enforcement orders in the *postacknowledgment* period.

CHANGING DIRECTION

As the land use program continued to evolve during the early 1980s, the United States entered its most severe recession since World War II— a recession particularly cruel to the interest-sensitive economies of the

Northwest. Moreover, by 1983, ten years after the program began, some local comprehensive plans had still not been acknowledged. With the economy in the depths of recession, and following two years of population loss, concern emerged that the program was inflexible, insensitive to the concerns of property owners, and detrimental to economic growth.

An initiative petition to rescind the Oregon Land Use Act, similar to petitions soundly defeated in 1974 and 1978, seriously threatened the program's survival in 1982. At various times during that year, polls indicated that the initiative would pass. Former Governor McCall, then visibly dying of cancer, implored voters to give the program one more chance. Those opposing the initiative launched an aggressive advertising campaign, portraying developers as greedy despoilers of wilderness areas. Those supporting the initiative accused the land use program of contributing to, if not causing, Oregon's economic malaise.

Just prior to the election, then–Governor Victor Atiyeh commissioned a task force to study the impact of Oregon's land use program on economic development (Governor's Task Force on Land Use in Oregon 1982). The task force was headed by a highly respected former legislator and eastern Oregon hog rancher, Stafford Hansel. The task force recommended significant changes in the process of land use regulation and in the content of land use plans. To assure that the LCDC would implement those recommendations, Governor Atiyeh convinced the commission to elect Hansel as its chair.

Following the recommendations of the task force, the 1983 legislature passed two bills that significantly altered the direction of the program. House Bill 2296 and Senate Bill 237 required the following: (1) accelerating the acknowledgment process, (2) streamlining the permit process, (3) defining policies to show how they encourage economic development, and (4) balancing land use interests more equitably in rural areas (Oregon DLCD 1984).

Accelerating the Acknowledgment Process

Legislation passed in 1983 greatly accelerated the acknowledgment process by easing acknowledgment standards. Before 1983, local government plans had to conform to the letter, and often the liberal interpretation, of each of the planning goals. Prior to 1983, therefore, special interest groups could successfully challenge many plans for inconsistency with just one statewide planning goal. Since many goals conflict, plans were unable to withstand challenge by "one goalers," the epithet used to identify interest groups aligned mainly against development using just one goal as their position.

Since 1983, however, local governments have been allowed to demonstrate "substantial," if incomplete, compliance with the applicable goals. The substantial compliance standard accelerated plan review largely by reducing the legal influence of one-goalers.

Streamlining the Permit Process

Another significant change removed building permits from quasi-judicial review unless the issuing local government was under an enforcement order. Prior to 1983, builders and citizens were never certain they could get a building permit even if they had met all local regulations; and once they had permits, they were never certain they could build for fear that neighbors would oppose them and have the permit voided by the courts. In 1983, the legislature removed building permits as reviewable under the goals, thereby enhancing both speed and certainty in the issuance of permits (Nelson 1984).

Fostering Economic Development

Legislation passed in 1983 was motivated primarily by concerns about the effects of planning on the Oregon economy; thus the legislation contained several provisions to encourage economic development. Specifically, comprehensive plans reviewed after 1983 had to contain: a detailed analysis of the local economy, an adequate supply of suitable sites for industrial and commercial use, constraints on sites zoned for commercial and industrial land to those compatible with proposed uses, and a public facility plan to service more industrial land. Whereas planning was once considered an impediment to economic development, economic development officials after 1983 argued that state land use planning and regulation enhanced Oregon's potential for economic development (1000 Friends 1982e).

Assuring Impartial Appeals

Another change involved the legal authority of LCDC. Prior to 1979, and before a land use plan had been acknowledged by LCDC, citizens and interest groups who opposed local land use decisions could take their appeals directly to LCDC. LCDC retained its own hearings officers, who routinely recommended that LCDC hold against applicants requesting approvals for development. In every case involving the conversion of rural land to urban land, LCDC decided against the applicant, although a few cases were later reversed by the court of appeals and the supreme court. To make the appeals process more impartial and to resolve other technical legal issues, the legislature created the Land Use Board of Appeals (LUBA) in 1979. At first, LUBA's decisions were reviewed by the LCDC before going on to state courts. The LCDC could change LUBA's recommended orders, essentially reversing them. The power to prevent development thus still rested with LCDC—a power that LCDC continued to exercise. Many observers were still not satisfied with the objectivity of LUBA's jurisdiction.

The 1983 legislature severed the legal ties between LUBA and LCDC. It made LUBA tantamount to a state land use court (similar to a tax court). Land use appeals now go directly to LUBA. Appeals from LUBA go directly to the Oregon Court of Appeals, then to the supreme court. LCDC no longer has review authority, but now must decide whether to argue before LUBA as an interested party only. Eliminating LCDC's role as an adjudicator of Oregon's land use laws enabled LCDC to choose which issues to contest; and this resulted in a more impartial appeals process.

Balancing Rural Interests

One of the most significant features of the 1983 legislation was the change in standards applied to local government decisions to convert rural land to nonfarm or nonforest uses. Prior to 1983, local governments had difficulty justifying nonfarm use on land outside urban growth boundaries (UGBs). To designate land outside the UGB for uses other than farming, local governments had to demonstrate through "compelling" evidence the "impossibility" of using the land for *farm uses*. The 1983 legislation changed this requirement to allow local governments to show the "impracticability" of preserving such land. It also allowed single-family home construction on certain, narrowly defined, "lots of record." There is no doubt that additional farmland was allowed to be developed because of this change, but there is also little doubt that the change in review standards helped salvage the entire statewide planning effort (Nelson and Recht 1988).

In large part because the legislature forced LCDC to ease the standards for acknowledgment, the 278th and final comprehensive plan was acknowledged on 7 August 1986, more than ten years after the original deadline. The planning phase of the program had come to a close. It had cost the state government more than $50 million.[10] There had been no accounting of the monetary cost incurred by local governments, either directly in planning or indirectly in defending themselves in law suits filed by developers and special-interest planning groups. But in spite of the monetary and political costs, the program had reached a milestone not reached by any other state: every acre of land in Oregon had become part of a state-approved comprehensive plan.

After entering the postacknowledgment period, LCDC focused much of its attention on assuring that comprehensive plans fostered economic development and that the programs of state agencies were consistent with local comprehensive plans. But following seven years of renewed economic growth, the pendulum began to swing once again away from economic development and toward growth management. As the Oregon economy gained momentum, in-migration once again outpaced out-migration, especially in the Portland metropolitan area, and once again placed development pressures on Oregon farmland. Thus in 1989, the legislature appropriated funds to DLCD to explore urban growth management issues and to propose new strategies for managing urban growth.

AN INTERPRETIVE LOOK BACK

In the course of about 70 years, land use regulation in Oregon has changed dramatically. Where it once entailed zoning at the option of city governments, today it includes citizen participation, comprehensive planning, state acknowledgment, periodic review, enforcement, appeals, LCDC, DLCD, LUBA, and more. Although each of the three legislative acts passed from 1969 to 1973 precipitated stark and revolutionary change, the process of planning was modified almost continuously in response to equally continuous social change.

Oregon's land use program rests on five major land use acts passed in response to specific land use problems. The City Planning and Zoning Enabling Act enabled cities to plan and zone in response to rapid urban growth. The County Planning and Zoning Enabling Act enabled counties to plan and zone in response to uncontrolled suburban growth. Senate Bill 10 required cities and counties to plan and zone, to control the urbanization of the Willamette Valley. The Coastal Zone Management Act established state participation in planning and zoning, to protect state interests in the coastal zone. Finally, Senate Bill 100 required local plans to meet statewide goals and guidelines, to assure that local plans serve state land use interests.

As a result of these five land use acts, Oregon now has in place an intergovernmental planning system, a system in which state and local governments jointly control land use. Comprehensive planning by local governments encourages participation in land use decision making by those most closely familiar with and affected by such decisions. Review of local comprehensive plans by the state prevents local governments from adopting plans that would be detrimental to larger statewide interests. While local planning with state review naturally creates tension between state and local interests, the tension has been tempered by an extensive body of administrative rules and judicial interpretations.

The intergovernmental structure of Oregon's program influences the objectives as well as the process of planning. Compared to purely local systems of land use control, combined state and local systems of control enfranchise a wider geographic constituency. Perhaps, then, the major structural difference between planning in Oregon and planning in other states is the ability of nonlocal interests in Oregon to participate in local land use decision making throughout the state.

Oregon's planning structure also affects how land use plans adapt to change. Requiring state acknowledgment or review, comprehensive plans in Oregon take longer to prepare and to change—when change is initiated by local governments. But, for the same reason, comprehensive plans serve as vehicles for expedient land use policy change—when change is initiated by state government.

The ability of state government to instigate sweeping change in land use policy has had both beneficial and detrimental effects. The state's ability to change the process and direction of planning enabled the state to use land use planning as a means of responding to the vagaries of the Oregon economy. As a result, the policy focus of LCDC has swung widely from conservation to development and perhaps back to conservation. While such an ability to change focus has enabled the state to maintain political support for the program, it has perhaps also undermined the purpose of state involvement in planning and regulation. This is a topic for subsequent chapters.

A STRATEGY FOR ANALYSIS

Although much has been written about Oregon's land use program, there have been no previous attempts to analyze its effects systematically—and for good reasons. First, land use planning addresses many, often competing, long-term goals. Thus identifying all the potential effects of planning is perhaps impossible—especially at the state level. Second, the instruments used to control land use and the intended effects of those instruments in Oregon have changed, thus rapidly depreciating the utility of any one study. Finally, planning in Oregon is performed by state and local governments; the counter example—in other states and before 1973—is planning by local governments. But because we can never know how local governments in Oregon would have planned without state participation, we can never know for certain how planning differs with state participation. And states differ in too many critical respects for rigorously comparing land use programs among them. Therefore, conventional policy analyses, with experimental or quasi-experimental controls, are not feasible.

In spite of these obstacles, we can derive many lessons from the Oregon experience. Economists, geographers, lawyers, political scientists, public administrators, and land use planners have explored the effects of Oregon's land use program on selected issues at particular times. The chapters that follow review the findings of nearly two decades of such exploration. The chapters proceed by introducing a selected land use issue, describing how Oregon has addressed the issue, reviewing studies exploring the issue, and discussing the policy lessons provided by the Oregon experience. While recognizing both the limitations of previous research and the bias of interpretation, the chapters proffer insights into the performance and prospects of state land use reform, insights perhaps valuable to those now beginning or considering similar land use reforms.

Notes

1. Oregon's annexation laws require a triple majority of support to succeed. This means that annexation must receive the support of the majority of residents, the majority of land owners, and the majority of land owners weighted by assessed value.

2. See Knaap (1987b), Plotkin (1987), Heiman (1988) and chapter 8 for more on the relationship between social structure and land use reform.

3. For more on the Oregon agricultural economy, see chapter 5.

4. The state had minor programs in land use policy from 1935 to 1939, when a state planning board provided local governments with recommendations on how to utilize, conserve, and develop natural resources, and again in 1955, when the state established a technical assistance program to administer federal funds under the "701" planning assistance program (BGRS 1984).

5. Also passed in 1973 was Senate Bill 101, which established important features of Oregon's farmland preservation program. See chapter 5.

6. See Little (1974), Leonard (1983), DeGrove (1984), and chapter 7 for more on Oregon state land use politics.

7. Although LCDC technically retained authority over all land use decisions, during the preacknowledgment period, the commission never became involved in day-to-day decisions. Instead, local governments had to write *findings* against the state's goals when making local land use decisions. After their plans were acknowledged, local governments had to meet only the standards of their own plans.

8. State authority over local land use action prior to acknowledgment had two positive but unintended effects. It provided an added incentive to local governments to have their plans acknowledged and it resulted in a large body of judicial interpretations of the land use statutes (Liberty 1989b).

9. The 1987 legislature changed the cycle of periodic reviews to range from four to seven years.

10. The total amount budgeted for DLCD and LCDC from 1973 through 1989 (eight biennial budgets) was $50,098,621. One-third of that came from the federal government for coastal zone management. Fifty-six percent of the total budget went directly to cities and counties as grants.

2

Urban Growth Boundaries and Urban Growth Management

B EFORE 1973 LAND USE was determined in Oregon as in every other
state: land use changed when private developers purchased land
and obtained building permits and urban services from local governments. After 1973 the process of land development in Oregon changed
dramatically. Following the passage of Senate Bill 100, every local government was required to prepare a comprehensive land use plan, every plan
had to be approved by the State Land Conservation and Development
Commission (LCDC), and every local government had to make land use
decisions consistent with its comprehensive plan. Urban growth boundaries
(UGBs), which now encompass all urban areas in the state, represent a key
component of urban-area comprehensive planning in Oregon.

This chapter explores the effects of UGBs on the land market and urban
development. The chapter begins by presenting urban economic theory,
which provides hypotheses about how UGBs might affect land value and
urban development. The presentation highlights how perceptions of UGBs
changed with experience and empirical research. After presenting theory,
the chapter reviews empirical evidence on the effects of UGBs on urban
land value and urban development. The chapter concludes with policy
lessons for Oregon and other states.

URBAN GROWTH BOUNDARIES

Urban growth boundaries separate urban land from *rural land* and are the
cornerstone of the Oregon land use program. The concept of the UGBs
originated in Salem, as that city and the counties of Marion and Polk

struggled to manage Salem metropolitan growth. This struggle led to the first urban development stop line adopted anywhere in the United States (Nelson 1984). In short, the UGB is a line that delineates where urban development may take place in a metropolitan area; land within the UGB may be developed for urban use; land outside the UGB may not.

Following the model pioneered in Salem, the architects of the statewide land use program included UGBs as a central feature. Goal 14 (Urbanization) is, "To provide for an orderly and efficient transition from rural to urban land use." To achieve this goal, LCDC requires that, "Urban growth boundaries shall be established to identify and separate *urbanizable land* from rural land" (Oregon LCDC 1990).

From the beginning the UGB concept featured an intergovernmental approach to urban growth management. Today, with state participation in the delineation, implementation, and enforcement of all UGBs, intergovernmental participation remains a characteristic feature of the growth-boundary system. Under state land use goals and guidelines, local governments may, at their discretion, use tax incentives and disincentives, fee and less-than-fee acquisition, zoning, and urban service programming to guide urban development within UGBs; local governments may not, however, under the force of state law, allow urban development outside an acknowledged UGB. Therefore, UGBs are enforced jointly by local governments and the state, while land use controls inside and outside UGBs are enforced only by local governments. This hierarchy of enforcement standardizes statewide the restrictions embodied in UGBs, while allowing variability in the management of growth within UGBs.

The primary function of UGBs was to help manage urban growth. Whereas other growth management instruments adopted in the early 1970s featured density zoning, development moratoria, and population caps, UGBs were intended, not to limit growth, but simply to manage the process and location of growth. By restricting urban development to a well-defined, contiguous area—the size of which is based on the best available information about urban development trends—UGBs were expected to accommodate urban growth without permitting urban sprawl.[1]

The objectives of UGBs, as specified by LCDC, include: preservation of prime farmland; efficient provision of public facilities; reduction of air, water, and land pollution; and creation of a distinctly urban ambience. When determining UGBs, local governments were required to make them large enough to meet the requirements for housing, industry and commerce, recreation, open space, and all other urban land uses until the year

2000. All land not contained within UGBs was subsequently designated for rural use until after 2000. Specifically, UGBs were to be established based on the following factors:

1. Demonstrated need to accommodate long-range urban population growth requirements consistent with LCDC goals
2. Need for housing, employment opportunities, and livability
3. Orderly and economic provision of public facilities and services
4. Maximum efficiency for land uses within, and on the fringe of, the existing urban area
5. Environmental, energy, economic, and social consequences
6. Retention of agricultural land as defined, with Class I being the highest priority for retention and Class VI the lowest priority, and
7. Compatibility of the proposed urban uses with nearby agricultural activities.

Although they appeared relatively simple in concept, UGBs proved difficult to implement. Part of the difficulty stemmed from uncertainty over the rate of urban development, which made it problematic for planners to determine exactly how much land to include inside a UGB. Too little *urban land* could cause land price inflation; too much would not contain urban sprawl. Such concerns led many local governments to overestimate demands for urban land and err on the side of UGBs that would perhaps turn out to be too big.

Implementation of UGBs introduced political problems as well. Although boundary delineation was intended to be a cooperative affair, turf battles often arose between cities and their county governments, and, in larger metropolitan areas, among city governments. Later, conflicts often ensued between local governments and the Department of Land Conservation and Development (DLCD), the administrative arm of LCDC. According to LCDC, local governments frequently sought to include more land inside UGBs than was justified by demographic and economic trends. In most cases, LCDC forced local governments to reduce the sizes of their UGBs. Although it is difficult to generalize about the impact of this interaction, it appears that the LCDC's review of UGBs resulted in less land becoming eligible for urban development than would have been eligible under a purely local land use program (Knaap 1989b).

Through the acknowledgment process, UGBs have become well known and widely accepted policy instruments in Oregon, although not all the technical and political problems have been solved. At this writing, the process of expanding, amending, or renewing UGBs has not yet been fully determined. Considerable controversy remains on what should be done with land immediately inside and outside UGBs. Although the art and science of growth management in Oregon have greatly improved through experience, there are still many unresolved problems with UGBs as growth management instruments.

THEORY OF UGB
IMPACTS ON LAND VALUE

Research on the effects of UGBs began soon after the tool was established. Although UGBs were multi-objective instruments, most research on the effects of UGBs focused on land value—for two probable reasons. First, most of the early analyses of UGBs were conducted by economists. According to conventional economic theory, instruments that influence land use or land allocation must affect land value. Based on economic reasoning, then, a test for UGB impacts on land value is, in effect, a test for UGB impacts on land use and land allocation. The second reason for focusing on the land value impacts of UGBs was the widespread speculation that the state land use program—and UGBs in particular—had contributed to, if not caused, the rapid escalation of Oregon's land and housing prices in the late 1970s.[2] Although UGBs were intended to constrain urban growth, they were not intended to raise housing costs. Thus, the influence of UGBs on land value was, and remains, a key political issue.

The economics and politics of the relationship between UGBs and land value deserve some emphasis. Because increases in land value, and thus housing cost, are politically unattractive, many supporters of land use planning insist that UGBs do not influence land value, or at least not very much (Liberty 1989b). If so, however, then by economic logic, UGBs do not influence urban growth and development, or at least not very much. Ironically, studies showing that UGBs do indeed influence land value, and thus serve as effective policy instruments, have not been well received by supporters of Oregon's land use program. Contrary to popular beliefs, such evidence indicates that UGBs *are* effective policy instruments.

UGBs as Supply Constraints

The first theoretical analysis of the effects of UGBs on land value was published by Whitelaw (1980) for the Urban Land Institute. Viewing UGBs as potential constraints on urban land supplies, Whitelaw argued that UGBs, if effective, would raise the value of unimproved urban land. Holding other things constant, the land values inside UGBs would be higher than land values outside UGBs. This effect occurs when those who would have bid for urban land outside UGBs are constrained to bid for land inside UGBs. UGBs, then, operate much like ordinary zoning constraints, increasing urban land value by reducing the supply of urban land below the market-prescribed level.[3]

Figure 2 illustrates the effects of UGBs as supply constraints. In figure 2, R_m represents the land value gradient for urban land in the absence of a UGB; R_g represents the land value gradient for urban land after the imposition of a UGB at u_2. Following the imposition of the UGB, land values at greater distances beyond the boundary fall because urban development is no longer allowed. At the same time, land values inside the boundary at u_2 rise, as those who would have bid for land outside the UGB are constrained to bid for land inside the boundary. The gap in the gradient R_g, then, offers a measure of the effects of the UGB: the greater the gap, the greater the impact.

If UGBs indeed restrict the urban land supply, and thereby result in a higher urban land value, then UGBs lead to higher-density development.

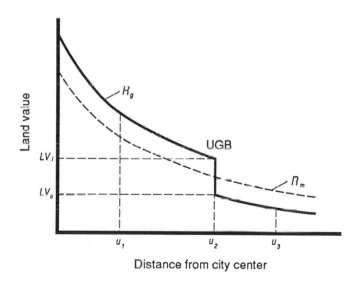

Figure 2. UGBs as Supply Constraints

This occurs as developers economize on the relatively more costly input, land, and substitute for land the relatively less costly input, capital. As a result, urban development inside the UGB becomes more capital-intensive and less land-intensive. Supply-constraining UGBs thus produce more compact and densely developed cities.[4]

UGBs as Timing Constraints

Knaap (1982, 1985) extended Whitelaw's analysis. Knaap observed that UGBs are imposed on an existing patchwork of zoning constraints. Therefore, because land on both sides of UGBs is zoned, the supply of urban land is constrained by zoning, not by UGBs. UGBs, according to Knaap, affect land value by specifying when existing zoning restrictions can be changed. Land zoned for rural use outside UGBs will remain so until at least the year 2000; land zoned for rural use inside the UGB may not. Thus UGBs affect land value only by influencing the expected date of zoning changes.

The effects of UGBs as timing constraints are illustrated in figure 3. In figure 3, R_u and R_r represent the land value gradients for urban and rural

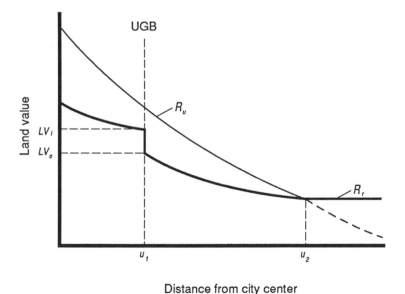

Figure 3.   UGBs as Timing Constraints

The Mathematics of UGBs as Timing Constraints

Knaap's theory of the influence of UGBs on land value can be illustrated with the following simple example. Suppose there are 100 parcels of land in the urban fringe currently in rural use but with potential for urban development next year. Suppose further that market conditions—including conditions imposed by local governments—would result in the development of one-half of the 100 parcels next year. Assuming a two-year time frame for simplicity, the land values of each of the 100 parcels could be expressed as follows:

1. $LV = R_r + 0.5[R_r/(1+i)^1] + 0.5[R_u/(1+i)^1]$

where, L = land value,
R_r = annual rent in rural use,
R_u = annual rent in urban use,
i = the real discount rate, and
$R_u > R_r$.

Here, the first term on the right-hand side captures the value of rural rents in the current year; the second two terms capture the discounted expected value of rents in the second year. Rents in the second year have a 50 percent chance of remaining at the rural level and a 50 percent chance of increasing to the urban level. The value of all 100 parcels, then, contains a speculative component equal to the expected value of future rents.

Now suppose that the UGB established with perfect certainty which 50 parcels will be converted to urban use next year and which parcels will not. The land values of parcels inside the UGB and outside the UGB can then be expressed as follows:

2. $LV_o = R_r + R_r/(1+i)^1$, and

3. $LV_i = R_r + R_u/(1+i)^1$

where, LV_o = the present value of land outside the UGB,
LV_i = the present value of land inside the UGB, and
therefore, $LV_i > LV_o$.

The value of the 50 parcels outside the UGB now equals the present value of rural rents for two years. The value of the 50 parcels inside the UGB now equals the value of rural rents in the current year plus the discounted value of urban rents in the second year. Thus the UGB, as an indicator of future urban use, can transfer speculative value from land outside UGBs to land inside UGBs, while not affecting the supply of urban land.

land, respectively, where the allowed use and thus land value are deter-mined by zoning. Urban land values are influenced by a number of fac-tors—such as location, neighborhood quality, and urban services—but not by the presence of the UGB. Because UGBs do not influence the future zoning of urban land, urban land values would be equal on both sides of a UGB (if land were zoned for urban use on both sides).

Land values in rural zones, however, are influenced by UGBs. This occurs because rural land inside UGBs may, through zoning changes, be-come urban land before the year 2000. Rural land outside UGBs, however, may not. Therefore, rural land values will be higher inside UGBs due only to expectations of sooner conversion to urban land. Thus, according to Knaap, UGBs affect land value only in rural zones via expectations con-cerning the timing of zoning changes.[5]

UGBs as Location Constraints

Nelson (1985a, 1985b, 1986b) extended Knaap's analysis by focusing on spillover effects between urban and rural land uses. Nelson, viewing exclu-sive farm use zoning outside UGBs as privately held greenbelts, suggested that urban residents near the UGB might enjoy the benefits of rural scen-ery, open space, environmental quality, and other rural amenities.[6] Simi-larly, farmers near the UGB might suffer congestion costs, pollution, and other urban disamenities. If so, Nelson argued, then these location-specific characteristics would be capitalized into land values. Holding other things constant, urban land values will be higher near rural land, and rural land values will be lower near urban land. Thus, according to Nelson, UGBs affect land value by specifying, for some period of time, the boundary between nonconforming land uses.

Figure 4 illustrates how land values might vary with distance from UGBs. In figure 4, land values inside the UGB fall with distance from the urban core until distance u_1; beyond there, land values increase with distance, as the value of proximity to the UGB more than offsets the decline in value due to distance from the urban core. Land values outside the UGB increase with distance from the urban core until u_3; beyond there, the decline in value of distance to the urban core more than offsets the increase in value due to distance from the UGB.

These theoretical analyses of UGBs suggest that they may affect land value and land allocation in three ways. First, UGBs can affect land value by restricting the supply of urban land. In this respect UGBs may increase

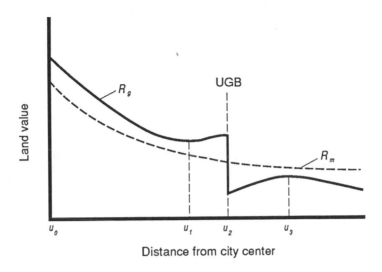

Figure 4.   UGBs as Use Constraints

the density of urban development by increasing the price of urban land. Second, UGBs can affect land value by specifying future zoning changes. In this respect UGBs may alter expectations concerning future land use, which in turn may alter current development decisions. Finally, UGBs can affect land value by specifying the boundary between nonconforming land uses. In this respect UGBs may define the location of future urban development, which may alter current location decisions.

EVIDENCE OF UGB
IMPACTS ON LAND VALUE

The empirical evidence concerning the effects of UGBs on land value is now sizable. Without exception, researchers have used the hedonic price approach to estimate the contribution to value of various land attributes. Hedonic price estimation uses statistical techniques to identify the influence of land characteristics on the market price of land.[7] The technique can identify, for example, how much land values on opposite sides of a UGB differ, holding other things constant.

An Illustrative Hedonic Price Equation

The hedonic price equation can be expressed as follows:

$$P = B_0 + (B_1)(X_1) + (B_2)(X_2) + (B_3)UGB + e$$

where, P = price per acre of land,
X_1 = various land attributes,
X_2 = local land use policies,
UGB = location relative to the UGB,
1 = outside,
e = a random error.

In the above equation, the B_i terms capture the contributions to value of various land attributes. For example, B_3 captures the price effects of UGBs; if B_3 is significant and negative, then land values are lower outside UGBs than inside UGBs.

The Salem-Area UGB in 1976

The first empirical analysis of the effects of a UGB on land value was conducted by Beaton et al. in Salem. By no coincidence, the concept of the UGB was born in Salem, the state capital. In the early 1970s, the Salem metropolitan area housed many state and federal offices, included several large unincorporated areas (one of which has since incorporated as the city of Keizer), extended over two counties, and grew rapidly. Managing Salem's growth thus required an intergovernmental approach. As a result, the Salem planning commission, along with the planning commissions of Marion and Polk Counties, adopted the UGB as part of the Salem-area comprehensive plan (figure 5). According to Leonard (1983), the Salem-area UGB was "masterminded" by Wes Kvarston, who later became the first director of DLCD.

Concerns over the effects of UGBs on land value created controversy when the Salem-area UGB was drawn. Planners faced angry property owners—some who wanted their property inside, and others who wanted their property outside, the UGB. Planners also encountered conflict between the city of Salem and Polk and Marion Counties. Most challenging to planners, however, were developers who claimed that the UGB would inflate land prices by restricting the supply of land (à la Whitelaw 1980). As a result, in 1974 the Mid-Willamette Valley Council of Governments adopted a UGB for the Salem area that contained 25 percent more land than necessary to achieve 100 percent buildout in the year 2000, based on urban

SOURCE: Nelson 1986b

Figure 5. Salem-Area Urban Growth Boundary, 1976

growth projections. This "market factor" was designed to facilitate choice in the marketplace and to prevent land price inflation.

To test whether the Salem-area UGB in fact restricted land supplies, the Mid-Willamette Valley Council of Governments in 1975 commissioned a study by Beaton, Hanson, and Hibbard (1977). Beaton et al. gathered data on 105 undeveloped parcels of land, located both inside and outside the Salem UGB, which had been sold at arm's length in 1976. These observations were then used to identify the determinants of land value. The results are reported in table 2.

By including four variables in addition to the UGB, Beaton et al. were able to explain approximately 40 percent of the variation in land values, but they could not attribute any of the variation to the UGB. That is, holding other things constant, they did not find land values inside the UGB statistically different from land values outside the UGB. From these results they concluded that in 1976 the UGB did not constrain the supply of urban land in the Salem metropolitan area.

Although the data used by Beaton et al. were limited, the results were plausible. In 1976, the UGB was a new planning instrument in Salem and had been drawn to include a 25 percent surplus of land. Thus the UGB had not constrained the supply of land nor had it influenced the expecta-

Table 2.   Determinants of Land Value, Marion and Polk Counties, 1976

Variable	Regression coefficient, price per acre (t)		
	1976 (N = 105; R^2 = 0.38)	1974 (N = 17)	1970 (N = 26; R^2 = 0.42)
Intercept	8,531.4 (7.33)	698.4 (0.15)	3,814.3 (4.71)
Time[a]	−17.9 (0.71)	599.7 (1.20)	−140.9 (1.82)
School[b]	−1,323.0 (2.73)	−1,095.0 (0.43)	−130.2 (0.42)
DSER[c]	−2,673.0 (3.95)	−2,944.0 (0.88)	31.94 (0.07)
DUGB[d]	−11.6 (0.02)	−733.6 (0.21)	−181.1 (0.33)
Class[e]	−2,690.0 (6.11)	−1,410.0 (0.85)	−592.5 (2.26)

[a]Travel time from central business district.
[b]Indicates if parcel is in 24J school district.
[c]Indicates if parcel is serviceable.
[d]Indicates if parcel is outside the UGB.
[e]Land classification.
SOURCE: Beaton et al. 1977

tions of participants in the land market. The availability of urban services, at the time, was the most significant indicator of development potential. In the Beaton study, therefore, the availability of sewer services was the most significant determinant of unimproved land values. Thus, in spite of the study's limitations, its conclusion that the UGB had no effect on land values was probably quite accurate.

The Beaton study was widely read and very influential. It provided supporters of the state land use program with valuable empirical evidence that UGBs could be drawn without increasing urban land value. Had the Beaton study found otherwise, UGBs may never have been used anywhere in Oregon outside Salem.

The Portland-Area UGB in 1980

The next empirical analysis of the effects of UGBs on land value was conducted in 1980 by Knaap (1982, 1985) in the Portland metropolitan area. Perhaps even more than in Salem, the construction and acknowledgment of the metropolitan Portland UGB involved a heated and protracted political process.[8]

The Portland metropolitan area encompassed nearly 30 units of government, but responsibility for delineating the metropolitan UGB belonged to the Columbia Region Association of Governments (CRAG). Based on the Beaton findings, CRAG included in the Portland metropolitan UGB 25 percent more land than they projected was necessary for urban development until the year 2000. LCDC, however, rejected CRAG's boundary, claiming it contained too much land. After removing only three square miles of land, CRAG resubmitted the UGB to LCDC. Then in 1979 CRAG was replaced by the Metropolitan Service District (Metro), a new and unique, elected, regional government with independent budgetary and land use authority.[9] As one of its first official acts, while the UGB was still being reviewed by LCDC, Metro adopted CRAG's UGB.

Although LCDC still believed that the Metro UGB was too large, it was anxious to proceed with the acknowledgment process and reluctant to antagonize an elected government representing over half the population of the state, including the state's largest city. Thus Metro and LCDC struck a compromise. LCDC would acknowledge Metro's UGB, but Metro would place a ten-year moratorium on residential development in areas designated as prime agricultural land. This in effect created an intermediate growth boundary (IGB) within the urban growth boundary. Land within the IGB

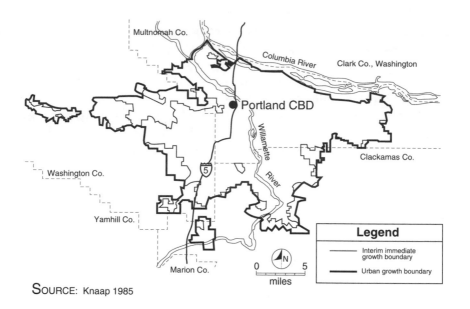

SOURCE: Knaap 1985

Figure 6. Portland-Area Urban Growth Boundaries, 1980

could be developed immediately; land within the UGB but outside the IGB could not be developed for ten years, and land outside the UGB could not be developed until the year 2000 (figure 6).

Although the UGB acknowledged by LCDC was larger than necessary under the specifications of Goal 14, it was smaller than either CRAG or Metro would have adopted alone. The revised UGB contained a 15.3 percent *market factor* of excess vacant land; enough, according to Metro (1979) "that the market will not be affected for some years into the future."

Funded in part by Metro, Knaap examined the effects of the Portland UGB on land value. Knaap gathered data on over 900 unimproved land sales recorded in fiscal year 1979–1980 in the Portland metropolitan area. Including ten explanatory variables, in addition to the UGB, Knaap was able to explain nearly 75 percent of the variation in land values. Knaap also included a variable to capture the effects on land value of the intermediate growth boundary, the result of the political compromise between Metro and the LCDC.

Knaap found the effects of the UGB significant in both Washington and Clackamas Counties. (Knaap had no observations from Multnomah County outside the UGB.) In a report submitted to Metro, Knaap (1981) states: "The predicted value of a raw acre of land 50 minutes from downtown Portland equals $35,697 if located inside the UGB, while the predicted value of the same acre falls to $19,688 if located outside the UGB." (See table 3.) Metro was surprised by the results. Because the UGB contained a large excess supply of land, Metro argued, the UGB could not possibly have influenced land values (Metro undated). Knaap replied that the UGB had been in place long enough to influence the expectations of participants in the land market and thus had affected land value even without affecting land supply (as in The Mathematics of UGBs as Timing Constraints, see previous box insert).

Knaap supported his argument by examining the influence of the IGB on land zoned for urban and rural use. At the time of the Knaap study, there were parcels of land outside the IGB that had already been committed and thus zoned for urban use, especially in Washington County. By demonstrating that the IGB influenced the value of land currently zoned for rural use, but not the value of land currently zoned for urban use, Knaap argued that the IGB (and thus the UGB) affects land value by specifying the timing of zoning changes, not the supply of urban land.

Knaap also found that land use instruments other than the UGB—such as the IGB, zoning, and sewer services—had different effects on land values in Washington and Clackamas Counties. Specifically, Knaap found that zoning and the IGB each influenced land values significantly in Washington County but not in Clackamas County. These findings Knaap attributed to the difference between locally enforced land use instruments and the state-enforced UGB. With supporting evidence from Metro (1979), Knaap argued that Washington County, which had large areas with access to sewer and water services, managed growth within the UGB by strictly enforcing its current and future zoning designations; these designations thus significantly influenced land values in that county. Clackamas County, however, managed growth within the UGB not by zoning, but by the availability of sewer services; thus—as in Salem—the availability of sewer services was the most influential determinant of land value in Clackamas County.

The Salem-Area UGB in 1977–79

With one prior study finding no UGB influence in Salem and another finding a significant UGB influence in Portland, Nelson (1985a 1985b,

Table 3. Determinants of Land Value, Washington and Clackamas Counties, 1979 to 1980

| Variable | Regression coefficient, price per acre $(t)^p$ | |
	Washington County (N = 267; R^2 = 0.81)	Clackamas County (N = 188; R^2 = 0.79)
Intercept	11.061	−5.571
Urban	0.267 (1.80)**	−0.407 (1.74)^{ns}
Nonurban UGB	−0.980 (4.10)***	−0.645 (2.50)***
Nonurban IGB	−0.944 (5.57)***	−0.258 (0.78)^{ns}
Urban IGB	−0.005 (0.03)^{ns}	−0.064 (0.28)^{ns}
Access to Portland CBD	−0.404 (2.36)***	−0.019 (0.12)^{ns}
Size of plot	−0.186 (2.85)***	−0.665 (10.12)***
Access to sewer	0.148 (1.71)**	0.470 (2.79)***
Platted	0.506 (4.23)***	0.084 (0.44)^{ns}
Outside incorporated city	−0.374 (3.61)***	−0.140 (1.11)^{ns}

Since both the dependent and independent variables are expressed in logarithmic terms, the coefficients can be interpreted as elasticities, i.e., percentage change.

** $p < 0.05$, one-tailed test.
*** $p < 0.01$, one-tailed test.
^{ns} p not significant.
n.a. not applicable.
SOURCE: Knapp 1981

Continued on next page

Table 3. *Continued*

Variable	Regression coefficient, price per acre $(t)^p$	
	Washington County ($N = 267$; $R^2 = 0.81$)	Clackamas County ($N = 188$; $R^2 = 0.79$)
Location in Portland	0.255 $(0.48)^{ns}$	n.a. n.a.
Tax rate	0.414 $(0.95)^{ns}$	−1.442 $(3.35)^{***}$
Median income	1.055 $(2.31)^{***}$	0.311 $(1.11)^{ns}$
Percentage white	−1.048 $(0.39)^{ns}$	6.278 $(1.34)^{ns}$
Slope of land	−0.108 $(0.50)^{ns}$	0.087 $(0.89)^{ns}$
Date of sale	0.085 $(1.73)^{**}$	0.057 $(1.16)^{ns}$
F	72.38	45.75

1986a, 1986b) returned to Salem to break the deadlock. Reevaluating the Salem UGB was a particularly appropriate research strategy. By doing so, Nelson was able to show that the effects of UGBs on land value varied not by metropolitan area, but instead by the extent to which participants in the land market perceived the UGB as a binding instrument. At the time of the Nelson study, the Salem UGB had not yet received acknowledgment from the LCDC, but participants in the Salem land market had become increasingly aware of the location and meaning of the UGB (Leonard 1983).

Nelson gathered data on 209 unimproved land sales between 1977 and 1979 from within, and to three miles beyond, the Marion County portion of the Salem UGB. Nelson included ten variables in addition to the UGB and was able to explain 58 percent of the variation in land values (table 4). Although Nelson's sales observations occurred only two years after those used by Beaton et al., Nelson found land values lower outside the UGB than inside the UGB—even after controlling for the availability of sewer service. Based on these results, Nelson concluded that in Salem it took less

Table 4. Determinants of Land Value, Marion County, 1977 to 1979

Variable	Regional cases ($N = 209$; $R^2 = 0.29$)	Rural north cases ($N = 42$; $R^2 = 0.38$)	Urban north cases ($N = 40$; $R^2 = 0.47$)
	Regression coefficient, price per acre $(t)^p$		
Intercept	1,214.10	−10,072.71	22,493.49
Parcel size, in acres	−126.43 (35.47)***	−34.78 (64.60)^{ns}	56.61 (78.29)^{ns}
Date of sale (no. of months after August 1977)	168.30 (42.03)***	58.36 (75.31)^{ns}	301.71 (98.49)***
Pasture production potential, in half-ton units	240.02 (116.70)**	907.13 (279.24)***	49.48 (455.70)^{ns}
Average family income of census tract, in $100	1.48 (13.45)^{ns}	0.61 (24.61)^{ns}	−25.47 (60.60)^{ns}
Seller participation in sale	−515.44 (651.52)^{ns}	1,365.49 (1,117.30)^{ns}	−364.88 (1,369.83)^{ns}
Enrollment in farm use tax program	−1,141.40 (972.32)^{ns}	−559.26 (1,348.17)^{ns}	4,727.72 (4,243.04)^{ns}
Adjacent to urban water and sewer	1,946.91 (1,148.62)**	n.a.	2,900.40 (3,006.78)^{ns}
Presence of greenbelt zoning	−1,649.35 (1,129.47)*	−3,439.73 (1,464.80)**	n.a.
Distance from downtown Salem, in 100-foot units	0.52 (6.09)^{ns}	−33.32 (12.26)***	−57.49 (32.09)**
Location within urban growth boundary	3,877.88 (1,380.09)***	n.a.	n.a.

n.a. not applicable
* $p < 0.10$, one-tailed test.
** $p < 0.05$, one-tailed test.
*** $p < 0.01$, one-tailed test.
^{ns} p not significant.
SOURCE: Nelson 1986b

Continued on next page

Table 4. Continued

Variable	Regional cases (N = 209) (R^2 = 0.29)	Rural north cases (N = 42) R^2 = 0.38	Urban north cases (N = 40) R^2 = 0.47
	Regression coefficient, price per acre $(t)^p$		
Distance from urban growth boundary, in 100-foot units squared	n.a.	280.95 (74.68)***	−150.29 (115.01)*
Distance from urban growth boundary, in 100-foot units squared	n.a.	−1.61 (0.55)***	2.97 (1.28)**
Standard error, in $	4,297.17	3,138.87	3,443.85
Degrees of freedom	10; 198	10; 31	10; 29
F	9.97	3.48	4.20

than two years for participants in the land market to capitalize the value of a UGB into land value.

Further, Nelson found that land values varied significantly according to their distance from the boundary. By including variables to capture distance to the UGB, Nelson showed that land values inside the UGB decreased with distance from the urban core—at locations greater than 5,000 feet from the UGB—as the value of proximity to the urban core exceeded the amenity value of proximity to the UGB. Within 5,000 feet of the boundary, however, land values rose with distance from the urban core, as the amenity value of proximity to rural land beyond the UGB began to exceed the value of proximity to the urban core.

Outside the UGB, Nelson found that rural land values increased with greater distance from the urban core—at locations less than 17,000 feet from the boundary —as the value of disamenities exceeded the value of proximity. In addition, at locations beyond 17,000 feet from the UGB, rural land values decreased with distance from the urban core, as the value of proximity again exceeded the value of the urban disamenities. These results support Nelson's theory that urban residents are willing to pay a premium for a location near the UGB and that rural land owners are willing to pay a premium for a location away from the UGB. Most important, Nelson's results demonstrated that placement of the UGB provides information about future urban form that is capitalized into present land values.

EVIDENCE OF IMPACTS
ON URBAN DEVELOPMENT

Nearly a decade passed before new research was conducted on the effects of UGBs on the urban land market. The 1980s failed to produce new research for two reasons. First, high interest rates associated with the economic recession of the early 1980s had dramatically reduced the rate of urban growth, thus there was little concern about either urban land supplies or urban growth management. Second, the Oregon planning and development community had become weary with conflict over where to place UGBs and had turned its attention to development issues inside and outside UGBs.

In 1989, following several years of renewed urban growth, the Oregon legislature appropriated funds for the DLCD to evaluate the effectiveness of the state's growth management program and to determine how growth management could be improved. The legislature was motivated by two factors. First, there was increasing anecdotal evidence that urban development was occurring outside UGBs, perhaps undermining their purpose. Second, the planning horizon for which the existing UGBs had been drawn was approaching fast; therefore the time had come to consider what to do as land within UGBs became fully developed.

In response to the legislature's request, DLCD commissioned ECO Northwest to study recent development patterns inside and outside UGBs. Using data on building permits, property tax assessments, and land subdivisions, ECO Northwest examined development activity in four metropolitan areas: Portland (metropolitan population about 1.1 million, located in the northern Willamette Valley), Medford (metropolitan population about 100,000, located in the Rogue River Valley of southern Oregon), Bend (metropolitan population about 75,000, located in the Three Sisters recreation area of central Oregon), and Brookings (metropolitan population 7,500, located on the southern Oregon coast).

ECO Northwest measured the type and amount of development from 1985 to 1989 in four subsections of each study area. These subsections were defined as follows: *urban areas* were inside UGBs and had a high percentage of existing development; *urbanizable areas* were inside UGBs and had a high percentage of vacant land; *urban fringe areas* were outside UGBs but within one to two miles of them; and *exurban areas* were more than two miles outside UGBs but within reasonable commuting distance to the central city.

ECO Northwest classified development inside UGBs and outside UGBs into two additional categories. Inside UGBs, they classified land as *cities* if the development was located inside an incorporated city, or as *unincorporated* if located in an unincorporated area. Outside the UGB, locations were classified as *resource area* if zoned for exclusive resource use and as *exception area* if the land was not.[10] ECO Northwest's measures of single-family development, multiple-family development, and subdivisions in each subarea of each metropolitan area are presented in tables 5, 6, and 7 below.

Single-Family Development

As shown in table 5, the patterns of single-family development, both inside and outside UGBs, varied markedly by study area. Within UGBs, single family development ranged from 37 percent in the Bend metropolitan area to 91 percent in metropolitan Portland. Inside UGBs, single-family development in *urban areas* ranged from 7 percent in the Bend study area to 53 percent in the Portland area. Outside UGBs, single-family development in *exurban areas* ranged from 6 percent around Portland to 58 percent around Bend.

Land Subdivision

As shown in table 6, the pattern of land subdivisions varied less within the study areas than did the pattern of single-family development. New subdivision lots outside the UGB ranged from 1 percent in the Portland metropolitan area to 17 percent in the Bend area. Inside UGBs, new subdivision lots in *urban areas* ranged from 15 percent in the Medford region to 67 percent in the Portland metropolitan area. Outside UGBs, almost no land in resource areas was subdivided.

Multiple-Family Development

As shown in table 7, multiple-family development differed by jurisdiction in total only. Most multiple-family development took place in the Portland metropolitan area. Nearly all multiple-family development occurred inside

Table 5. Single-Family Development, Selected Urban Areas in Oregon, 1985 to 1989

Location	Percentage in selected categories			
	Portland	Medford	Bend	Brookings
Inside UGBs				
Inside primary UGB	90.0	34.6	33.6	55.7
Urban area	53.3	11.4	7.2	n.a.
Urbanizable area	35.9	23.2	26.4	n.a.
City	61.7	33.6	20.9	36.4
Unincorporated	29.1	1.0	12.7	19.3
Other UGBs	0.8	38.3	3.5	n.a.
Subtotal	90.8	72.9	37.1	55.7
Outside UGBs				
Urban fringe	3.4	2.5	4.4	14.7
Exception area	n.a.	1.4	2.9	13.7
Resource area	n.a.	1.1	1.5	1.0
Rest of exurban area	5.8	24.6	58.4	30.0
Exception area	n.a.	14.5	48.2	28.4
Resource area	n.a.	10.0	10.2	1.2
Subtotal	9.2	27.1	62.8	44.2
TOTAL	100.0	100.0	100.0	100.0

SOURCE: ECO Northwest and Newton Associates 1991

UGBs, except in Brookings, where 18 percent took place outside the UGB, in the urban fringe along the coast. Within UGBs, most multiple-family development took place in previously developed urban areas.

Based on these results, ECO Northwest concluded that, "Urban growth *can* be largely contained in urban growth boundaries. . . . But the policies of the statewide planning program have not, by themselves, ensured such containment." Where over 95 percent of residential development in the Portland metropolitan area took place within the UGB, development inside the UGBs of the Medford (73 percent), Bend (37 percent), and Brookings (56 percent) areas was much lower. ECO Northwest further concluded that, around Portland, patterns of development were similar in Clackamas County and in Clark County, which is in Washington State.

Table 6. Approved Subdivision Lots, Selected Urban Areas in Oregon, 1985 to 1989

	Percentage in selected categories			
Location	Portland	Medford	Bend	Brookings
Inside UGBs				
Inside primary UGB	90.0	34.6	33.6	55.7
Urban area	66.7	14.6	42.9	n.a.
Urbanizable area	29.7	81.4	40.2	n.a.
City	64.6	100.0	n.a.	83.9
Unincorporated	31.7	0.0	n.a.	14.7
Other UGBs	1.3	n.a.	n.a.	n.a.
Subtotal	98.9	96.1	83.2	98.7
Outside UGBs				
Urban fringe	1.0	3.3	4.2	0.0
Exception area	n.a.	3.3	4.2	0.0
Resource area	n.a.	0.0	0.0	0.0
Rest of exurban area	0.2	0.5	12.6	1.3
Exception area	n.a.	0.5	10.8	1.3
Resource area	n.a.	0.0	1.9	0.0
Subtotal	1.2	3.9	16.8	1.3
TOTAL	100.0	100.0	100.0	100.0

SOURCE: ECO Northwest and Newton Associates 1991

ECO Northwest identified other troublesome development patterns, especially in Medford, Bend, and Brookings. In these three study areas, the development densities inside UGBs fell considerably below planned densities. And in all study areas, single-family development took place in multiple-family zones. Such development patterns inside UGBs, ECO Northwest warned, could cause UGBs to become filled with low-density development and require expansion much sooner than planned. ECO Northwest also showed that considerable residential development took place outside UGBs, in both exception and resource zones. Although residential development in fringe areas amounted to less than 15 percent of the total, noted ECO Northwest, the location of these developments could adversely affect opportunities for future UGB expansion.

Table 7. Multiple-Family Development, Selected Urban Areas in Oregon, 1985 to 1989

Location	Percentage in selected categories			
	Portland	Medford	Bend	Brookings
Inside UGBs				
Inside primary UGB	99.0	47.8	88.1	82.2
Urban area	64.5	44.4	38.3	n.a.
Urbanizable area	34.2	3.4	49.8	n.a.
City	71.5	47.8	71.0	82.2
Unincorporated	27.4	0.0	17.1	0.0
Other UGBs	0.2	52.2	11.2	0.0
Subtotal	99.2	100.0	99.3	82.2
Outside UGBs				
Urban fringe	0.2	0.0	0.7	17.8
Exception area	n.a.	0.0	0.7	17.8
Resource area	n.a.	0.0	0.0	0.0
Rest of exurban area	0.5	0.0	0.0	0.0
Exception area	n.a.	0.0	0.0	0.0
Resource area	n.a.	0.0	0.0	0.0
Subtotal	0.7	0.0	0.7	17.8
TOTAL	100.0	100.0	100.0	100.0

SOURCE: ECO Northwest and Newton Associates 1991

DISCUSSION

The research to date demonstrates that land values differ on opposite sides of UGBs and that development patterns differ in various metropolitan areas. These differences offer important insights on the effectiveness of UGBs as statewide growth management instruments.

UGB Effects on Land Values

The empirical evidence indicates that UGBs can affect land values in a manner consistent with economic models. Although tests for price effects have been performed in only two metropolitan areas, the consistency of the results strongly substantiates the models. In short, the results imply that UGBs take some time to affect land values, that the effects are manifested in expectations about future urban development, and that the effects vary with distance from the UGB. The evidence shows that UGBs can be influential land use instruments with predictable and measurable impacts on land values.

The evidence further reveals that UGBs can influence the expectations of land market participants and thus can influence land allocation. Individuals are willing to pay more for agricultural land inside UGBs than outside, based on expectations of more rapid urban development. Individuals are also willing to pay more for urban land near UGBs but less for agricultural land near UGBs, reflecting expectations about the future location of the urban-rural boundary. These findings have significant implications concerning both the efficiency and equity of the land market.

From an efficiency perspective, UGBs can provide information about future development which, if accurate, could improve the short-term efficiency of the urban development process. For example, if it is known that urban development will soon take place on agricultural land inside a UGB, then investments in agricultural production are unlikely unless they amortize before the expected date of urban development. Similarly, investments for continued agricultural use of rural land outside the UGB become more likely, even if they do not amortize until after UGB expansion. Further, urban residents who wish to reside near the urban-rural border will know where they must bid on land. And those who wish to farm away from the urban-rural border know the same. Thus the dynamic efficiency of the urban development process is potentially enhanced as information about future land use policy is capitalized into land values and market participants react accordingly.[11]

The effects of UGBs on urban land supplies, however, remain uncertain. The involvement of LCDC in the planning process resulted in more tightly drawn UGBs than local governments would have constructed on their own (Knaap 1989b). Even so, urban development within UGBs cannot take place until local governments have approved the zoning, issued building permits, and provided urban services. These instruments—and not UGBs—constrain the supply of urban land. Whether less land has been developed as a result of UGBs and whether UGBs will in the future restrict the supply of urban land will not be known for some time; the latter depends largely on national housing trends and on the rate of development supported by local governments.

Because UGBs affect land values, UGBs affect equity. With the imposition of a UGB, wealth is transferred from people who own land outside the boundary to those who own land inside it. Wealth is also transferred from those who own urban land at a distance from the UGB to those who own urban land near it; and from those who own agricultural land near the boundary to those who own agricultural land further from it. Thereby, UGBs redistribute wealth. But it is unclear whether this form of wealth redistribution is more or less equitable than that which would occur without UGBs. Wealth transfers also occur in the absence of UGBs.[12] But because the process of establishing UGBs enfranchises a larger geographic constituency, wealth transfers due to UGBs are less likely to benefit a disproportionate few. Moreover, since UGBs designate zoning changes far in advance of development, wealth transfers related to UGBs are more explicit than without them, and the wealth accrues gradually over time.

Based on the evidence from Portland and Salem, UGBs will eventually influence land values, but the same cannot be said for the package of land use controls imposed by local governments. The empirical results imply that the influence of local land use instruments varies by jurisdiction. Judging by impacts on land values, urban development inside the UGB is controlled by zoning in Salem, by urban service provision in Clackamas County, and by the combination of zoning, intermediate growth boundaries, and urban service provision in Washington County. Thus, when local governments have chosen to enforce land use controls inside UGBs, such controls have also proven influential on land values. But when local communities have not strongly enforced local controls, their effects have been insignificant. Thus, based on studies conducted in Portland and Salem, state participation in the land use program appears to have contributed to the significance and predictability of the effects of UGBs, but not to the package of land use controls over which local governments exercise discretion.

UGB Effects on Urban Development

Recent research on urban development patterns by ECO Northwest provides evidence consistent with earlier studies of UGB impacts on land values. The evidence suggests that development at urban densities—single-family development in subdivisions and multiple-family development—has been contained within UGBs. But the pattern of development, both inside and outside the UGBs, varies by jurisdiction, and development patterns in some jurisdictions raise concerns over the long-term effectiveness of UGBs.

According to state planning goals and guidelines, local governments must facilitate development inside UGBs and restrict development outside

UGBs. But the means by which they meet these guidelines vary markedly—and urban development patterns vary markedly as a result. In all metropolitan areas examined by ECO Northwest, land was developed inside UGBs at densities lower than planned, and land was developed outside UGBs at densities higher than planned. If this trend continues, the effects of the UGBs will be the opposite of their intended effects: UGBs will become filled with low-density urban development and precluded from expansion by high-density rural development.[13] As a result, any short-term efficiency gains in the process of development will be lost in inefficient development patterns.

UGB Effects on Long-Term Urban Growth

To provide for long-term development opportunities, planning beyond the horizon of the existing UGBs must begin soon. One option is to expand UGBs into areas previously committed to exurban use, that is, into exception areas. This option will increase the supply of urban land and reduce pressure for development on rural land. But this option further encourages low-density development on urban land and hig-density development on what was previously rural land. This option also does not resolve long-term urban expansion issues.

A second option is to impose minimum density restrictions inside the UGB, to impose maximum density restrictions outside UGBs (in areas designated as urban reserves), and to expand the UGB incrementally into these areas. Inside UGBs minimum lot sizes would have to be small enough to encourage more compact urban development. Outside UGBs lot sizes would have to be large enough to accommodate future land subdivision. Development approvals on such lots might also require the applicant to record a shadow plat, which indicates plans for future land subdivision and development. This option would assure high-density urban development within UGBs and low-density rural development outside UGBs with explicit plans for future urban redevelopment. UGBs would expand incrementally into urban reserve areas but only with LCDC approval. But this option would also expand the role of LCDC in land use planning and regulation.[14]

A third option is to construct new, longer-term UGBs around existing UGBs. If new UGBs were drawn around existing UGBs, while maintaining the existing boundaries until the year 2000, short-term effectiveness would not be lost, and no serious disruptions in the land market would need to take place. Land within the existing UGBs would become developed as planned, and land outside existing UGBs would remain undeveloped until the year 2000. After the year 2000, urban development would occur outside the existing UGBs but only within the new UGBs, until the sunset date of the new UGBs. In effect, urban areas would be encompassed by a set of UGBs, each with clearly specified sunset dates.

Preserving the restrictions of the original UGBs, even as the expiration date approaches, provides important benefits. First, planners could design new comprehensive plans for land inside the new UGBs. In fact, such planning could be done with far more knowledge than available when planning for the existing UGBs. Second, counterproductive political conflict over transfers of wealth near the urban-rural border would be minimized. Existing public policy would remain in force until the prescribed expiration date, and the future urban-rural border could be placed at locations currently far from speculative influence. Third, participants in the land market would continue to make long-term development decisions consistent with carefully designed public land use policy. Speculators would purchase and hold land outside the UGB on the expectation of future urban development. Facilitating such efficient behavior by participants in the land market is perhaps the greatest potential contribution of UGBs and urban growth management in general.[15]

LESSONS FROM OREGON

Although the term urban growth boundary describes a policy instrument perhaps unique to Oregon, the policy dimensions embodied in the UGB are commonplace, thus the policy lessons from UGBs in Oregon are widely applicable. Comprehensive planning is now common, and requires foresight with respect to capital improvements, urban services, roads, land use, and more. In short, comprehensive planning requires planning for future development. Except in places where city boundaries are so extensive as to enable urban areas to grow over the planning horizon within municipal borders, comprehensive planning requires planners to delineate future urban borders. Many states currently enable cities to plan for development outside their incorporated areas. Although the boundaries around comprehensive plans in other states may not receive the emphasis they receive in Oregon, such boundaries serve in part as urban growth boundaries.

The evidence from Oregon suggests that UGBs facilitate intergovernmental coordination. Establishing a UGB in Oregon requires city, county, and state agencies to address issues concerning the rate and location of future urban development. But the difference between Oregon and other states may be less in substance than style. In California, for example, disputes between cities over future development and annexation are settled by Local Agency Formation Commissions (LAFCOs) (Fulton 1989). Although certainly different from the LCDC, LAFCOs essentially establish regional urban growth boundaries. In many other states, cities independently enter into annexation agreements with other cities, counties, special districts, and state agencies, which effectively designate urban growth boundaries for each city (Lewis 1989). Florida communities are obliged to design urban service limits within which short-term urban development will be accommodated. In short, the purposes served by UGBs in Oregon, and perhaps the effects on urban land markets and allocation, may differ from other states only in name.

The evidence from Oregon also suggests that UGBs, or other instruments that specify future urban use, can affect current land values and allocation. If future land use designations are firm, well known, and represent a public commitment to future development, then participants in the marketplace can make investment decisions consistent with public plans, thus resulting in a more efficient development process. If future use designations are not well known or, even worse, unreliable, then the potential for this kind of dynamic efficiency is lost.

In spite of similarities in purpose, however, differences in process matter. The process by which UGBs are established and enforced influences their size, their location, and thus their effect on urban land markets. State participation in the establishment and enforcement of UGBs has resulted in greater consistency in their effects on land values and development patterns. Land values and development densities are higher inside UGBs than outside UGBs. Further, as a result of state participation in the construction and implementation of UGBs, urban growth boundaries in Oregon are more circumspect than they would have been if local governments had drawn them on their own. Whether UGBs will create more compact and densely developed cities in the long term, however, remains uncertain.

Finally, the evidence from Oregon suggests that UGBs have limited ability to manage urban growth. Although development at urban densities in Oregon has been contained within UGBs, development densities inside UGBs are lower than planned and development densities outside UGBs are higher than planned. Thus, as planners and policy makers in Oregon have only recently discovered, meeting long-term growth management objectives will require more than short-term growth management instruments.

Notes

1. As opposed to other growth management instruments adopted in the 1970s—e.g., population caps, development quotas, and facilities programming (Scott 1975)—UGBs were not intended to slow either the rate or total quantity of development. As an instrument to be used ostensibly for protecting farmland, UGBs were drawn with generous supplies of urban land.
2. See chapter 3 for more on UGB effects on housing costs.
3. For more theory on zoning, see Ohls, Weisberg, and White (1974) and Courant (1976).
4. For more on land values and urban structure, see Mills and Hamilton (1987, 96–124).
5. See Capozza and Helsley (1989) for a more developed exposition of land as a capital asset.
6. For more on green belts and land values, see Correll et al. (1978).
7. For more on hedonic estimation, see Sullivan (1990, 345–6).
8. See Leonard (1983) for more detail on UGB politics.
9. For more on Metro, see Bollens and Schmandt (1982).
10. See glossary for definition of resource area and chapter 5 for more on exception areas.
11. Dynamic efficiency refers to the efficient utilization of land and land-based investments through the process of land use change.
12. See Fischel (1985), and Hagman and Juergensmeyer (1986) on the distributive effects of land use controls.
13. Although planned density targets will be exceeded, densities inside UGBs will remain higher than densities outside UGBs.
14. See Fischel (1988a) for a discussion on state participation in an incremental growth management process.
15. See Schaeffer and Hopkins (1987) for a discussion on the economics of planning information.

3

Land Use Controls as State Housing Policy Instruments

HOUSING ISSUES HAVE COME to the forefront of U.S. urban policy in the 1990s. According to a recent review of the state of the nation's housing (Joint Center for Housing Studies 1989), U.S. citizens are having increasing difficulty finding suitable, affordable housing. Homeownership, once the key to financial and social stability, has become increasingly difficult for many Americans to obtain, especially young Americans. Trapped in a rental market in which rents have risen faster than incomes, a large number of Americans has been forced into homelessness. Although the Joint Center report offers few specific policy recommendations, its authors conclude that housing problems have reached crisis proportions and deserve immediate attention.

How best to address housing problems remains an important policy question. Constrained by budget deficits, the federal government has eliminated all but a few housing programs and reduced funding levels for those that remain—leaving state and local governments to solve the problem. They have responded in a number of ways. Some cities and states provide financial assistance to low-income residents; some subsidize construction of low-income housing; others directly engage in housing construction (Christensen et al. 1988). Some do all three. But for political and budgetary reasons, state and local governments have limited ability to resolve growing housing problems.

In the face of political and budgetary constraints, state and local governments have sought indirect means of intervening in the housing market. Many have turned to land use planning and regulation. Land use plans and their implementing ordinances prescribe the location, height, width, depth, density, and type of housing constructed. And they remain the exclusive responsibility of state and local governments. As a result, land use controls offer state and local governments a vehicle for altering the performance of the housing market.

Many analysts of state and local land use controls, however, argue that the controls contribute more to the cause than to the solution of housing problems. In a comprehensive review of the effects of land use controls on the housing market, William Fischel (1988b) concludes the following: "Growth controls and other aggressive extensions of land use regulations probably impose costs on society that are considerably larger than the benefits they provide. The higher housing prices associated with communities that impose growth controls are more likely the result of wasteful supply constraints than benign amenity production." In addition, Robert Ellickson (1982) levied sharp and influential criticism on local land use policies that expressly seek to provide housing relief for the poor.[1] Thus the efficacy of addressing housing problems by land use planning and regulation is far from certain.

This chapter examines the influence of statewide land use planning on the housing market in Oregon. The chapter begins by presenting a conceptual framework for analyzing the effects of land use controls on the housing market. Using microeconomic theory, this presentation addresses two issues: the influence of land use controls on the housing market and the influence of land use controls on the mix and density of housing development. The chapter then describes how Oregon's state housing policy was established through the intergovernmental process of planning. Next, the chapter examines how state housing policy influenced the content of local land use plans and the housing market in Oregon. The chapter concludes with a discussion of the efficacy of using statewide land use planning as a housing policy instrument.

LAND USE CONTROLS AND THE HOUSING MARKET IN THEORY

The influence of land use controls on several important aspects of the housing market is easier understood in the context of a general conceptual framework. For at least three reasons microeconomic theory serves this purpose well. First, the variables of primary interest—housing price, housing density, and housing mix—are determined mainly by economic forces. Second, housing in the U.S. is produced, in general, by a relatively large number of producers for profit—even in a planned and regulated housing market. Thus the housing market satisfies, to a reasonable degree, the critical assumptions of microeconomics. Finally, the field is well known to planners and policy analysts, thus it clarifies the logic of the analysis and conclusions.

Land Use Controls, Housing Price, and Housing Starts

By necessity, housing development is a public-private enterprise—it requires contributions by many participants, including land developers, builders, realtors, financial institutions, and local governments. In various combinations, and at various points in the production process, these participants provide the inputs necessary for housing development. The multiplicity of participants in the development process and the durability of the housing stock contribute to the complexity and cyclical sensitivity of the housing market (Goldberg and Chinloy 1984).

The complexity of the development process notwithstanding, housing production can be analyzed in a simple supply-and-demand framework.[2] The quantity of housing demanded is determined by its price, the income level of local residents, and the relative attractiveness of the local area to new residents.[3] Other things being equal, the quantity of housing demanded in a region decreases with the price and increases with income and attractiveness. The quantity of housing supplied is determined by the price of housing and by the cost of housing inputs— i.e., land, labor, capital, and materials. Other things being equal, the quantity of housing supplied increases with the price and decreases with the cost of housing inputs.

Land use controls influence the housing market primarily through the market for land. A parcel of land cannot be used for housing construction until the parcel has been zoned for residential use and provided with access, urban services, and a building permit. These attributes of the land input are provided by local governments. Thus, regardless of the physical supply of land available for sale, the supply of land available for housing construction is jointly determined by the decisions of private landowners and the decisions of local governments. The decisions of local governments regarding the provision of requisite urban services, then, affect the supply, and thus the price, of land. The price of land, in turn, affects the price of housing.[4]

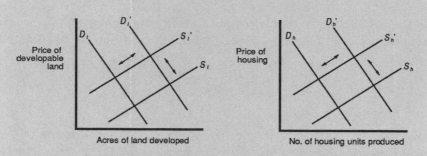

The Effects of Land Use Controls on Land and the Housing Market

By restricting the provision of urban services, land use controls can shift the supply of developable land from S_i to S_i', decreasing the amount of land developed and increasing land price. Subsequently, the supply of housing shifts from S_h to S_h', decreasing the number of housing units produced and increasing housing price.

Alternatively, by increasing the attractiveness of the local area, land use controls can increase the demand for housing from D_h to D_h', increasing the number of housing units produced and increasing the price of housing. Subsequently, the demand for developable land increases from D_i to D_i', increasing the amount of land developed and increasing the price of developable land.

Both supply and demand effects increase the price of land and housing; supply-side effects also decrease the rate of housing development, however, while demand-side effects also decrease the rate of housing development.

The supply-and-demand model provides a framework for analyzing the influence of land use controls on the housing market. Land use controls influence the supply of urban services. If the rate at which these services are provided falls, then the supply of developable land falls, which increases the price. As the price of land increases, housing becomes more expensive to produce, and housing prices increase. Alternatively, of course, land use controls could increase the rate at which urban services are provided and have the opposite effect on land and housing prices. According to microeconomic theory, then, land and housing prices provide insights into the restrictiveness of land use controls (see box insert).

In addition to supply-side effects, however, land use controls can also affect demand (Fischel 1988b). An important purpose of land use planning and regulation is to improve the quality of the residential environment. People like to live in high-quality environments. Thus, in places where land use plans can improve the urban environment, the demand for housing will rise, which will also increase the housing price.

Land use policy can thus increase land and housing prices in two ways, with widely different welfare effects. This adds complexity to the interpretation of price effects.

Land Use Controls, Housing Density, and Housing Mix

Besides influencing housing production and price, land use controls can influence the density and mix of housing construction. If land use controls restrict the supply of developable land, then the land value and housing price increase, slowing the rate of housing construction. The density of housing construction, however, may also increase. As land price increases relative to other input prices, housing producers will economize on the relatively more costly input, land, and use more of the less costly inputs, capital and labor. As a result, housing is produced with less land, i.e., at greater density (more housing per acre of land, see box insert on page 74).

Housing density and housing mix are, of course, related. Multiple-family housing is typically more densely constructed than single-family housing. Thus, if land use controls increase the density of housing development, the relative share of multiple-family housing will increase. If land use controls decrease the density of development, the share of multiple-family housing will decrease. The density and mix of housing development, therefore, also provide insight into the influence of land use controls.

State versus Local Land Use Controls

The previous discussion provides a simple framework for understanding the effects of land use controls on the housing market. The discussion made no distinction between the level of government at which land use is controlled. The level of government—e.g., state versus local government—may make a difference, not so much in how land use controls affect the housing market, but instead in how land use is controlled.

When land use is controlled at the local level, land use decisions are made in the interests of local constituents, to whom housing developments

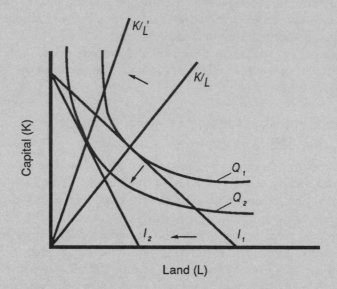

The Effects of Land-Supply Constraints on Housing Density

If land use controls decrease the supply of developable land and increase the price of land, the isocost line shifts from I_1 to I_2. As a result, the quantity of housing units produced is reduced from Q_1 to Q_2. In addition, the capital-to-land ratio changes from (K/L) to $(K/L)'$. That is, housing is built with more capital per unit of land, or at a higher density. A decreasing land price, of course, would have the opposite effects on housing construction and on density.

are not equally attractive. Some housing development, such as high-density housing, is undesirable because it adds more to local public costs than to revenues. Other types of housing, e.g., multiple-family housing and mobile homes, are undesirable because they are perceived as detracting from the quality of the community. Since land use controls can restrict inputs to production of these types of housing, land use controls can be used to exclude such development. This practice has been labeled exclusionary zoning (Babcock and Bosselman 1973, Mallach 1984).

As a result of exclusionary zoning, occupants of high-density or multiple-family housing—primarily low-income residents—are forced to reside in central cities, where they suffer high tax burdens and increased costs for commuting to suburban employment centers. Further, if all or many local governments practice exclusionary zoning, the housing densities can fall throughout an entire metropolitan region, resulting in widespread traffic congestion and urban sprawl. The incentives faced by local governments to practice exclusionary zoning, and the resultant effects of exclusionary zoning on housing cost, traffic congestion, and urban sprawl, provide the foundation for much of the criticism of local land use planning (Fischel 1988b).

Since the motive for practicing exclusionary zoning stems primarily from the pursuit of parochial interests, a possible remedy for exclusionary zoning is regional or statewide planning (Popper 1981a, Johnson 1982). Under regional or statewide planning, land use decisions can be made from a state or regional perspective, thus high-density and other locally undesired land uses can be allotted to jurisdictions in some equitable fashion (Listokin 1976). State laws in New Jersey, California, Massachusetts, and Oregon require various forms of such allocation systems (Sidor 1984a, 1984b). (See box insert on page 76.)

In review, land use controls have the potential to influence the housing market in several ways: by restricting the supply of housing inputs, by decreasing the supply of housing, and by increasing housing price. Theoretically, at least, land use controls can also do just the opposite. On the demand side, land use controls can increase the attractiveness of a community, thereby increasing housing demand and increasing housing price. Finally, land use controls can influence housing density by changing the price of land relative to other inputs and by imposing minimum lot (or maximum density) requirements.

Under a system of purely local land use controls, local governments have an incentive to zone out undesirable housing types, thereby forcing such types of housing into jurisdictions less capable of exclusion—usually the central city. Alternatively, a state or regional system of land use planning has the potential to overcome exclusionary motives, reduce housing costs, and provide for a greater variety of housing types.

LAND USE CONTROLS AS HOUSING POLICY INSTRUMENTS IN OREGON

The state of Oregon has many public programs and policies that influence the housing market. Some, such as the first-time homeowner program

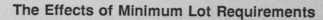

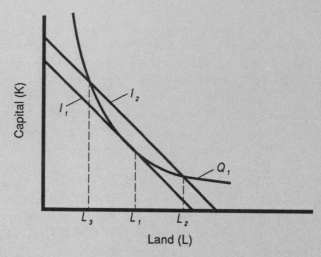

Here, the cost-minimizing expenditure level—the level of producing housing services equivalent to Q_1 under the existing input price—is depicted by I_1. The cost-minimizing lot size is thus L_1. If local land use controls impose minimum lot requirements, L_2 (or impose maximum-density constraints, resulting in higher lot sizes), then the cost of providing the same level of housing services increases to I_2. As a result, land use controls requiring excessive use of raw land can increase overall housing costs and contribute to urban sprawl. Removing minimum lot requirements, perhaps through state or regional land use planning, can thus result in lower housing costs and higher-density housing construction.

The ability to reduce housing cost and increase housing density by removing lot-size constraints, however, is limited. Reducing the minimum lot size from L_1 to L_3 (or further increasing allowed density) will have no effect on housing cost or housing density because, under current market conditions, the market-determined lot size is L_1.

administered by the Oregon Housing Division, influence the housing market directly; others, such as Oregon's heavy reliance on property taxes, influence the housing market indirectly. Since the adoption of Oregon's state land use program, the state has had an agency with the ability—in fact, a mandate—to address housing issues through land use planning: the

Land Conservation and Development Commission (LCDC). As a result, land use planning in Oregon has been used extensively as a housing policy instrument.

Oregon's Goal 10, "To provide for the housing needs of citizens of the state," says:

> *Buildable land* for residential use shall be inventoried and plans shall encourage the availability of adequate numbers of housing units at price ranges and rent levels which are commensurate with the financial capabilities of Oregon households and allow for flexibility of housing location, type and density. (Oregon LCDC 1990)

Although the language sounds bland, the goal has attracted considerable attention. Housing policy has the potential to affect nearly everyone. For many people, their home is their largest financial asset. Moreover, housing policy affects a highly active and influential interest group in state and local land use politics: the housing industry, including builders, realtors, banks, and other financial institutions. As a result, housing issues in Oregon remain a continuous source of controversy.

Establishing Housing Policy through the Planning Process

Although housing was an important component of state land use objectives from the very beginning, LCDC had little on which to base its housing policy. The housing and urbanization goals, though central to state-level housing policy, provided few specific guidelines with which to evaluate local comprehensive plans. Those guidelines that were specific, i.e., land use inventories and housing needs projections, were procedural rather than substantive. The substance of LCDC's housing policy thus had to be formed and articulated through the acknowledgment process, a process that attracted the attention of many interest groups and required local governments, LCDC, and the courts to make critical policy decisions (Morgan 1984a).

An early expression of LCDC's housing policy came out of the review of the Columbia River Association of Governments's (CRAG, now the Metropolitan Service District) urban growth boundary. When CRAG sought to include a 25 percent excess supply of land inside the Portland metropolitan urban growth boundary to provide developers choice in the marketplace and to prevent land price inflation, LCDC rejected it. The agency also rejected the "market factors" of all other plans that followed. Instead, LCDC required that urban growth boundaries contain only sufficient land supplies to exactly meet projected development to the year 2000. In articulating its CRAG decision, LCDC expressed a clear policy favoring high-density urban growth.[5]

The next influential housing policy decision by LCDC occurred in 1978, in *Seaman v. City of Durham*, even before Durham submitted its comprehensive plan for review. In 1977, the city had amended its zoning ordinance to reduce the density of permitted development. The change affected 19 landowners who petitioned the decision to LCDC. The petitioners argued that the zoning change violated the housing goal by excluding low-income residents. In a decision that closely paralleled the *Mount Laurel* decision in New Jersey (Sidor 1984a), LCDC determined that Durham's zoning policy effectively excluded low-income residents and thus did not meet the requirements of Goal 10. Later this decision was codified in a memorandum from LCDC to local governments and subsequently passed into law by the legislature (ORS 197.295 to 197.307). The memorandum required all communities in the Portland metropolitan area to plan for a 50/50 mix of single-family/multiple-family development and an overall housing density of six, eight, or ten units per acre, depending on the size of the community. This rule has become known as the Metropolitan Housing Rule (see box insert on page 79).

The next significant expression of LCDC's housing policy came when LCDC reviewed the plan submitted by the city of St. Helens. Perhaps in part to retain local autonomy over development decisions, and perhaps to circumvent the implementation of the state's housing goals, many local governments placed multiple-family and mobile-home land in conditional-use zones; development approvals in such zones could be conditioned on vague, discretionary, and unpredictable standards. This strategy effectively retained for local governments the ability to delay unwanted types of housing development—sometimes indefinitely.

LCDC closed this loophole, however, in its St. Helens decision. In reviewing St. Helens' comprehensive plan, LCDC required the city to clearly specify the conditions under which conditional uses would be allowed. Further, LCDC proclaimed, the conditions necessary for high-density development must not have the effect of discouraging needed housing types. As a result of the St. Helens decision, local governments are no longer able to place their share of high-density development in conditional-use zones and thereby prevent high-density housing via the application of vague or prohibiting conditions (see box insert on page 80).

Metropolitan Housing Rule

New Construction Mix

Jurisdictions other than small developed cities must designate sufficient buildable land to provide the opportunity for at least 50 percent of new residential units to be attached single family housing or multiple family housing. (OAR 660-07-030)

Minimum Residential Density Allocation for New Construction

(1) The Cities of Cornelius, Durham, Fairview, Happy Valley and Sherwood must provide for an overall density of six or more dwelling units per net buildable acre. These are relatively small cities with some growth potential (i.e. with a regionally coordinated population projection of less than 8,000 persons for the active planning area).

(2) Clackamas and Washington Counties, and the cities of Forest Grove, Gladstone, Milwaukie, Oregon City, Troutdale, Tualatin, West Linn and Wilsonville must provide for an overall density of eight or more dwelling units per net buildable acre.

(3) Multnomah County and the cities of Portland, Gresham, Beaverton, Hillsboro, Lake Oswego and Tigard must provide for an overall density of ten or more dwelling units per net buildable acre. These are larger urbanized jurisdictions with regionally coordinated population projections of 50,000 or more for their active planning areas, which encompass or are near major employment centers, and which are situated along regional transportation corridors.

(4) Regional housing density and mix standards as stated in OAR 660-07-030 and 660-07-035(1), (2), and (3) do not apply to small developed cities which had less than 50 acres of buildable land in 1977 as determined by criteria used in Metro's UGB Findings. These cities include King City, Rivergrove, Maywood Park, Johnson City and Wood Village. (OAR 660-07-035)

The CRAG, *Seaman,* and *St. Helens* decisions define the essence of LCDC's housing policy. The policy clearly favors compact urban growth and inclusionary zoning. According to LCDC, UGBs must contain sufficient, but not excessive, land to provide housing at an affordable price for all Oregon residents. Each city must zone its fair share of land for high-

Clear and Objective Standards Rule

Clear and Objective Approval Standards Required

Local approval standards, special conditions and procedures regulating the development of needed housing must be clear and objective, and must not have the effect, either of themselves or cumulatively, of discouraging needed housing through unreasonable cost or delay.(OAR 660-08-015)

density, multiple-family, manufactured, and government-assisted housing. And comprehensive plans must contain sufficient detail so as not to cause undue delay in the process of housing development.

Although LCDC's housing policy seeks to include a variety of housing types and to foster housing construction at the lowest possible cost, the policy stops short of requiring the types of financial incentives required in other states. California and New Jersey, for example, require local governments to provide density bonuses, land writedowns, development fees, or other financial incentives for the construction of low-income housing. Such incentives are not required in Oregon, although some cities offer them. LCDC requires local governments to remove, as much as possible, land use constraints to high-density housing; LCDC does not require local governments to assist developers in overcoming financial constraints.

Changing the Content of Local Comprehensive Plans

While state housing policy has been established through the proceedings of the celebrated cases noted above, what remains uncertain is whether the cases are representative of larger LCDC efforts. That is, without further analysis, it is uncertain whether LCDC changed the comprehensive plans of a relatively minor number of obstinate local governments or of a large number throughout the state.

LCDC's housing policy enforcement record was examined by Knaap (1990). In reviewing LCDC's acknowledgment files, Knaap found evidence of active intervention and enforcement of state housing policy. Of the 53 comprehensive plans submitted by cities with populations over 5,000, only one plan satisfied the requirements of Goal 10 in its first review—the plan submitted by the city of Portland. LCDC determined that the original plans of all other jurisdictions violated Goal 10.

There were three common reasons why LCDC rejected local comprehensive plans for violations of Goal 10. First, LCDC felt that local governments had allocated insufficient land for high-density development. This problem was most severe in the Portland metropolitan suburbs. In response to this problem, LCDC issued a technical memorandum to Portland-area governments articulating its fair-share policy. Further, the agency issued an enforcement order to Happy Valley (a Portland suburb) for refusing to comply with LCDC's density directives. Under the enforcement order, LCDC forbade the city to approve any "applications for subdivisions, partitions, and residential building permits which do not achieve a minimum density of six dwelling units per acre" (Morgan 1984b, 788). Low-density zoning, however, was also prevalent outside the Portland metropolitan area. Thus, according to LCDC, exclusionary zoning was not limited to metropolitan suburbs.

Second, LCDC felt that local governments did not clearly specify the conditions under which conditional uses would be approved. That is, LCDC applied its St. Helens policy often. This issue arose most often in cases when mobile homes were conditionally allowed on single-family lots. In response, local governments either removed the conditional-use designations or specified more precisely what was necessary to satisfy the zoning conditions.

The third most common violation of Goal 10 was procedural. Many local governments, especially smaller rural governments, had not satisfactorily completed a buildable lands inventory or a needs assessment. In these cases the local government simply had to complete a pre-planning analysis to the satisfaction of LCDC.

Although Knaap's review of LCDC's files was informal, two things became clear. First, LCDC pursued a consistent housing policy that it forcefully implemented through review of local comprehensive plans. Second, the housing policy that LCDC chose to enforce was not the same policy that would have been chosen by local governments on their own. That is, LCDC enforced a high-density, fair-share housing policy—one that would not have been pursued by local governments themselves, except perhaps by the city of Portland. Judging by the influence of LCDC's review of local comprehensive plans, Oregon's statewide land use program has forced local governments to practice inclusionary zoning and to plan for spatially constrained urban growth.

More specific analysis of the content of comprehensive plans was conducted by 1000 Friends of Oregon, which examined the content of com-

prehensive plans prepared by several jurisdictions in the Portland metropolitan area in 1978 and again in 1982 (1000 Friends 1982a). Since many
of these jurisdictions revised their comprehensive plans between 1978 and
1982 in response to, or in preparation for, acknowledgment review, the
study provides a before-and-after view of the influence of state review.

As shown in table 8, changes in plans of jurisdictions in the Portland
area resulted in an increase in overall planned density. The planned density
in single-family zones increased from 3.4 units per acre to 5.3 units per
acre. The planned density in multiple-family zones increased from 17.4
units per acre to 20.3 units per acre. Overall planned density increased
from 4.4 units per acre to 9.4 units per acre. As a result of higher-density
zoning, the number of potential housing units inside the Portland-area
UGB increased by 34,000 units. According to 1000 Friends, this was done
largely by up-zoning vacant, undeveloped land to higher densities, not by
up-zoning single-family neighborhoods.

The planned mix of housing types also changed. In 1978 land zoned for
single-family use represented over 92 percent of the net buildable acres and
over 70 percent of all units. By 1982 these uses had dropped to 73 and 41
percent, respectively. In this period the total amount of land zoned for
single-family use fell by over 3,500 acres, but, due to the increased density,
the total number of potential single-family units increased by 32,000. Land
zoned for multiple-family use increased by 6,500 acres, and the number of
potential multiple-family units increased by 172,000.

Despite such pervasive increases in overall planned density, 1000 Friends
found considerable variation in planned densities among jurisdictions, in-
dicating that local governments had preserved diversity in their approaches
to comprehensive planning. In 1982, the average lot size of land zoned for
single-family housing (for jurisdictions with 500 or more acres of buildable
land) ranged from 6,400 square feet in unincorporated Multnomah County
to 11,200 square feet in Tigard. In general, lot sizes remained larger in the
suburban areas than in the older central cities, although the variation between central city and suburbs decreased. The most significant reduction in
lot size of single-family land occurred in the unincorporated areas of
Clackamas and Washington Counties, which contained over 50 percent of
all buildable single-family land. A significant amount of large-lot single-
family zoning, however, remained.

Changes in multiple-family zoning also varied markedly by jurisdiction.
To meet state requirements, some communities increased allowable densi-

Table 8.   Residential Units Allowed by Zoning, Selected Portland-Area Communities, 1978 to 1982

| Size | No. of residential units per net buildable acre (UNA)[a] (percentage) | | | | | |
| | 1978 zoning | | | 1982 comprehensive plans | | |
	Single-family	Multiple-family	Total	Single-family	Multiple-family	Total
Net acres	26,946 (92.4)	2,219 (7.6)	29,165	23,412 (72.7)	8,795 (27.3)	32,207
No. of units	90,651 (70.1)	38,670 (29.9)	129,321	123,145 (40.8)	178,337 (59.2)	301,482
Density (UNA)	3.4	17.4	4.4	5.3	20.3	9.4

[a]Net buildable acres allocates 15 percent of land area to streets and open area.
SOURCE: 1000 Friends 1982a.

ties on existing multiple-family land; others zoned new land for multiple-family use. Most chose the latter approach.

The research by Knaap and by 1000 Friends demonstrates that state housing goals have had significant impacts on the content of local comprehensive plans. The state exercised its review authority and attempted to increase the supply of land zoned for multiple-family use and decrease the supply of land zoned for single-family use with the purpose of increasing the density of urban development and thereby increasing housing opportunities for low-income residents. Whether the state succeeded in meeting its ultimate goal, however, remains uncertain. Without, for example, financial incentives, Oregon's approach is rather passive. Further, the constraints on total land supply imposed by UGBs raise the possibility of land and housing costs being higher than necessary.

EVIDENCE OF IMPACTS ON
THE OREGON HOUSING MARKET

Identifying the impacts of state planning on the housing market in Oregon is difficult. An ideal test of impact requires detailed information on the housing market with and without state planning. Identifying specific causes of impact requires similar data on housing inputs. Data on what would have been, of course, are not available, and useful cross-section data on existing land and housing market conditions are almost equally scarce. As a result, nearly all studies measuring the impacts of statewide planning on the housing market suffer from incomplete data, and thus all require cautious interpretation.[6]

Impacts on Housing Price and Starts

One of the most frequently cited studies on the effect of Oregon's land use program on the housing market was funded by the Weyerhouser Corporation, where managers were concerned about the impact of state planning on the market for lumber and wood products (Beaton 1982). Relying primarily on secondary sources of data, Beaton drew two conclusions. First, land use controls appear to influence land value in the state. Second, land and housing prices in Oregon are not excessive compared to other western states. While the Beaton conclusions appear contradictory, close inspection of the evidence supports them.

Drawing on evidence provided by Knaap (1982), Beaton concluded that interjurisdictional differences in the provision of local government services and local zoning constraints are indeed capitalized into land value, as suggested by the model presented earlier. Specifically, Beaton demonstrated that land value in the Portland metropolitan area was higher for properties within 200 feet of a sewer line, properties in incorporated cities, and properties in platted subdivisions (see table 3 in chapter 2). Further, the land value of properties in multiple-family zones was higher than the value of properties in single-family zones. Finally, land value in both single- and multiple-family zones was higher in high-density zones than in low-density zones. These results suggest that zoning by local governments in the Portland metropolitan area in 1980 constrained the supply of high-density and multiple-family land below market-determined levels (Beaton 1982, 49). As a result, Beaton concluded, land value indeed reflects the influence of local land use policy.[7]

Next, drawing on data published by the Urban Land Institute and the Portland Metropolitan Home Builders Association, Beaton showed that the price of land in Portland comprised an increasing share of housing costs over the period 1976 to 1980. Further, he showed that Portland's land price grew more rapidly from 1975 to 1980 than in most U.S. cities. Beaton interpreted his results as evidence of the increasing restrictiveness of the regulatory environment, or as evidence of a reduction in the supply of developable land.

Using data on median home price in Oregon communities, Beaton next analyzed the determinants of housing price. Using multiple regression analysis, he was able to explain very little intrastate variation in housing price due to variation in income, population, or housing production. He did, however, find a significant relationship between housing price and population growth. Based on the latter result, Beaton hypothesized that housing price was best explained by housing demand, and he explored this hypothesis further by adding demand data from national sources. The addition of national variables, including income, interest rates, and national housing prices, significantly increased the explanatory power of his model. Beaton concludes: "Demand variables are still the driving force in housing markets, but . . . these are national or at least regional factors which tend to transcend a given state, and most certainly a given city" (Beaton 1982, 40).

More recent, but circumstantial, evidence is provided in table 9. As shown, the median housing price in the Portland metropolitan area had been roughly comparable to the national average until the year 1982. Since then Portland's median housing price has fallen below the national average every year. However, the median housing price in Portland has always been lower than other western U.S. cities'.

Figure 7 offers additional insight. The vertical axis measures the ratio of the median housing price in Portland to the median housing price in the U.S.; the horizontal axis measures the ratio of housing starts in Portland to housing starts in the nation. The figure thus depicts the intersection of the demand and supply curves for housing in Portland relative to the rest of the nation.

As shown, from 1976 to 1980, Portland's median single-family housing price rose relative to the national average, without related increases in housing starts. It is possible that local land use policies contributed to housing-price increases in this period, as most land use plans in the Portland metropolitan area had not come under acknowledgment review. The fall in relative prices and starts from 1980 to 1983 vividly illustrates the effects of declining demand for housing in Oregon during the early 1980s. The recession reduced housing demand in Portland relative to the rest of the nation, which resulted in falling relative price and starts.

The increase in relative starts from 1983 to 1988 illustrates the recovery of demand for housing in Portland after 1983. As the demand for housing recovered during the late 1980s, however, relative prices did not rise to

Table 9.   Median Housing Price, Portland, Western Census Region, and U.S., 1976 to 1990

| | Median single-family home price | | |
Year	Portland[a]	West[b]	U.S.[b]
1976	33,212[c]	46,100	38,100
1977	40,342[c]	57,300	42,900
1978	50,811[c]	66,700	48,700
1979	59,900	77,400	55,700
1980	62,900	89,300	62,200
1981	66,500	96,200	66,400
1982	65,000	98,900	67,800
1983	63,000	94,900	70,300
1984	62,500	95,800	72,400
1985	61,500	95,400	75,500
1986	62,900	100,900	80,300
1987	63,000	113,200	85,600
1988	64,000	124,900	89,300
1989	70,000	139,900	93,100
1990	79,700	139,600	95,500

[a]SOURCE: University of Portland 1992.
[b]SOURCE: National Association of Realtors 1991.
[c]Estimated from average sales values.

their previous levels. This suggests that supply was able to meet demand at a lower relative price in the 1980s than in the 1970s. The state land use program may have enabled relative housing starts to increase without relative increases in price; however, without further analysis it is impossible to rule out alternative explanations. The housing market cycle, illustrated in figure 7 for example, remarkably resembles cycles in the national economy that stem from adaptive inflationary expectations.[8]

The available evidence on housing price and starts in Portland thus supports the conclusions drawn by Beaton. Movements in relative housing starts in Portland reflect most clearly changes in the demand for housing. Changes in relative price—which fell throughout the 1980s—offer little evidence of constrained housing supply. In fact, the available evidence suggests just the opposite.

Overall, then, the evidence on the relationship between land use planning and housing price is fairly conclusive. Local differences in land use

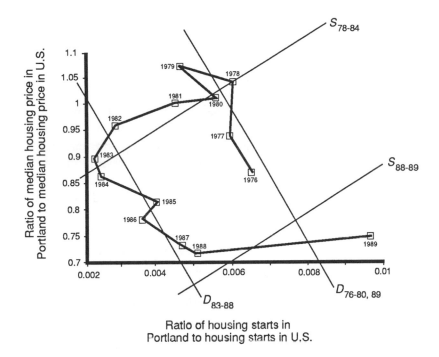

Figure 7. Portland PMSA Housing Market, 1976 to 1989

policy are capitalized into land value and potentially affect housing value accordingly; but demand-side variables, which stem largely from regional economic performance, appear to dominate movements in housing price and starts. In terms of the model of the housing market presented above, the evidence suggests that movements in the aggregate demand for housing in the state during the 1980s dominated the influence of aggregate supply. Thus, although state land use policies may have altered the location, density, and type of housing in Oregon, they do not appear to have constrained supply relative to demand.

Impacts on Housing Mix

Two recent studies examine the effects of land use controls on the density and mix of residential development in Oregon (ECO Northwest and Newton Associates 1991, 1000 Friends 1991). ECO Northwest studied residential development in the Portland, Medford, Bend, and Brookings metropolitan areas; 1000 Friends examined residential development within the Portland metropolitan area, especially in those jurisdictions subject to LCDC's metropolitan housing rule.

In examining the mix of housing development from 1985 to 1989, ECO Northwest found considerable differences among metropolitan areas in the regions' percentages of multiple-family housing development. As shown in table 10 the share of multiple-family housing units ranged from 9 percent in Bend to 52 percent in Portland. The number of multiple-family housing units constructed in Portland easily exceeded the total of multiple-family housing units approved in the other three metropolitan areas.

The 1000 Friends study found considerable variation in the multiple-family share of housing starts among Portland-area jurisdictions subject to the metropolitan housing rule. As shown in table 11, the share of multiple-family starts ranged from 29 percent in Sherwood to 78 percent in Forest Grove. Although the metropolitan area as a whole met the 50 percent multiple-family requirement, several jurisdictions within the metropolitan area did not. Comparing the number of multiple-family starts from 1985

Table 10. Residential Development, Selected Urban Areas in Oregon, 1985 to 1989

Region	No. of units approved (percentage)		
	Single-family	Multiple-family	Total
Portland	20,721 (48)	22,434 (52)	43,155 (100)
Medford	1,955 (88)	268 (12)	2,223 (100)
Bend	4,300 (91)	428 (9)	4,728 (100)
Brookings	497 (71)	202 (29)	699 (100)

SOURCE: ECO Northwest and Newton Associates 1991

Table 11. Building Permits Issued, Selected Portland-Area Communities, 1985 to 1989

Jurisdiction	No. of units approved (percentage)	
	Single-family	Multiple-family
Clackamas Co.	861	1,575
	(34)	(66)
Lake Oswego	1,459	1,500
	(49)	(51)
Milwaukie	232	264
	(47)	(53)
Oregon City	74	232
	(24)	(76)
West Linn	969	173
	(85)	(15)
Wilsonville	514	1,169
	(31)	(69)
Multnomah Co.	438	207
	(68)	(32)
Gresham	1,140	2,230
	(34)	(66)
Portland	2,531	2,303
	(52)	(48)
Washington Co.	3,851	4,894
	(44)	(56)
Beaverton	1,778	4,324
	(29)	(71)
Forest Grove	102	359
	(22)	(78)
Hillsboro	1,050	970
	(52)	(48)
Sherwood	59	24
	(71)	(29)
Tigard	1,667	1,504
	(53)	(47)
Tualatin	716	801
	(47)	(53)
TOTAL	17,441	22,529
	(44)	(56)

SOURCE: 1000 Friends 1991

to 1989 to the number of multiple-family starts in plans prior to the adoption of the metropolitan housing rule, 1000 Friends concluded that "the demand for multiple family housing units during 1985–89 could not have been realized in some Portland communities under pre-Housing Rule zoning" (1000 Friends 1991).

Data from other sources, however, cast doubt on the influence of the Metropolitan Housing Rule on actual housing development. Table 12 pre-

Table 12. Building Permits Issued, Phoenix, Portland, San Francisco, and Seattle, 1970 to 1990

Year	Percentage of multiple-family units approved			
	Phoenix[a]	Portland[b]	San Francisco[c]	Seattle[c]
1970	36	52	73	45
1971	38	57	69	30
1972	40	56	65	21
1973	38	46	73	28
1974	40	33	43	30
1975	10	29	43	34
1976	18	37	49	40
1977	17	36	27	40
1978	30	41	60	57
1979	37	40	55	51
1980	45	38	56	62
1981	47	39	63	52
1982	47	40	74	50
1983	53	20	61	42
1984	64	28	58	53
1985	55	52	58	58
1986	45	43	68	54
1987	34	45	66	57
1988	30	42	55	59
1989	13	63	60	54
1990	16	48	58	56

[a]Includes MSA as per 1985 definition.
[b]Includes Clackamas, Multnomah, and Washington Counties.
[c]Includes PMSAs as per 1985 definition.
SOURCES: U.S. Dept. of Commerce 1971; U.S. Dept. of Commerce 1991

sents the ratio of multiple-family housing starts to total housing starts in the Portland, Seattle, San Francisco, and Phoenix metropolitan areas from 1970 to 1990. As shown, the percentage of multiple-family starts in the Portland area did increase markedly after 1984; but the share of multiple-family housing starts was also high in Portland during the early 1970s, long before the Metropolitan Housing Rule was adopted. What is more, the pattern of multiple-family starts in Portland is not discernibly different from the pattern in other western cities. In fact, the share of multiple-family starts over the last four years in Portland approximately equals the average of other western cities. While these data do not rule out the possibility that the Metropolitan Housing Rule has had an effect, they demonstrate that multiple-family housing starts are highly cyclical, and thus may more closely reflect the influence of financial markets than land use plans.[9]

Impacts on Housing Density

ECO Northwest and 1000 Friends also examined the density of residential development from 1985 to 1989. As shown in table 13, the density of single-family development between 1985 and 1989 inside UGBs varied from 2.0 units per acre in Bend to 5.0 units in Portland, while the density of single family development allowed in the region by planning and zoning varied from 5.6 units per acre in Medford to 7.6 units per acre in Portland. In all the metropolitan areas, however, the densities of single-family development fell substantially below the densities allowed by planning and zoning. The number of single-family lots created by land subdivision fell 33 percent short of the allowed density in Bend, 56 percent short in Brookings, 66 percent short in Portland, and 75 percent short in Medford.

The study by 1000 Friends also examined the density of single-family and multiple-family development within the Portland metropolitan UGB in each of the types of jurisdictions specified in the Metropolitan Housing Rule. As shown in table 14, residential land was developed at 9.58 units per acre in jurisdictions required to zone for an average of 10 units per acre; 8.42 units per acre in jurisdictions required to zone for 8 units per acre; and 3.09 units per acre in the jurisdiction required to zone for 6 units per acre. Also as shown in table 14, jurisdictions in all three classifications came closer to reaching planned density levels in multiple-family zones than they did in single-family zones. Overall, single-family density reached 66 percent of the density planned, while multiple-family density reached 90 percent of the density planned.

Table 13. Actual and Planned Single-Family Density, Selected Urban Areas Inside UGBs, 1985 to 1989

No. of lots per net acre

Location	Actual				Allowed			
	Portland	Medford	Bend	Brookings	Portland	Medford	Bend	Brookings
Urban area	5.0	3.6	2.5	3.6	7.2	6.3	6.6	6.0
Urbanizable area	5.0	4.7	1.6	3.1	8.3	5.2	5.4	7.3
City	5.0	4.2	2.2	3.6	7.2	6.5	6.8	6.0
Unincorporated	5.0	n.a.	1.5	3.1	8.5	n.a.	4.0	7.3
Primary UGB	5.0	4.2	2.0	3.5	7.6	5.6	6.0	6.2

n.a. = not available.

Source: ECO Northwest and Newton Associates 1991

Table 14. Development Density in Selected Portland-Area Communities by Housing-Rule Classification, 1985 to 1989

Density class	No. of units per acre		
	Single-family	Multiple-family	Total
10 units/acre	5.0	21.0	9.6
8 units/acre	4.8	18.0	8.4
6 units/acre	2.4	14.0	3.1
All	4.9	19.7	9.0

Source: 1000 Friends 1991

DISCUSSION

Research on the effects of statewide land use planning provides clear evidence of the program's impact on the content of local comprehensive plans. As a result of state review, UGBs are more circumspect than local governments would themselves have drawn; urban services are better planned and coordinated[10]; and residential land is zoned for higher-density development. But evidence of the planning effort's impact on the housing market is more ambiguous.

This ambiguity in Oregon—and in other states—reflects, in part, limitations in data and in research design. It is possible to examine differences in land and housing values within states and to isolate their sources. But because states differ in so many critical respects, it is nearly impossible to do such studies across states. Similar limitations apply to differences in housing density and mix, which create uncertainties in interpretating research results.

A continuing source of controversy, for example, concerns the impact of UGBs on land and housing values. Land value in Oregon differs on opposite sides of a UGB; however, housing value in Oregon cities differs little from the housing value in other cities in the western U.S. There are at least two viable explanations for this paradox. First, UGBs may simply redistribute speculative land values without affecting the overall supply and thus the use value of urban land (see box insert, An Illustrative Hedonic Price Equation, in chapter 2). Second, the housing price in other western states, to which Oregon's housing price is compared, may also have been influenced by land use controls (Black and Dunau 1981). Thus UGBs and other land use controls may increase land and housing values in Oregon, but not more than in other western states. Land use controls in Oregon are imposed statewide, which is the reason Oregon receives so much publicity for them; but it is not clear that land use controls imposed at the state level are more restrictive of residential development than similar controls imposed at the local level. In fact, the available evidence suggests just the opposite.

The more current source of controversy concerns the influence of land use controls on housing density and mix. Recent research by 1000 Friends of Oregon demonstrates that the percentage of multiple-family housing has increased since adoption of the Metropolitan Housing Rule. One Thousand Friends attributes the rise to the rule. But the share of multiple-family development was as high in Portland during the early 1970s as it was during the late 1980s, and the share of multiple-family housing during both periods did not exceed similar shares in other western cities. Further, the overall density of housing construction—even during the recent multiple-family boom—fell significantly short of the allowed density.

There are several possible reasons why unambiguous changes in the content of comprehensive plans in the Portland metropolitan area have ambiguous impacts on housing density and housing mix. First, comprehensive plans before 1973 were not binding. Although little land was planned or zoned for high-density or multiple-family use before 1973, perhaps developers were not held to the low-density zoning that did exist. Thus, despite substantial changes in land use plans, actual changes in the regulatory environment may have been slight. Second, although comprehensive plans after 1978 contained additional land zoned for high-density and multiple-family use, zoning typically imposes maximum, not minimum, density constraints. The Metropolitan Housing Rule encourages but does not require high-density or multiple-family development.[11] Finally, although the Metropolitan Housing Rule made multiple-family and high-density housing possible, it did not make it profitable. In the absence of constraints on urban land supplies, the land price remained low; and low land price creates incentives to use more land in housing development. Thus, while the Metropolitan Housing Rule may have altered the regulatory environment, it did not alter the economic environment in which housing was developed—at least not in ways that foster higher-density development (cf., box inserts, pages 74 and 75).[12]

The lack of conclusive evidence—either positive or negative—on the impact of statewide planning on the housing market, however, must be viewed in historical context. Although Oregon's land use program has been in place since 1973, the legal and administrative structure for implementing the program has only recently been organized. In that regard, the state is further ahead in meeting its housing goal than it is in meeting other goals. What is more, the period in which the state housing policy has been in place has been volatile for the housing industry, thus the policy may not yet have been tested appropriately. If the housing market in Oregon had grown as expected when local comprehensive plans were prepared, the influence of state housing policy might have been quite different. Unfortunately, because of the near collapse of the Oregon housing market in the early 1980s, it is not clear whether the market failed to put pressure on meaningful land use controls or whether political and economic pressure rendered land use controls meaningless. Time will tell. At this point, however, the influence of Oregon's land use program on housing price, starts, density, and mix remains highly uncertain.

LESSONS FROM OREGON

By Oregon state law, local land use plans must address the housing needs of residents. Over the course of nearly two decades, Oregon's statewide land use program has spawned an extensive set of statutes, administrative rules, and judicial interpretations specifying how comprehensive plans must address housing issues. These statutes, rules, and interpretations form the basis of Oregon's housing policy. The statewide land use program thus provides the means by which state government promulgates state housing policy.

Through the process of acknowledgment review, the state is able to force local governments to plan in accordance with its housing policy, one which favors compact urban growth and inclusionary zoning. With the assistance of influential interest groups and the state judiciary, LCDC has been able to change considerably the content of local comprehensive plans. Urban growth boundaries are tighter than they otherwise would have been. And local governments—at least in the Portland metropolitan area—can no longer practice exclusionary zoning.

Despite state policy favoring compact urban growth, state land use planning and regulation does not necessarily lead to higher land and housing costs. Contrary to widespread expectations, Oregon's planning program has not resulted in excessively high housing costs. While it may never be known whether housing price would have been lower without state land use planning, it is clear that statewide planning has not caused residents to suffer housing costs that are higher than those of neighboring states—indeed Oregon's housing costs continue to be lower.

Statewide land use planning also does not clearly lead to a wider mix of housing types or to higher-density housing development. While regulations prohibit local governments in the Portland metropolitan area from practicing exclusionary zoning, the percentage of multiple-family housing starts in the area is no higher now than it was in the early 1970s or than it was in other western cities in the late 1980s. Although the state's inclusionary zoning policy may have facilitated the multiple-family housing boom in the late 1980s, inclusionary zoning appears to be neither a necessary nor a sufficient condition for increasing the share of high-density, multiple-family housing.

Finally, in Oregon and elsewhere, resolving the problem of affordable housing will likely require more than a policy that requires inclusionary zoning. The lackluster performance of the Oregon economy, the increase in allowed densities within UGBs, and the coordination of planning for urban services has likely increased the supply of housing relative to demand—and reduced housing costs. But according to microeconomic principles, increasing the supply of developable land lowers land and housing costs and encourages developers to build large, low-density housing for those who are able to purchase housing that has been produced for profit. The evidence from Oregon suggests that statewide land use planning has not altered these fundamental economic principles.

Notes

1. Ellickson views exclusionary zoning requirements as a tax on housing that benefits a minority at the expense of the majority.
2. See Mercer and Morgan (1982) and Segal and Srinivansan (1985) for more on supply and demand for housing.
3. A major determinant of the attractiveness of a local area to new residents is the availability of local employment.
4. In conventional economic theory, the direction of causation runs the other way, i.e., the value of land is determined by the value of housing. The direction of causation can, however, be reversed, such as with the forward shifting of a tax.
5. See discussion in chapter 2.

6. An important data limitation on housing price and cost stems from the difficulty of holding constant the unit of housing. That is, the housing price has increased over the years but so have the size and quality of the housing stock. The studies reviewed and the data presented in this chapter are not adjusted for changes in the size and quality of the housing stock and must be interpreted accordingly.

7. The Beaton results have been confirmed by studies in several other locations. For example, see Fischel (1988b).

8. See Gordon (1981, 202–3).

9. Although the report by 1000 Friends argues that the Metropolitan Housing Rule did contribute to the rise of multiple-family housing starts from 1985 to 1989, it lists two caveats "which suggest that sustained development of greater than 50 percent multiple family is not possible through the planning horizon:

   Caveat I: Construction permits for multiple family approvals peaked in 1985 and 1989. These two years 'prop up' the new construction mix during the study period. . . . Coupled with the recent 'cooling off' of the multifamily market, this gives us reason to doubt whether Metropolitan Housing Rule objectives for housing mix will be met through the planning period.
   Caveat II: Even if all remaining land, so designated, is developed for multiple-family use—and at maximum densities—housing opportunities foregone preclude development of at least 50 percent multiple family through the planning horizon. Critical multiple-family housing opportunities were foregone because a significant amount of single-family housing developed on land zoned 'multiple family.'"

10. For more on urban services, see chapter 4.

11. See note 9, Caveat II.

12. In a survey of planners and project engineers by 1000 Friends (1991) to determine why densities fell short of planned densities, market demand was chosen as more influential than site constraints, regulatory constraints, facility or service inadequacy, and citizen opposition.

4

Urban Services Planning and Management

P LANNING FOR URBAN SERVICES is an integral part of land use planning as a whole. Land cannot be successfully urbanized until it offers essential services, including access, shelter, water supplies, and wastewater removal, often collectively referred to as "infrastructure." Although buildings for shelter are usually provided by private developers or contractors, the remaining essential urban services are typically provided by numerous and diverse public or semipublic agencies. The challenge of providing and maintaining adequate public services has been persistent and difficult, and planners are still uncertain about how best to meet it. By the mid-1980s the inadequacy of urban infrastructure had reached crisis proportions (Porter and Peiser 1984), a crisis reflecting the inability of local governments to meet rapidly rising service demands.

Demands for urban infrastructure continue to rise at a rapid rate for two reasons. First, continuing urban growth creates a need to serve ever more land, especially in rapidly growing regions. Second, increasingly stringent environmental standards require expanded capabilities to remove and treat urban wastes. This requires, for example, more and better sewage treatment plants, landfills, and stormwater retention capacity.

For several reasons, local governments have failed to supply urban services in pace with rising demands. First, financial support for urban infrastructure from the federal government, which rose rapidly during the 1970s, fell equally rapidly in the fiscally constrained 1980s. This quick entry and exit of federal dollars left local governments with large and aging stocks of public facilities and few resources with which to maintain or expand them.

Second, property tax revolts swept the nation, placing strict limitations on the largest source of revenues for most local governments. Finally, rising factor costs, especially the cost of debt, rendered public services increasingly costly to provide.

Caught between rising demands, falling revenues, and rising costs, local governments sought new approaches to infrastructure planning and finance. Some local governments made urban growth contingent upon provision of essential public services, thereby slowing the rate of urban growth. Others adopted new methods of infrastructure finance—such as tax-increment financing, system development fees, and developer exactions—thereby shifting the costs of infrastructure to new residents. Still others established new institutions for providing urban services, such as local improvement districts, municipal service districts, and regional service agencies. Some local governments combined several of these approaches. In the process, however, the planning and management of urban services became a critical element in land use planning.

This chapter examines the planning and management of urban services in Oregon. It begins with a discussion of conceptual issues in providing public services. This discussion identifies unique characteristics of urban services and goals for planning and managing them. Next the chapter describes the development and implementation of Oregon's Goal 11, Public Facilities and Services. The chapter continues with a review of studies on the performance of a regional service district, focusing on the differences in land value, urban development, and local government finance among service regions. The chapter concludes with lessons from Oregon on public facility planning and management.

CONCEPTUAL ISSUES IN PUBLIC SERVICE PLANNING AND MANAGEMENT

The conceptual foundations of public service planning and management stem from four fundamental characteristics of public services. First, public services are provided by a large number of disparate sources, which requires coordination among and between providers. Second, urban public services depend on capital-intensive public facilities, thus public services exhibit significant economies of scale. Third, public services are immobile, causing costs to vary significantly based on distance from central facilities. Finally, public service facilities are durable and operate over extended periods of time. These characteristics create unique problems both in providing public services and in establishing objectives for public facility planning.

Interagency Coordination

Urban development entails supplying diverse and essential public services—from a variety of private and semiprivate providers—to new parcels of land. Fostering intergovernmental coordination is therefore a fundamental goal of public service planning (Lim 1983).

Economies of Scale

When land is developed at low densities, some services can be provided on a parcel-by-parcel basis. Residential developments at less than one unit per acre, for example, are often possible on septic systems, private wells, and private roads. Due to environmental constraints, however, development at high densities requires large, central facilities, such as water pumping stations, sewage treatment plants, and integrated road networks.

These large facilities, however, represent substantial capital costs, thus fixed costs are high relative to the costs of operation. That is, once a capital facility has been built, the cost of expanding services to additional parcels of land is relatively low. In economic parlance, the marginal costs are less than the average costs of providing urban services for a significant range of customers.[1]

This cost structure creates the conditions for a natural monopoly: a single or small number of providers can supply public services at lower costs than many competing providers in a given area. Unfortunately, unregulated, profit-maximizing monopolies often charge prices in excess of their marginal and average costs, resulting in monopoly profits and inefficient public service provision. To realize the benefits of scale economies and to avoid the inefficiencies of monopoly pricing, public intervention is required. As a result, most public services are provided by either regulated monopolies or public agencies. Capturing the benefits of the system's economies of scale while avoiding monopoly pricing is therefore one objective of public services planning and management.

Economies of Geographic Scope

Capital facilities necessary for providing urban services are both large and immobile; as a result, the costs of providing services vary by the location of the customer. In general, service costs rise with distance from central facilities. For example, the costs of transmitting water, wastewater, and power vary widely by location. Locating development—and clustering it—near treatment plants, with careful scheduling for extension of interceptor sewers, can reduce the marginal cost of sewer service (Downing 1973). The unit cost for servicing high-density development is therefore lower than the unit cost of servicing low-density development (Windsor 1979; Frank 1989). The precise nature of the spatial variation in costs depends, of course, on the characteristics of individual facilities (Frank 1989).

Consider the distribution of drinking water from a central treatment plant. If the load at a treatment plant doubles because the service area doubles in density, then all the pipes in the system need to be enlarged. But if the treatment plant load doubles because the service area doubles in size, then all the distribution pipes have to be extended in length and the existing pipes have to be doubled in size to handle the extra flow. Further, to maintain adequate flow at the fringes of the system, the water has to be pumped at a higher pressure, which requires that all the pipe joints be upgraded. Increasing treatment plant load while holding density constant also exacerbates the problem of "peaking." The fewer the customers on a given line, the higher the ratio of peak demand to mean daily demand. Capturing these economies of location requires development at a certain level of density, and thus represents another important objective in public facility planning and management.

Public Service Finance

The need for large capital facilities affects the financing, as well as the scale and location, of public services. Constructing public facilities requires large capital investments at the time of construction; yet once the facility has been constructed, the facility provides services for an extended period of time. Thus the explicit costs of providing a certain urban service vary significantly over the life of a particular facility. Spreading capital costs evenly over time, therefore, requires diligent saving before construction of a new facility, making principal and interest payments after construction, or receiving intergovernmental construction grants.

Although many public facilities were once financed by construction grants from the federal government, such funding has become increasingly scarce. Local governments' saving up for investments in capital facilities has become nearly equally uncommon. And debt has become increasingly costly and difficult to obtain. Thus as urban areas have expanded and the need for new or larger public facilities has grown, finding appropriate financing methods has added to the problem of planning and managing public services.

In sum, the nature of public services presents a complex problem in land use planning. Public services are necessary for urban development. But assuring that they are provided efficiently, by a disparate set of public agencies, requires considerable planning and intergovernmental coordination. Assuring that public services are provided at appropriate scales and locations requires planning the sizes of facilities, the scopes of the service areas, and the densities of the service areas. Finally, assuring that funds are available for public facilities requires careful financial planning over a considerable time horizon.

PUBLIC FACILITIES PLANNING AND MANAGEMENT IN OREGON

Public facility planning and management has played an increasingly prominent role in Oregon's land use program. Goal 11, the public services and facilities goal, was among the original 14 goals adopted by LCDC in 1974. To meet the requirements of Goal 11, local governments had to demonstrate that urban services were provided in urban areas and not extended into areas designated for rural use. When adopted, the public services goal was intended to help contain urban growth. In the 1980s, however, as planning objectives changed from urban containment to urban development, new administrative rules were adopted, requiring local governments to use public facility planning to facilitate urban growth. More recently, in the fiscally constrained 1990s, Goal 11 became a vehicle for addressing increasingly difficult problems in financing urban services.

Goal 11: Public Facilities and Services

Goal 11 of the statewide land use goals and guidelines requires local governments, "To plan and develop a timely, orderly and efficient arrangement of public facilities and services to serve as a framework for urban and rural development." The goal is clarified as follows:

> Urban and rural development shall be guided and supported by types and levels of urban and rural public facilities and services appropriate for, but limited to, the needs and requirements of the urban, urbanizable and rural areas to be served. A provision for *key facilities* shall be included in each plan. (Oregon LCDC 1990)

Goal 11 addresses three types of land: urban, urbanizable, and rural. In general, Goal 11 requires that public services be provided in a manner commensurate with, and appropriate for, the type and intensity of development in a given area. Goal 11 defines urban and rural facilities and services as follows:

> *Rural Facilities and Services*—refers to facilities and services which the governing body determines to be suitable and appropriate solely for the needs of rural use.
>
> *Urban Facilities and Services*—refers to key facilities and to appropriate types and levels of at least the following: police protection; sanitary facilities; storm drainage facilities; planning, zoning and subdivision control; health services; recreation facilities and services; energy and communication services; and community governmental services. (Oregon LCDC 1990)

Although Goal 11 clearly expressed the intent of public facility planning, it left a fundamental question unanswered: what levels of services are appropriate for various types of land use? Lacking explicit guidance prior to 1975, communities were empowered to approve development regardless of the availability of public facilities. Between 1975 and 1985, LCDC decisions and judicial interpretations held that development within UGBs could not be denied for want of adequate public facilities unless it involved zone changes or plan amendments, or resulted in premature development of urbanizable areas (Nelson and Knaap 1987).

After 1985 the attitude towards public facility planning and programming changed. In the late 1980s, a case was taken before the Land Use Board of Appeals (LUBA) by neighbors opposing approval of a new development within an urban service area on the grounds that the local public schools would not have capacity to accommodate students generated by the development.[2] The case pushed Oregon's public facility policy towards Florida-style "concurrency," in which facilities and services needed to support new development are required to be in place concurrent with development (Starnes 1991). Subsequent cases have given greater latitude to the application of this concept in Oregon. At present, water, sewer, and road capacity must be available to accommodate new development (ORS 197.752), but capacity in other public facilities, such as schools, parks, fire, and police, need not be available concurrent with development as long as the jurisdiction has a plan to expand these services within a reasonable period of time.

Administrative Rules for Public Facility Planning

Although local governments had to demonstrate that public services were available or would soon be provided to existing urban areas, public facilities planning for future urban development received little attention in the early years of the process. Plans approved prior to 1985 were not required to include public facility plans to accommodate anticipated growth. Local governments were also not required to demonstrate financial capacity to pay for needed facilities. Although a proposal during the initial hearings on establishing planning goals during 1974 by the LCDC's first vice-chairman, Steven R. Schell, would have required capital improvement plans with financial components to assure provision of facilities within UGBs, the proposal was not adopted. Not until the acknowledgment phase was nearly over were local governments explicitly required to demonstrate that they would make public services available to accommodate future development within UGBs.

In 1985, administrative rules were adopted requiring local governments to prepare, adopt, and submit public facility plans for all urban areas with populations greater than 2,500 (OAR 660-11-000 to 660-11-050). Oregon defines a public facility plan as a support document (or set of documents) to a comprehensive plan that describes the water, sewer, and transportation facilities necessary to support the land uses specified in the plan. The local government responsible for preparing the public facility plan must be established via a *growth management agreement* for the urban area. Public facility plans are to be prepared before the responsible government's first periodic review.

Public facility plans must contain:

- An inventory, describing the location, capacity, and condition of existing facilities
- A list of proposed projects, including type, location, and capacity
- Rough cost estimates for proposed projects, to generally establish the fiscal requirements of the comprehensive plan's designated land uses and to assist in reviewing existing funding mechanisms
- Policy statements, identifying the providers of every system and project
- Estimates of the timing of each public facility project, which must be commensurate with the comprehensive plan's projected growth estimates, and
- A discussion of the funding mechanisms for each project and their ability cover costs. (OAR 660-11-005)

The role of public facility planning after 1985 was to facilitate the conversion of urbanizable land into urban land. In theory, facility expansion to accommodate urban development was not to be allowed in urbanizable areas until areas already provided with facilities were fully developed. Only then would roads, water and sewer systems, and other facilities and services be extended into urbanizable areas. In practice, this was difficult to implement for two reasons. First, many landowners in urbanizable areas could not be deprived of development rights essentially because that action resembled a constitutional "taking" of private property without just compensation, which applies even if development is merely postponed. This issue was often resolved through interim zoning mechanisms that allow low-density development on a case-by-case basis. For example, a home might be allowed on a two-acre tract provided it is located in such a fashion as to enable economical subdivision of the tract at some future time. Thus throughout the state, *redivision plans,* also known as "concept plats," are on file in local government offices and are used in planning future facility extensions.

Second, local governments lacked guidance from LCDC regarding when and where to extend urban facilities and services into urbanizable areas. In theory, all urbanizable areas have tentative engineering plans showing the location and timing of facility extensions. When the urban area becomes "built out," part of the urbanizable area is "opened" for development through rezoning and facility extensions. In practice, if a developer can demonstrate that the supply of buildable land is exhausted and that facility extensions opening new areas for development would result in contiguous development patterns, then development of urbanizable areas is usually allowed.

The approach toward urban growth management prescribed by Goal 11 and its companion administrative rule, differs markedly from the approach taken in other states. Whereas local governments in other states, such as Florida, use public facilities to dictate the pace and direction of urban growth, the long-term pace and direction of urban growth in Oregon are pre-established by land use designations—principally the UGB. Thus, the framework for achieving long-term efficiency in the scale and geography of urban services is established by the UGB. As a result, public facility planning serves not as the "linchpin" in the development process (Starnes 1991), but as an instrument for managing short-term urban growth within the UGB.

New Directions in Public Facility Finance

The administrative rule amplifying the requirements of Goal 11 did much to improve the planning for public facilities in urban areas. The rule helped to improve coordination among public facility providers, to establish a framework for extending urban services within UGBs, and to identify future facility needs. It also required local governments to plan the timing and funding of future capital facility projects. However, the rule said that plans for future capital facilities projects are expressly not considered land use decisions, and thus cannot serve as a basis for appeal (ORS 197.610(1) and ORS 197.835(4)). That is, because financial resources for constructing new capital facilities remain generally beyond the control of local governments, long-term plans for capital facilities represent hopes for, rather than commitments to, meeting public facility needs. Thus, even though local governments throughout the state began to prepare extensive capital improvement plans, the crisis in capital facility financing remained.

Factors leading to the national crisis in urban infrastructure have affected communities in Oregon as they have communities in other states. Federal funding for urban infrastructure continues to decline. The state's ability to finance urban services has been crippled by economic recessions and property tax revolt. And while growth in Oregon was slow in the 1980s, it is projected to grow rapidly again in the 1990s. Capital facility planning did not alter these fundamental trends. Not surprisingly, then, the ability of local governments in Oregon to meet public facility needs remains strained.[3]

Required capital facility planning did help identify public facility needs; and as local governments identified needs, state agencies reexamined their roles in meeting them. *Making the Right Turn: Protecting the Public Investment in Oregon's Roads and Bridges,* a report prepared for the Oregon Department of Transportation (Price Waterhouse 1986), projected a need for Oregon cities and counties to invest nearly $20 billion before the year 2004 to meet the state's road system requirements (see table 15).

An Assessment of Funding for Sewerage and Drinking-Water Facilities in the State of Oregon, conducted for the Oregon Health Division (ECO Northwest et al. 1989), projects a need for cities and counties to invest $3.5 billion in sewer and water systems before the year 2008 (see table 16). A review of these and other studies, entitled *Local Government Infrastructure Funding in Oregon,* prepared for the LCDC (Center for Urban Studies 1990), revealed that state agencies provide financing for about one-fifth of the identified needs for road, sewer, and drinking water projects. But even with this level of state support, about one-half of projected public facility needs remains underfunded (see table 17).

Table 15.   Estimated Expenditure on Road Systems by City and County, 1987 to 2004

Type	Expenditure, in $ million		
	Counties	Cities	Total
Operations & maintenance	2,878	1,892	4,770
Repair & preservation	3,874	1,361	5,235
Construction & expansion	1,092	586	1,678
Backlog[a]	5,947	2,017	7,964
TOTAL	13,791	5,856	19,647

[a]Existing requirements for repair, preservation, construction, and expansion.
SOURCE: Price Waterhouse 1986, 12

The LCDC report also showed that local governments raised revenues for public services from a variety of sources, including property taxes, user fees, system development charges, and intergovernmental grants. These sources were found sufficient for meeting the operating costs of most public services, excluding schools, parks, and police and fire service. None of these sources, however, was found suitable to pay the capital costs of public service facilities. Rate payers generally refused to allow public service providers to accumulate savings by charging rates that exceed operating costs. Also, Oregon voters throughout the state rejected bond levies necessary to issue general obligation bonds, and the electorate recently passed a property tax limitation referendum further constraining the use of property-tax financed debt. Finally, by state statute, system development charges (often known as exactions) may recover only the actual cost of off-site capacity related to new developments. As a result, the report concludes, local revenue sources are inadequate to meet local public facility needs. The study recommends that the state of Oregon expand its role in assisting local governments finance infrastructure.

The state's ability to provide financial assistance, however, is also limited. Although the state has greater bonding potential than most local

Table 16.   Estimated Expenditure on Sewer and Water Systems in Oregon, 1988 to 2008

Type	Expenditure, in $ million		
	Current	Future	Total
Sewer	1,003	569	1,572
Water	760	1,141	1,901
TOTAL	1,764	1,710	3,473

SOURCE: ECO Northwest et al. 1989

governments, the state's bond rating is lower than some communities', which makes the state's interest rates higher. The state also has a broad tax base, but that is limited because Oregon has no sales tax. As a result, policy makers are exploring institutional alternatives for addressing public service needs. ECO Northwest et al. (1989), for example, reviewed several institutional arrangements for providing sewer and water services, including county service districts, sanitary districts and authorities, water supply authorities, and joint operating agencies. *Safety on Tap: A Strategy for Providing Safe Dependable Drinking Water in the 1990s*, published by the Oregon Health Division, recommends that "DLCD dedicate new resources for public facilities planning and that individual systems become eligible for technical assistance grants to examine regionalization options" (35). Further, the report states

> The periodic review process and the current requirement for public facility planning can provide a framework for a planning and coordination effort involving water providers throughout the state. Since state law already requires cities to prepare facility plans and designates counties as the coordinator for planning by various governments and districts, cities and counties could become responsible for effective water supply planning. This would provide a way to achieve better water system coordination and reduce the economic impacts of new drinking water regulation.

In sum, Oregon's approach to public service management and planning evolved in response to ever-changing economic conditions. From 1974 to 1985, local governments were required only to see that public services were provided in a manner consistent with the objectives of urban growth management. Since 1985, the state has required local governments to prepare public facility plans to facilitate urban development within urban growth

Table 17. Estimated Annual Expenditure on Infrastructure, and Sources of State Funding

Infrastructure type	Expenditure, in $ million
County and city roads	764
Water	136
Sewer	79
TOTAL	979

State aid	Amount, in $ million
Gas tax (FY 89–90)	154
Wastewater treatment grants	33
Other	18
TOTAL	205

Gas tax revenues are reported for most recent year since they have been increasing. State aid in other programs fluctuates from year to year, so averages are reported.
SOURCE: Center for Urban Studies 1990

boundaries. Today the state is exploring how public facility plans can serve as the basis for institutional reform to resolve problems in public facility finance.

EVALUATING THE PERFORMANCE OF REGIONAL SERVICE DISTRICTS

For historical reasons, public services in Oregon are provided by a variety of organizations, including city and county governments, special service districts, local improvement districts, and intergovernmental councils—big and small. Some of these institutional forms are more suited than others to provide public services in the current economic environment. Thus, enhancing efficiency may require institutional changes (ECO Northwest et al. 1989, Oregon Health Division 1991). Recent studies examined differences among service-providing organizations in interagency coordination and the impact of services on land value, urban growth rate, and fiscal health. These studies give insight into the prospects for institutional reform in public services provision.

The Portland metropolitan area, excluding the city of Portland itself,[4] provides an opportunity to compare the performance of alternative institutional arrangements for providing urban services. The area, which includes more than 30 cities and significant unincorporated settlements over 3 counties, has 17 regional sewer service agencies. Sixteen of them serve most of the urban portions of Clackamas and Multnomah Counties; the other agency—the Unified Sewerage Agency (USA)—serves urban Washington County and portions of western Clackamas and Multnomah Counties (see figure 8).

The USA was formed in 1969 to bring 26 separate sewer districts under central control. The agency is governed by the Washington County Commissioners, but has a budget separate from the county at large. The USA provides sewer and stormwater service to 12 cities in the metropolitan area and to unincorporated parts of 3 counties. With respect to sewer services, then, metropolitan Portland consists of two identifiable sewer planning and

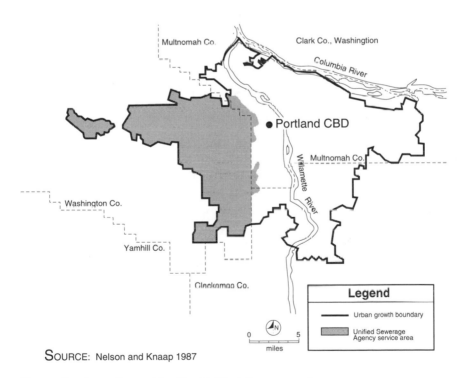

SOURCE: Nelson and Knaap 1987

Figure 8. Area Served by the Unified Sewerage Agency

delivery regions: a western region, served by USA, one centralized agency, and an eastern region, served by 16 separate sewer agencies.

Regional Sewer Service and Interagency Coordination

A study funded by the Portland Metropolitan Home Builders Association explored differences between the USA and the remaining regional sewer service providers in the metropolitan area from a developer's perspective (Bolen 1979). The study revealed that between 1976 and 1978, it took from 3 to 25 months, or an average of 10.3 months, for 15 selected subdivisions to be approved in Clackamas and Multnomah Counties, which comprise most of the eastern sewer planning region in the Portland metropolitan area. Subdivisions in Washington County, which makes up most of the USA service region, obtained approval in 4 to 20 months, or an average of 9 months, for 10 selected cases. Subdivision permits were awarded roughly six weeks more quickly in Washington County than elsewhere in the metropolitan area.

Sewer connection fees for single-family units ranged from $350 to $1,800 and averaged just under $800 in the decentralized sewer region, but they were a flat $680 within the USA region. Sewer connection fees for multiple-family units in the decentralized region ranged from $350 to more than $1,250 per unit and averaged $700. But, again, the fee was a flat $680 per unit in the USA region. Sewer connection fees generally were less complicated to administer and lower in the USA region than in the decentralized sewer region.

Interviews with builders revealed that many were often frustrated in dealing with the smaller service providers. In one case, three sewer districts were operated out of the same office but each had slightly different administrative procedures, which were sometimes difficult for developers to keep clear. A number of smaller sewer agencies relied on consulting engineers for technical matters. Often, developers needed to make special appointments with those consultants, paying them directly (or through an agency) for their time and information. Sometimes smaller agency offices were not open during regular business hours, did not possess routine information, such as maps of interceptor sewers, and had trouble tracking down their consulting engineers in a timely manner to answer basic questions or to make appointments. This was especially troublesome for developers working in areas that had several sewer agencies within close proximity to each other. Sometimes, as well, the sewer agency not only was located in a separate building away from city planning offices, but was administered by an independent and elected governing body. This separation generated confusion between local plans and local sewer capacities, frustration between the sewer providers and planning officials, and frustration for many builders, who could not always interact effectively with the smaller agencies.

In contrast, the USA serves a large area from a central office that is always open during business hours. Developers could visit the office without an appointment and inspect and obtain copies of maps and plans (free or for a small printing charge). There was almost always at least one engineer in the office during business hours to answer questions from drop-ins. Developers also could easily make appointments with agency engineers and administrators. Furthermore, the agency was housed in the county courthouse, which also housed planning and building permit agencies of the county (but not of the many cities within the region). The governing body of the USA was the Washington County Board of Commissioners, which greatly expedited coordination of the USA not only with other county agencies, but also with the many cities affected by the USA.

In sum, Bolen found that the USA was superior to its subregional counterparts from the perspective of developers. Not only did the USA provide sewer service at a lower cost and in less time, but the USA was better able to facilitate coordination between the developer and the sewer provider and coordination between the sewer provider and other government agencies.

Regional Sewer Service and Urban Land Value

Nelson and Knaap (1987) compared the USA to the remaining regional service providers in the Portland metropolitan area from the perspective of the land market. They argued that if the USA offered better service performance than the other providers in the Portland metropolitan area, such differences would be reflected in land values. That is, developers would be willing to pay more for land within the USA service region than for land outside it; and if the land market is reasonably competitive, such increased willingness to pay by developers would be capitalized into land values.

Using data and models similar to those reported by Knaap (1985), Nelson and Knaap (1987) focused specifically on variables reflecting the influence of public services (see table 18). They found that parcels located within 300 feet of the nearest interceptor sewer line were approximately 14 percent higher in price than comparable parcels more than 300 feet away.

Table 18. Determinants of Land Value, Urban Areas of Clackamas, Multnomah, and Washington Counties, 1979 to 1980

Variable	Regression coefficient $(t)^p$ ($N = 764$; $R^2 = 0.595$)
Intercept	6.150
Distance from Portland city center in driving time during peak commuting hours	−0.233 (2.77)***
Presence of multi-family zoning for more than 17 units per acre	0.856 (6.31)***
Presence of multi-family zoning for less than 17 units per acre	0.560 (5.58)***
Presence of single-family zoning for more than 4.4 units per acre	0.451 (5.63)***
Location of parcel in a subdivision plat	0.494 (6.77)***
Median family income of census tract of the parcel	0.681 (5.10)***
Month in which parcel was sold	0.008 $(1.38)^{ns}$
Presence of 25%+ slopes	0.062 $(0.81)^{ns}$
Property tax rate per $1000 of valuation	−0.094 $(0.44)^{ns}$
Size of the parcel, in acres	−0.358 (10.89)***
Presence of sewer interceptor within 300 feet	0.175 (4.58)***

** $p < 0.05$, one-tailed test.
*** $p < 0.01$, one-tailed test.
ns p not significant.
SOURCE: Nelson and Knaap 1987

Continued on next page

Table 18. *Continued*

Variable	Regression coefficient $(t)^p$ ($N = 764$; $R^2 = 0.595$)
Location of the parcel within the 10-year intermediate growth boundary	0.531 (6.77)***
Location of parcel within Portland city limits	−0.274 (3.64)***
Location of parcel outside corporate limits of any city	−0.184 (3.56)***
Percentage of white population in census tract of parcel	0.258 (1.73)**
Location within Unified Sewerage Agency	0.316 (6.52)***
F	68.64

This suggests that proximity to an interceptor line enhances property values both inside and outside the USA. Further, Nelson and Knaap found that the effects on land value of proximity to a sewer line were slightly, but not significantly, higher inside the USA.

What is more, Nelson and Knaap found that location within the USA service region had a significant and positive effect on land value. Land values within the USA region were about 32 percent higher than land values elsewhere. These findings suggest that participants in the land market indeed view the performance of the USA as superior to the performance of other service providers, and that such performance differences are capitalized into land values.

Regional Sewer Service and Urban Growth

As Nelson and Knaap explored differences in land value due to sewer service, Kamara (1984, 1987) explored differences in rate of urban growth due to urban services. Using census tracts as units of analysis, Kamara addressed two issues: the influence of urban services on the location of metropolitan-area growth and the influence of centralized sewer service on the location of metropolitan-area growth.

Kamara gathered data on geographic, socioeconomic, and public service characteristics for each census tract in the Portland metropolitan area for 1970 and 1980 and organized the data into groups comprising Clark, Clackamas, Multnomah, and Washington Counties. With these data Kamara tested a model that specified the number of housing starts as a function of seven independent variables for each census tract (see table 19).

As shown in table 19, all of the variables measuring increases in public services had positive effects on housing production except percentage change in lane-miles of arterial street networks, which was insignificant. Based on these results, Kamara concluded that urban services variables best explain variation in the number of housing starts in a given region. That is, accord-

Table 19. Determinants of Residential Construction, Urban Fringe of Portland MSA, 1970 and 1980

Variable	Regression coefficient $(t)^p$	Beta	R^2
Net vacant land	0.24 (4.20)***	0.32	0.10
Median family income	1.95 (3.41)***	0.26	0.03
Percentage increase in sewer and water services	0.16 (3.94)***	0.30	0.27
Percentage increase in septic tanks and cesspools	0.14 (2.00)***	0.15	0.02
Distance to Portland CBD	0.03 (2.74)***	0.25	0.03
Percentage change in lane-miles of arterial street networks	1.23 (5.13)***	0.43	0.16
Future changes in lane-miles of arterial street networks	−0.39 (−1.72)^{ns}	−0.16	0.04

*** $p < 0.01$.
ns p not significant.
SOURCE: Kamara 1987

ing to Kamara, infrastructure is the most important determinant of residential development.

Kamara also found that Washington County grew faster than either Multnomah or Clackamas County during the 1970s, attracting about 88,000 of the nearly 172,000 new residents in the metropolitan area, or more than half of the decade's population growth, while accounting for little more than 6,000 acres, or less than half, of the metropolitan area's nearly 14,000 acres converted to urban uses during the decade. Over that period, Washington County surpassed Clackamas County in total population, and its relative growth, Kamara inferred, stems from the formation of the Unified Sewerage Agency in 1972. Based on these findings, Kamara concluded that "a regional service district fosters more fringe-area urban growth than a number of smaller ones, probably suggesting that within a county, the larger the area covered by one district, the more economical the service to the consumer" (Kamara 1984, 163).[5]

Regional Sewer Service and Fiscal Structure

Extending the work by Nelson and Knaap and the work by Kamara, Nelson (1987) explored the influence of regional sewer service on regional fiscal structure. If regional sewer service results in higher land values and accelerates urban growth, Nelson argued, such benefits should be reflected in the fiscal health of local governments. To support his argument, Nelson presented data on population, land development, sewer service, residential growth, and property value, by county, from 1970 to 1980. Tables 20, 21, and 22 present and update Nelson's findings.

Table 20. Population by County, Oregon Portion of Portland MSA, 1970 to 1990

County	1970 population	1990 population	Change, 1970–1990	Percentage change	Percentage change in metro area
Clackamas	166,088	278,850	112,762	67.9	38.1
Multnomah	554,668	583,887	29,219	5.2	9.9
Washington	157,920	311,554	153,634	97.3	52.0
TOTAL	878,676	1,174,291	295,615		

SOURCES: U.S. Dept. of Commerce 1983; U.S. Dept. of Commerce 1991

Table 21.   Real Property Value by County, Oregon Portion of Portland MSA, 1971 and 1986

County	1971 assessed valuation, in $ million (percentage of region)	1986 assessed valuation, in $ million (percentage of region)	Change 1971–1986, in $ million (percentage of region)
Clackamas	1,513 (19.8)	8,618 (23.1)	7,105 (24.0)
Multnomah	4,679 (61.3)	18,863 (50.7)	14,184 (47.9)
Washington	1,442 (18.9)	9,750 (26.7)	8,308 (28.1)
TOTAL	7,634	37,230	29,597

SOURCE: U.S. Dept. of Commerce 1972; U.S. Dept. of Commerce 1987

The distribution of population growth in the metropolitan area between 1970 and 1989 is illustrated in table 20. As Nelson noted, the total amount of buildable urban land in 1970 in Clackamas and Washington Counties was roughly equivalent. That is, both had allocated nearly the same total amount of land for urban development. Nelson also noted that the entire urbanizable area of Washington County, but only very small portions of Clackamas and Multnomah Counties, are served by the USA. Based on these observations, Nelson suggested that the USA caused Washington County to grow faster than Clackamas County.

Nelson also reported assessed property value and changes in assessed property value in the three metropolitan counties on a total and per capita basis. Tables 21 and 22 present and update Nelson's data. As shown, total and per capita property values in Clackamas County exceeded those in Washington County in 1972; in 1987, however, total and per capita property values in Washington County exceeded those in Clackamas County.

Based on his review of the data, Nelson offered a three-part conclusion. First, a regional service district offers development savings that are capitalized into land values. Second, a regional service district is better able to attract urban-area growth. Third, the combined effects of development savings and induced growth alter the metropolitan tax base in favor of governments in the regional service district.

Table 22.   Real Property Value per Capita, Oregon Portion of Portland MSA, 1971 and 1986

County	1971 assessed valuation per capita, in $	1986 assessed valuation per capita, in $	Change, 1971–1986, in $	Percentage change, in $
Clackamas	9,310	33,546	24,236	260.3
Multnomah	8,436	33,268	24,832	294.4
Washington	9,131	35,925	26,794	293.4
Totals	8,688	34,000	25,312	

SOURCE: U.S. Dept. of Commerce 1972; U.S. Dept. of Commerce 1987

DISCUSSION

The objectives of public facility planning in Oregon are closely linked to the objectives of urban growth management. Public facility planning was once used largely to prevent urban development outside UGBs and more recently has been used to facilitate development inside UGBs. While the emphasis of public facility planning has perhaps changed, the objectives have not; for the best way to prevent development outside UGBs is to facilitate development inside UGBs, and vice versa. To implement this double-edged objective, Oregon crafted its own concurrency doctrine: local governments are required to assure concurrency within UGBs and are prevented from doing so outside UGBs. This doctrine changes concurrency, in the view of local governments, from a growth-control instrument into a growth-control responsibility. How this doctrine will work in an era of fiscal restraint, however, remains to be seen.

Oregon's concurrency doctrine also adds to the role of UGBs as policy instruments. Since public facilities must be planned in the context of UGBs, UGBs must be drawn with consideration of the scale and scope economies of public services. Failure to do so results in inefficient provision of public facilities. At the same time UGBs must be drawn in consideration of other planning goals—such as resource conservation and environmental protection. As a result, the objective of UGBs, as well as the objectives of public facility planning, extend beyond interagency coordination, economies of scale, economies of scope, and sound financial management.

The objectives of public facility planning and management alone, however, can perhaps be pursued through institutional reform. The studies reviewed here provide consistent evidence that public service provision by a regional service agency offers measurable benefits, benefits consistent with those discussed at the beginning of the chapter. A regional service provider brings under central control a number of distinct service agencies providing similar services. Research by Bolen (1979) suggests that such central control facilitates coordination among levels of government and coordination between the public and private sectors. Research by Nelson and Knaap suggests that land values are higher in areas served by a regional service agency, perhaps because the regional agency is better able to capture economies of scale. The available research thus offers consistent evidence that regional service providers indeed offer administrative and scale efficiencies.

Similarly, research by Kamara and by Nelson suggests that regional service providers are better able than other institutions to realize efficiencies in managing the geographic and financial aspects of service provision. Kamara demonstrates that regional service agencies are powerful magnets of urban growth and are therefore able to reach efficient density levels quickly and thus prevent or minimize inefficient urban sprawl. Kamara's findings suggest that regional service providers are better able to use public facilities to manage urban growth. Research by Nelson suggests that regional service providers offer promise for solving problems in infrastructure finance. The comparative fiscal strength of Washington County reflects both the fiscal benefits of strong and consistent urban growth and the ability of the USA to manage its own financial problems.

These findings, regarding the USA in metropolitan Portland, strengthen the case for institutional reform. The USA demonstrated superior performance because it was better able to achieve its basic objectives. Specifically, the USA was better able to coordinate various service providers with private developers, to capture economies of scale, to manage the geography of urban development, and to manage its own finances. All but the latter are possible through effective intergovernmental public facility planning. The ability of the USA to manage its own financial resources, however, stems largely from its ability to issue revenue bonds at reasonable interest rates. Disjointed urban service providers, even if well managed and planned, are unlikely to achieve similar financial capabilities.

In spite of the weight of evidence supporting regional service provision, the call for widespread institutional consolidation does not necessarily follow. Widespread consolidation of public service providers enhances the potential of administrative inefficiency as well as efficiency. Service agencies too large and powerful can exhibit diseconomies of scale, bureaucratic ineptitude, and monopoly pricing. Competition must balance concentration. Unlike Portland, many other Oregon cities are too small to capture the benefits of regionalization without forsaking the benefits of intergovernmental competition. For such communities smaller districts that are well planned and supported with state resources may be more appropriate.

What is more, the benefits of regional service provision have been measured in only one metropolitan area and with research designs that compare one provider to all other providers. From such studies it is not clear whether the benefits would exist if all services were to be regionalized or whether the regional service agency in Portland gained purely at the expense of other service providers.

Even in communities that cannot or will not reform institutions that provide public services, however, Oregon's planning requirements are likely to play an increasing role in public service provision. Not only will the planning requirements establish a framework for interagency coordination and urban growth management, but they will also play an important role in public facility finance. Because all state agencies must coordinate programs that affect land use with DLCD and local comprehensive plans, state agencies that fund public facilities can coordinate only with comprehensive plans. Thus a sound and acknowledged public facility plan will become a prerequisite for receiving state aid for public facilities and will thereby establish a critical link between state and local governments and between capital facility planning and capital facility finance.

LESSONS FROM OREGON

Public facilities are essential for effective land use and thus play a key role in the land development process. The need for large capital facilities in providing urban services, however, creates special planning problems in the scale, location, and financing of public services. Oregon's planning program requires local governments to confront these problems directly and in coordination with one another.

Goal 11 of Oregon's land use goals requires local governments to provide public facilities in a manner commensurate with the level of development. Although Oregon's land use laws stop short of Florida-style concurrency requirements, local governments in Oregon must provide urban-scale facilities in urban areas and rural-scale facilities in rural areas.

While the definitions of urban-scale and rural-scale continue to evolve through the judicial process, requisite facilities for urban development are generally limited to sewer, water, and transportation services. Oregon's narrow interpretation of requisite services for urban growth limits the number of agencies capable of preventing or delaying urban development.

Goal 11 also requires local governments to plan for the extension of public facilities into urbanizable areas within urban growth boundaries. Administrative rules require public facility plans to accommodate urban growth to the urban growth boundary. As a result, the urban growth boundary—and not the availability of urban services—serves as the primary instrument for urban growth management and as the determinant of urban form. Heavy reliance on UGBs for directing urban growth simplifies the task of public facility planning but may cause problems when efficiencies in the scope and scale of public facilities are not considered in drawing urban growth boundaries.

While public facility plans help coordinate and direct the location of urban growth within UGBs, plans alone cannot solve problems in public facility finance. Although public facility plans must identify potential sources of revenue for capital facilities, many sources of revenue remain beyond the control of local governments, thus plans for future public facilities are not binding. And though revenues from existing sources are adequate to cover operating costs, they are inadequate for financing capital costs. Thus the state will most likely have to provide local governments with increasing financial assistance. Here again, however, planning can play an important role. Because state agencies must comply with local comprehensive plans, comprehensive plans can serve to structure the allocation of state funds for local capital improvement.

Perhaps most significantly, Oregon offers experience in a promising new approach to service provision and finance. The evidence suggests that the Unified Sewerage Agency in Washington County holds significant advantages over other sewer-service providers in the Portland metropolitan area. Evidence based on differences in land value, development rate, and tax base suggests that economies of scale, interagency coordination, and urban growth management are better captured by regional service agencies. Although many political, institutional, and physical obstacles prevent the realization of such benefits for all public services throughout the state, the evidence from the USA suggests that better planning and management of public services can deliver measurable results.

Notes

1. See any standard microeconomics text, such as Nicholson (1990).
2. See *Dickas v. City of Beaverton* in box insert, Key Oregon Court Cases, in chapter 1.
3. The Oregon Economic Development Department expressed the problem as follows: "Unless we are able to develop tax and fee structures that smoothly finance necessary investments in infrastructure and public services, the state risks entering the next century with overburdened and deteriorating facilities" (OEDD 1989).
4. In 1980, the USA provided service to about 250,000 people, and the other agencies, combined, served about 700,000 people. The city of Portland alone provides sewer service to about 370,000 people, but it is not considered a regional agency because its service area has been largely built out for several decades, and metropolitan growth on the Oregon side of the Columbia River is mostly in suburban Multnomah, Clackamas, and Washington Counties, which are served by other agencies.
5. Similar evidence on the growth effects of regional sewer service in Dallas, Texas, is provided by Peiser (1981).

5

Protecting Oregon's Farmland

U NDERLYING THE 19 GOALS of Oregon's planning program are two
fundamental objectives: to facilitate efficient development and to
preserve natural resources. Oregon's natural resources are large in
number, rich in diversity, and spectacular in beauty. They include rugged
coastlines, forested mountain ranges, spacious rangelands, and fertile river
valleys. While each is the focus of one or more statewide land use goals, the
natural resource most central to Oregon's land use program is land suitable
for farming.

Farmland in Oregon is scarce, highly productive, and often located near
urban areas. As a result, the use of farmland—whether for agricultural or urban purposes—is a continuing source of controversy and a primary focus of
Oregon's land use program. This chapter reviews Oregon's experience with
farmland preservation. It has six parts. The first part discusses the reasons for
preserving farmland and the policy instruments available for doing so. The
second describes Oregon's farm economy and the threats to its survival. The
third part describes how land use plans and policies in Oregon are used to
preserve farmland. The fourth reviews research on the effectiveness of Oregon's
farmland program. The fifth discusses the research results and their implications. Finally, the sixth part offers policy lessons.

THE FARMLAND PRESERVATION ISSUE

Farmland is a national resource but receives little national protection. The
foremost piece of national legislation is the 1981 Farmland Protection
Policy Act, which directs the U.S. Department of Agriculture to see that
federal agencies take no action that would contribute to loss of farmland
(Daniels 1990). For the most part, however, farmland issues are addressed

by the states. Farming takes place in every state, and as urban areas grow
and decentralize, farmland in every state disappears. Product diversity notwithstanding, the reasons for protecting farmland are similar throughout
the country and have produced relatively similar farmland protection
programs.

Economic Reasons for Preserving Farmland

In the absence of farmland preservation programs, the preservation of farmland is left to the land market. Under a market system, farmland remains in
farm use until someone pays the owners more for their land than it is
worth to farm it. If the land market works well, then land remains in farm
use until it is more valuable to society in urban use. But the market for
agricultural land may not work well and, for several reasons, may lead to
excessive conversion of farmland to urban use. These reasons include external benefits, inefficient public pricing, urban spillovers, and the impermanence syndrome.

First, the market price of farmland may not reflect external benefits,
benefits to individuals other than the farmer. For example, farmland may
provide social benefits, such as flood control, air and water purification,
and scenic open space, which are enjoyed by society at large. Farmers,
however, receive no compensation for these social benefits. Thus the value
of farmland to the farmer may not reflect the true value of farmland to
society and the public interest that may be served by preserving it.

Inefficient pricing of urban services is another reason that the market
may not work well for farmland. To convert farmland to urban use, farmland must be provided with urban services, such as potable water, wastewater disposal, access, and shelter. Conversion of farmland to urban use is
efficient if urban land users are willing to pay more for the farmland than
farmers—after paying for all requisite urban services. But most urban services are provided by local governments, often at less than full cost. Those
services not provided by local governments, such as housing, are subsidized
through the federal income tax. In addition, farmers of large acreages may
pay exceptionally high property taxes for urban services—such as schools,
sewers, and other essentially urban services—from which they benefit very
little. Such inefficiencies in public prices and subsidies can lead to excessive
conversion of farmland.[1]

A third reason that the market might convert too much farmland stems
from conflicts between farmers and urban residents. Five common conflicts

at the urban-rural border create friction between farmers and urban residents. First, farming activities may be viewed as nuisances by some nonfarm residents. These residents may thus seek to impose restrictions on applying fertilizers, disposing of manure, slow-moving farm vehicles on commuter roads, pesticide and herbicide use, irrigation, and other activities (Berry 1978). Second, crops and livestock may be damaged by automobiles, industrial activity, dumping, and litter (Prestbo 1975). Third, urban neighbors may destroy crops or equipment, harass farm animals, or steal tree crops, berries, and vegetables (Berry, Leonardo, and Bieri 1976). Finally, urban governments sometimes use eminent domain to acquire farmland for public uses, such as roads and reservoirs. These conflicts reduce farm productivity and may cause farmers to forsake farming and sell their land for urban development (Schmisseur et al. 1991).

Farmland may be excessively converted to urban use for another reason: the "impermanence syndrome" (Keene et al. 1975; Currier 1978). The impermanence syndrome occurs when farmers believe that urban development will absorb farms in the near future, causing disinvestment in farm operations, crop conversions to those requiring less investment, and land sales to hobby farmers. As a result, investment in farm capital declines and farm productivity falls. The critical mass of farmland and farming needed to sustain the agricultural economy can be undermined by such actions (Berry 1976; Daniels and Nelson 1986; Daniels 1986; Lapping and FitzSimmons 1982).

In sum, market imperfections, including those cited above, can result in excessive conversion of farmland to urban use. These market imperfections serve as the conceptual foundations for programs in farmland preservation.

Programs for Preserving Farmland

To protect farms and farmland, state and local governments have adopted a variety of farmland protection instruments. These include property tax incentives, right-to-farm laws, agricultural or open space zoning, and others.[2] All of these instruments are effective to some degree; unfortunately, all have shortcomings and some may do more harm than good (Nelson 1990a, 1990b).

Tax incentive programs are a common tool for encouraging farmland preservation. Such programs typically reduce property taxes on land in farm use and impose penalties for farmland development, such as the repayment of taxes saved from tax incentive programs. Tax incentive programs can, however, have perverse effects. For example, they may make farmland more attractive to speculators. Farmland may be "saved" from development in the short term, but by preventing the otherwise timely conversion of urban fringe farmland, urban development can be pushed further into the rural landscape. The result is the very kind of urban sprawl that farmland preservation programs seek to prevent (Forkenbrock and Fisher 1983; Boehm and McKenzie 1981).

After tax incentive and disincentive programs, agricultural zoning is the most common farmland preservation instrument (USDA 1981). There are two general types of agricultural zoning: nonexclusive and exclusive. Nonexclusive zoning usually imposes minimum lot sizes ranging from about 10 to 640 acres and allows a wide range of conditional uses, such as commercial recreation, industrial activities related to agricultural use, and planned developments. Such zoning can also have perverse outcomes, however (Daniels and Nelson 1986; Nelson 1983). Families who want small-acreage tracts near urban areas often must purchase large farms but then use only the few acres they really wanted. This reduces the number of viable commercial farming operations, and the local agricultural economy suffers (Nelson 1983, Daniels 1986, Daniels and Nelson 1986).

Exclusive farm use zoning prohibits nonfarm activities in farming districts. It may or may not stipulate a minimum lot size for land division or allow dwelling units. Land divisions are approved only when there is evidence showing that partitioning will improve farm performance. *Farm dwellings* are allowed only if demonstrably needed to support farming operations, although nonfarm dwellings are allowed as a conditional use in certain low-production areas. Commercial recreation and industrial activities are restricted to *marginal lands* or to relatively small areas significantly affected by nearby urban development. This approach holds promise for maintaining farm productivity but by itself does not prevent the purchase of existing farms by urban households or the speculation of farmland near urban areas.

Right-to-farm laws protect farmland by shielding farmers from nuisance complaints by urban residents who move into farming areas. Lawsuits based on nuisance charges can result in disinvestment or termination of viable commercial farming (Hagman and Juergensmeyer 1987). Right-to-farm laws discourage such lawsuits by granting farmers specific legal rights (USDA 1981; Lapping, Penfold, and MacPherson 1983; Leutwiler 1986; Lapping and Leutwiler 1987; Penfold 1988). These laws have several deficiencies, however: they do not prevent farmers from converting land to urban uses or from selling land to speculators; they may not extend to successors-in-interest; they do not protect nuisance suits brought against operators who change agricultural intensity, no matter how insignificant the change may appear (Lapping and Leutwiler 1987); they may not protect farmland that is fallow one year from complaints registered by new residents against intensive operations in the next year. For these reasons, right-to-farm laws alone are not likely to be effective in preserving farmland in the long term (Leutwiler 1986).

Tax incentives, agricultural zoning, and right-to-farm laws are thus used in various combinations throughout the country. More often than not, however, these programs are administered by separate and uncoordinated agencies. Tax incentives, for example, are administered by state departments of revenue, agricultural zoning by county zoning boards, and right-to-farm laws by state and county courts. The success of these programs is limited, therefore, not only by the reach of each policy instrument, but also by the lack of coordination among instruments. Success is further limited by the lack of clearly specified policy objectives and the administrative inability to use the best instrument for each objective.

THE OREGON AGRICULTURAL ECONOMY

In many places farmland protection programs serve primarily to preserve open spaces, essentially for the benefit of urban residents (Fischel 1985). To some extent, Oregon's farmland preservation policies are no different (Leonard 1983; DeGrove 1984; Daniels 1986; Daniels and Nelson 1986). But Oregon's farmland program is designed to protect more than open space; specifically, the program is designed to protect and enhance the agricultural sector of the Oregon economy.

As in most states, farm income and employment in Oregon have fallen in recent decades. In 1988, agriculture employed only 4 percent of the labor force and generated only 2 percent of personal income in the state (U.S. DOC, Bureau of Economic Measurement Division 1991). But the agricultural sector plays a larger role in the Oregon economy than employment and income figures alone suggest. Because agricultural products are often processed within the state, then exported, farming is a basic industry, which creates jobs and income through a multiplier effect. Based on the multiplier effect, Schallau (1989) estimates that the agricultural sector supports approximately 15 percent of the Oregon economy. Based on similar logic, Beaton and Hibbard (1991) claim agriculture supports 20 to 25 percent. Regardless of the precise share of the economy supported by agriculture, however, this sector clearly remains important.

Oregon's agricultural sector uses but a fraction of the state's land base. As shown in table 23, the federal government owns 32 million of the state's total 62 million acres, most of which are managed for forest use. Of the remaining privately held lands, approximately 17 million acres, or 29 percent of all Oregon lands, were used as farmland in 1987; only 4 million acres, or approximately 7 percent of all Oregon lands, were used as cropland, which is considered the most productive farm use.

In 1989, these 17 million acres generated nearly $2.7 billion in gross farm income (Beaton and Hibbard 1991). As shown in figure 9, the largest share of sales from 1983 to 1987 was in cattle, followed by specialty horticulture (i.e., nursery stock and Christmas trees). Oregon's agricultural sector is one of the most diversified in the nation, which makes its importance difficult to characterize. For example, Oregon ranks relatively low among states (24th) in dollar value of the leading single-commodity product (cattle). At the same time, however, Oregon is a national leader in many specialized commodities, such as grass seed, filberts, nursery crops, snap beans, peppermint oil, and Christmas trees (Cornelius 1989).

Table 23.   Land Use in Oregon, 1989

Classification	No. of acres, in thousands	Percentage of land in state
Federally owned	32,122	51.70
Water	673	0.01
Nonfederally owned	29,332	47.21
TOTAL	62,127	100.00
	Farmland	
Cropland	4,356	7.01
Other farmland	13,344	21.48
TOTAL	17,800	28.65

SOURCE: Beaton and Hibbard 1991

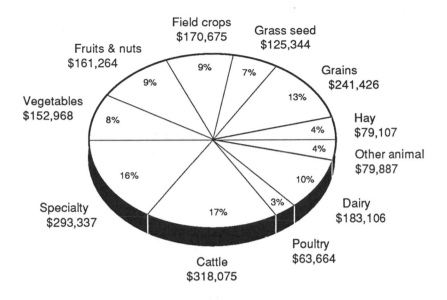

Field crops
$170,675

Grass seed
$125,344

Fruits & nuts
$161,264

9%

9%

7%

Vegetables
$152,968

8%

Grains
$241,426

13%

Hay
$79,107

4%

4%

Other animal
$79,887

16%

10%

Specialty
$293,337

17%

3%

Dairy
$183,106

Cattle
$318,075

Poultry
$63,664

SOURCE: Cornelius 1989

Figure 9. Annual Farm Sales by Commodity Group, 1983 to 1987

Despite statewide diversity, the farm economy in specific regions of Oregon is highly specialized. The coastal region specializes in dairy products; southern Oregon specializes in livestock and pears; the Columbia Basin specializes in grains, potatoes, and hay; and eastern Oregon, the leading region in total agricultural production, specializes in wheat and cattle. The Willamette Valley, however, is where agriculture is most diversified and the soil is most productive (Oregon Dept. of State 1983).

The valley stretches 100 miles north to south and averages about 40 miles east to west. It contains 83 percent of the state's prime farmlands and produces 48 percent of the state's agricultural goods (Beaton and Hibbard 1991). But the Willamette Valley is also home to more than 2 million of the state's 2.8 million residents. Much of Oregon's planning program, therefore, was designed to address urban-rural conflicts there. Indeed, early drafts of Senate Bill 100, the Oregon Land Use Planning Act, focused entirely on the Willamette Valley (Leonard 1983).

FARMLAND PRESERVATION
PROGRAMS IN OREGON

Programs to protect farmland in Oregon are longstanding. In 1961 the
Oregon legislature created a farm tax deferral program and enabled counties to zone land for exclusive farm use (EFU). But since EFU zoning was
not necessary to qualify for farm tax deferral, and was rarely imposed by
county governments, farm tax deferral became little more than a subsidy
program for real estate speculators (Leonard 1983). Lacking an effective
protection program, farmland continued to disappear at an alarming rate.
In 1973 alone, for example, 30,000 acres of farmland in the Willamette
Valley gave way to urban use.

As this trend continued, especially in the Willamette Valley, the state
adopted a sweeping new program to protect farmland. The program was
established by two bills passed in 1973. Senate Bill 100 established a program requiring local governments to construct urban growth boundaries
(UGBs) and to place all farmland outside them in exclusive farm use zones.
Senate Bill 101 set the parameters of EFU zoning, established rights to
farm, and created tax incentives for farming in EFU zones. Together these
bills created the most comprehensive farmland protection program in the
nation.

Goal 3: Agricultural Lands

The foundations of Oregon's farmland program are expressed in Goal 3 of
the state land use goals and guidelines, "To preserve and maintain agricultural lands."

> Agricultural lands shall be preserved and maintained for farm use, consistent with
> existing and future needs for agricultural products, forest, and open space. These
> lands shall be inventoried and preserved by exclusive farm use zones (pursuant to
> ORS Chapter 215). Such minimum lot sizes as are utilized for any farm use zones
> shall be appropriate for the continuation of the existing *commercial agricultural enter-
> prise* within the area.
>
> Conversion of rural agricultural land to urbanizable lands shall be based upon
> consideration of the following factors: (1) environmental, energy, social and eco-
> nomic consequences; (2) demonstrated need consistent with LCDC goals; (3) un-
> availability of an alternative suitable location for the requested use; (4) compatibility
> of the proposed use with related agricultural land; and (5) the retention of Class I, II,
> III and IV soils in farm use [classified by the Soil Conservation Service]. A governing
> body proposing to convert rural agricultural land to urbanizable land shall follow the
> procedures and requirements set forth in the Land Use Planning goal for goal excep-
> tions. (Oregon LCDC 1990)

Goal 3 establishes two major tenets of Oregon's farmland program. First, it requires, not just enables, local governments to place farmland in exclusive farm use zones. Second, it establishes explicit and standard criteria for determining what constitutes farmland.

Goal 3 defines farmland in accordance with the soil classification system of the U.S. Soil Conservation Service. All areas in western Oregon with soils classifications I to IV, and all areas in eastern Oregon with soils classifications I to VI, constitute farmland under Goal 3. This designation also includes "other lands" of lesser quality found amidst or near prime farmland where the soil conditions, climate, irrigation, existing land use patterns, energy supply, and accepted farming practices indicate potential for agricultural use. According to Goal 3, all lands meeting those broad criteria are to be zoned for exclusive farm use by local governments.

Exceptions

In establishing the definition of farmland, state leaders recognized that thousands of acres of land meeting the criteria were already subdivided and developed or could not be actively farmed for other reasons. To address this and similar problems, the land use goals included a provision for *exceptions*. The exception clause (in its original form) stated:

> When, during the application of the statewide goals and plans, it appears that it is not possible to apply the appropriate goal to specific properties or situations, then each proposed exception to a goal shall be set forth during the plan preparation phases. . . . If the exception to the goal is adopted, then the compelling reasons and facts for that conclusion shall be completely set forth in the plan and shall include:
>
> (a) Why these other uses should be provided for;
> (b) What alternative locations within the area could be used for the proposed uses;
> (c) What are the long term environmental, economic, social and energy consequences to the locality, the region or the state from not applying the goal or permitting the alternative use;
> (d) A finding that the proposed use will be compatible with other adjacent uses. (Oregon LCDC 1974)

Local governments (primarily county governments) were required to determine which lands qualified for exception status; LCDC then reviewed those determinations on a case-by-case basis. The exception clause thus created a procedure for zoning land outside of UGBs for rural use other than farming.

Senate Bill 101

According to Goal 3, all farmland outside UGBs not specifically excepted must be placed in EFU zones. The restrictions placed upon those lands were established in Senate Bill 101, which states:

(1) Open land used for agricultural use is an efficient means of conserving natural resources that constitute an important physical, social, aesthetic and economic asset to all of the people of this state, whether living in rural, urban or metropolitan areas of the state.

(2) The preservation of a maximum amount of limited supply of agricultural land is necessary to the conservation of the state's economic resources and the preservation of such land in large blocks is necessary in maintaining the agricultural economy of the state and for the assurance of adequate, healthful and nutritious food for the people of this state and nation.

(3) Expansion of urban development into rural areas is a matter of public concern because of the unnecessary increases in costs of community services, conflicts between farm and urban activities and the loss of open space and natural beauty around urban centers occurring as a result of such expansion.

(4) Exclusive farm use zoning as provided by law, substantially limits alternatives to the use of rural land and, with the importance of rural lands to the public, justifies incentives and privileges offered to encourage owners of rural lands to hold such lands in exclusive farm use zones. (quoted in Leonard 1983, 67)

Senate Bill 101 established several key elements of Oregon's farmland preservation program. Specifically, Senate Bill 101

- Required county governing bodies to review all land partitions in EFU zones that create one or more parcels less than 10 acres in size
- Made all land in EFU zones eligible for farm tax deferral
- Excepted all land in EFU zones (except for the farm dwelling and one acre surrounding it) from special levies for sewer and water districts, and
- Prohibited local governments from enacting laws that would unreasonably restrict farm operations.

Adjustments and Refinements

While Senate Bills 100 and 101 established the foundations of Oregon's farmland preservation program, continuing controversies in implementing the program led to several adjustments and refinements. In 1983, for example, the legislature stipulated that new nonfarm dwellings in agricultural zones are not eligible for farm property tax deferral, thus removing an important financial incentive for exurban sprawl. The 1983 legislature also required each county to report its land use decisions regarding resource lands to the legislature. Most of the adjustments to the farmland program, however, concern two continuing sources of controversy: What constitutes farmland? And what should be allowed on such land?

According to Goal 3, all land not contained within an urban growth boundary must be zoned for *resource use* unless the relevant county, and subsequently LCDC, certifies that the land meets the criteria for an exception. But the original criteria for exception were difficult to meet because they required "compelling reasons and facts." This test was largely responsible for many plans failing to receive LCDC acknowledgment well into the early 1980s.[3] This was politically embarrassing since all plans were to have been approved by 1976. As a result, the 1983 legislature and then–Governor Victor Atiyeh pressured LCDC to be more flexible.

Responding to legislation passed in 1983, the LCDC revised Goal 3 to streamline the exception process and to ease exception standards. The key revision changed the criteria for an exception from a test based on "compelling reasons and facts" to a test demonstrating it "impracticable" to apply the relevant preservation goal because the land had been irrevocably *committed* to nonresource uses. Besides adding to the Oregon planning lexicon, the change eased exception criteria and accelerated the acknowledgment process.[4] By 1985, all plans were acknowledged. But the change in standard allowed exception lands to become scattered throughout the state—especially in the Willamette Valley. A map of these lands, prepared by 1000 Friends of Oregon, is titled the "Map of Shame" (figure 10).

Additional legislation passed in 1983 required LCDC to allow local governments to identify marginal lands, lands of low farming productivity that would not be subject to the same restrictions as prime agricultural lands. In response LCDC amended Goal 3 to allow counties to relax land use standards on marginal lands if they enforced more stringent standards on primary lands (Eber 1984). Few counties, however, chose this option. After further prodding by the legislature in 1987 and 1989, LCDC funded pilot studies in six counties to establish criteria for secondary lands and to adopt appropriate land use restrictions for them. The pilot studies were recently completed, but no consensus has formed among policy makers and the land use community (Pease 1990).

As new controversies arose concerning exception and secondary lands, old controversies concerning what should be allowed on primary lands continued to fester. At first, the LCDC allowed local governments to establish minimum lot requirements to preserve resource lands. Some eastern counties created 320-acre minimum lot districts, while some western

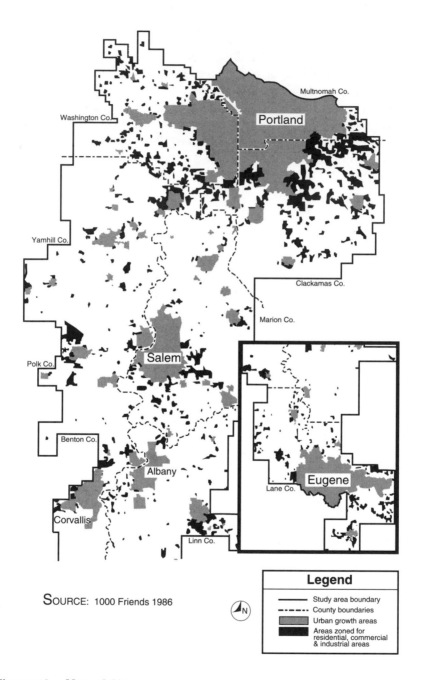

SOURCE: 1000 Friends 1986

Legend

— Study area boundary
-·-·- County boundaries
▨ Urban growth areas
▰ Areas zoned for residential, commercial & industrial areas

Figure 10.   Map of Shame

counties created 10-acre minimums. Most counties settled on 20- to 40-acre minimums. Minimum lot requirements were essentially designed "for the continuation of existing commercial agricultural enterprise." Counter-productive parceling and home construction were prohibited, but the standards for land divisions and home construction were not clearly defined (Daniels and Nelson 1986).

Since 1982, however, a combination of judicial rulings, legislative actions, and improved local administration has clarified and tightened the standards for new residences and land divisions in EFU and forest districts (Daniels and Nelson 1986, Oregon LCDC 1989, Nelson 1992). As a result, the only way to secure a land division or building permit is to demonstrate—in a quasi-judicial setting, typically with agricultural experts—that the resulting change will maintain or improve agricultural production. Thus by 1985, all counties in the Willamette Valley had effectively forsaken minimum lot requirements in favor of performance standards in EFU zones.

The Regulated Landscape

After many years of adjustment and refinement both in the content of plans and in the regulations to implement them, the land use plans of all counties were finally acknowledged. The outcome is illustrated in table 24. Of the state's approximately 28 million acres in private holdings, about 2 million are located within UGBs. The remaining 25.8 million acres are in a variety of resource and rural districts, including 16 million acres in exclusive farm use and 8.8 million acres in primary forest use zones. Nearly 90 percent of all privately owned land is restricted to resource activities. In all, 58.6 million acres, or 95 percent, of the state's land base is either publicly owned or restricted to resource use. Only 5 percent is zoned for nonresource activities, including the 3.3 percent contained within UGBs.

Approximately 3 percent of all privately owned land outside UGBs is set aside for hobby (noncommercial) farming, ranchettes, and other quasi-rural uses. An outgrowth of the exception process, this setaside is an important, though often overlooked, component of Oregon's farmland preservation program (Gustafson, Daniels, and Shirack 1982). Counties have set aside more than 300,000 acres within the Willamette Valley alone for such development. Statewide, more than 700,000 acres are included in quasi-rural districts.

Table 24. Designated Land Use in Oregon, 1986

Classification	No. of acres in thousands	Percentage of land in state	Percentage of privately owned land
Publicly owned	33,750	54.80	——
Privately owned	27,837	45.20	——
TOTAL	61,587[a]	100.00	——
	Privately owned land, location		
Inside UGBs	2,048	3.33	7.36
Outside UGBs	25,789	41.87	92.64
	Privately owned land, use		
Exclusive farm use	16,036	26.04	57.61
Primary forest use	8,771	14.24	31.51
Rural residential	710	1.15	2.55
Commercial	10	0.02	0.04
Industrial	46	0.07	0.17
Rural service centers	29	0.05	0.10
Other	189	0.31	0.69

[a]Excludes area of water.
SOURCE: Oregon DLCD 1986

EVIDENCE OF IMPACTS

The comprehensive and ambitious scope of Oregon's farmland protection program is known throughout the nation. Less well known, even in Oregon, however, are the impacts of these instruments on Oregon's farmland and farm economy.

Research evaluating the effectiveness of Oregon's farmland preservation program has taken three general approaches. One approach uses data on home construction and land divisions in rural areas to examine the record of local implementation. A second approach uses data on land values at the border between land use zones to examine land use conflicts and land speculation.[5] The third approach uses data from the U.S. census of agriculture to examine changes in farmland, farms, and farm productivity.

Building Permits and Land Subdivisions

Although Senate Bills 100 and 101 created a statewide farm preservation program, the implementation of the program was left to local governments, especially county governments. To monitor implementation, LCDC required local governments to document decisions on building permits and land partitions in EFU zones. These documents subsequently served as the basis for research on the local administration of EFU zoning.

Much of the early research on EFU zone administration was conducted by 1000 Friends of Oregon, the land use watchdog group. On three occasions 1000 Friends reviewed county decisions on applications for dwellings and land partitions (Liberty 1989a). As shown in table 25, 1000 Friends found that in the late 1970s and early 1980s counties approved a large number, and a high percentage, of applications for both dwellings and land partitions in EFU zones. According to 1000 Friends, the majority represented "inappropriate approvals," defined as cases where the county omitted or misapplied the statutory basis for the decision. From these findings, 1000 Friends concluded, "County administration of EFU zoning has failed" (Liberty 1989a).

Spurred in part by 1000 Friends, the 1983 legislature required counties to report EFU decisions to the LCDC and required LCDC to submit analyses of the data to the Joint Legislative Committee on Land Use. The data reported by LCDC in 1987 and 1989 are presented in table 26. In analyzing these data, the 1987 LCDC report concluded, "Although no cumulative impact can be determined now, a continuation of this approval

Table 25. Approval Rate for New Farm Dwellings and Farm Divisions, 1981, 1982, and 1985

	Percentage of applications approved		
Type	1981	1982	1985
Farm dwellings	96	96	95
Nonfarm dwellings	90	85	91
Farm use divisions	75	89	90
Nonfarm use divisions	73	94	81

Source: Liberty 1989a

Table 26. New Residential Dwellings on Exclusive Farm Use Lands, 1985 to 1988

Type of Dwelling	No. of units approved		No. of units denied	
	1987–88	1985–86	1987–88	1985–86
New farm dwellings	205	230	9	0
Replacement farm dwellings	65	79	1	0
New farm-worker dwellings	103	97	8	8
Replacement farm-worker dwellings	18	21	1	1
New nonfarm dwellings	279	264	36	17
Replacement nonfarm dwellings	34	60	0	1
TOTAL new dwellings	587	591	53	25
TOTAL replacement dwellings	117	160	2	2

Source: Liberty 1989a

rate for all types of dwellings and land divisions is a cause for concern" (Liberty 1989a).

While perhaps providing legitimate cause for concern, these findings alone did not demonstrate that the farmland preservation program was not working, or that it was being administered improperly. Since the criteria for farmland divisions and farm dwellings were contingent upon performance standards—e.g., that land divisions or dwelling construction were necessary for more effective commercial farming—a test for effective administration required an examination of land use performance. Under legislative directive, LCDC commissioned research to examine land use in EFU zones following a division or dwelling approval (Pacific Meridian Resources Associates 1991).

Pacific Meridian Resources Associates found evidence of lax local enforcement. After reviewing the findings of Pacific Meridian, LCDC concluded the following (Oregon DLCD 1991a):

• The majority of dwellings approved in EFU areas are not being used in conjunction with commercial farm use, defined as operations making at least $10,000 in annual income from farming; three-fourths of the farm operations with new dwellings gross less than $10,000 annually

- Sixty-two percent of owners with new dwellings work less than 40 hours per week on the farm; 20 percent spend under 20 hours per week on the farm
- Fourteen percent of farm dwelling approvals report that they have no farm management in place or that all the land is leased out
- Farm operations with new dwellings on under 40 acres are unlikely to be managed for commercial farm use; all of the farm operations with no gross receipts are under 40 acres in size
- Fifty-four percent of farm operations under 80 acres in size on which dwelling units have been permitted report no farming receipts; about 90 percent of farm operations under 160 acres in size report no farming receipts
- More than half (358) of farm operations approved for new dwelling units statewide (667) are found in the Willamette Valley.

Based on these findings DLCD concluded that the current statutory standard for approving building permits in EFU zones was not working and should be changed to better identify dwellings for persons whose principal work is farming and managing farmland on a daily basis. Specifically, DLCD recommended standards based on quantifiable measures, such as farm income, farm investment, and farm productivity.

After reviewing the findings by Pacific Meridian on land use parcels in EFU zones, DLCD concluded:

- A majority of approved farm parcels are not managed as farms nor are they appropriate for commercial agriculture
- One-third are not managed as farms or are completely leased out
- Almost two-thirds of the operations associated with partitions gross less than $10,000 annually
- Almost half of the owners of the farm operations with partitions work less than 40 hours per week on the farm; over one-third work under 20 hours per week
- The lowest incidence of demonstrated farm management is on operations with newly approved parcels.

Thus DLCD has concluded that the statutory standards for land divisions are not working. According to LCDC, the existing standard—which requires the continuation of existing commercial agricultural enterprise in the area—is vague and immeasurable. In its place DLCD recommends standards based on minimum lot sizes, incentives to encourage consolidation of existing parcels, and other stipulations, such as deed restrictions against building.

Agricultural Land Value

As 1000 Friends and LCDC explored local implementation, Nelson (1988, 1989) explored the impacts of EFU and exurban (for exception land) zoning on land value. According to Nelson, to be effective, EFU zoning must alter expectations concerning development potential. These expectations, in turn, must affect land value. If land values are not affected, Nelson argued, then EFU zoning does not serve as an effective policy instrument. Thus, according to Nelson, land values offer information on how EFU and exurban zoning affect development expectations.

Nelson's theoretical framework is illustrated in figure 11, which depicts the rent gradient for land in relation to distance from the exurban border in exclusive farm use zones and in exurban zones. R_m illustrates the rent gradient for land in the absence of agricultural zoning or if the zoning were not effective. If the zoning is effective, Nelson hypothesized, then land value will be affected as follows:

1. Land values in EFU zones will fall relative to land values in exurban zones, as the demand for developable land is transferred from the former to the latter. That is, land values in EFU zones will fall from R_m to R_f, and land values in exurban zones will rise from R_m to R_x. If land values are not affected this way, then expectations about developing land within EFU zones have not been reduced.
2. Land values in exurban zones will rise near the exurban border because land values reflect the value of proximity to farmland, such as enhanced privacy, scenery, and open space. That is, land values in exurban zones between the EFU/exurban border and d'' would rise from R_x to R_x'. If this effect is not found, then exurban residents do not value proximity to land in EFU zones or they expect such land to be developed in the near term.
3. Land values in EFU zones may fall, rise, or remain constant based on proximity to exurban zones, depending on how such proximity affects farm productivity and expectations about future land use. Three outcomes are possible: (a) land values in EFU zones may fall with proximity to exurban zones if such proximity adversely affects farm productivity; (b) land values in EFU zones may rise with proximity to exurban zones if proximity to exurban zones creates expectations of

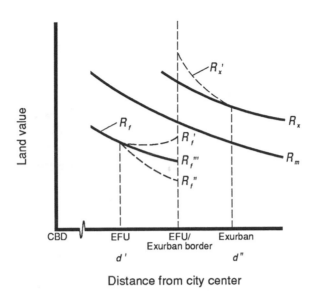

Distance from city center

Figure 11.   Relationship Between UGBs and Rural Land Value

future development; or (c) land values in EFU zones may not change with proximity to exurban zones if proximity affects neither neighboring farm productivity nor expectations concerning future exurban use (or if productivity effects exactly offset expectation effects). As shown in the figure, land values in EFU zones between d' and the EFU/exurban border could change from R_f to R_f', R_f'', or R_f'''.

Nelson tested his hypotheses using data on land sales in Washington County from 1983 to 1986. Of the 458,000 acres in Washington County, roughly one-half is forest land; the rest is equally divided among farmland, urban land, and exurban land. In 1983 the county adopted land use planning policies designed to contain urban development within an urban growth boundary and to preserve prime agricultural land in EFU districts. The policies also preserved prime forest land in districts subject to forest and conservation restrictions. Exurban development is limited to "rural residential" or nonexclusive "agriculture/forest" zones with minimum lot sizes of 5, 10, and 20 acres. The study area included all EFU land and exurban land in 5- to 20-acre minimum lot size districts.

Nelson's sample included 150 arms-length sales of undeveloped land; 41 of the sales were in EFU zones and 109 were in exurban zones. To identify the influence on land value of proximity to the exurban border, Nelson divided his sample into three subsets: the first included parcels in exurban zones; the second, parcels in EFU zones near exurban zones with 5- to 10-acre minimum lot size restrictions; and the third subset included parcels in EFU zones near exurban zones with 20-acre minimum lot size restrictions. Dividing the set of parcels in EFU zones into subsets distinguished by the density of allowed use in exurban zones enabled Nelson to explore whether density in exurban zones influenced development expectations in neighboring EFU zones.

Nelson's results are presented in tables 27, 28, and 29. In general, Nelson found the influence of agricultural zoning consistent with his expectations. In the pooled sample (table 27), he found land values lower in EFU zones, suggesting that EFU zoning indeed lowers or eliminates development expectations. In the exurban sample alone, he found that land values rose with proximity to (and fell with distance from) the exurban border, suggesting that exurban residents indeed value proximity to land in exclusive farm use zones. In the EFU sample, he found that land values in EFU zones rose with proximity to 5- to 10-acre minimum exurban zones (table 28) and fell with proximity to 20-acre minimum exurban zones (table 29), suggesting that the value of proximity to exurban zones depends on the allowed density of adjacent exurban zones.

From these results, Nelson concluded: (a) that EFU zoning is effective at reducing development expectations and thus at preserving land for farm use; (b) that exurban residents value proximity to EFU zones and thus also expect that they will not be developed[6]; and (c) that speculation on land in EFU zones varies by the allowed density of neighboring exurban zones. Farm productivity is adversely affected by exurban zoning, even with 20-acre minimum lot sizes. But where neighboring land is zoned for exurban use at 5- to 10-acre densities, the effect is to fuel land speculation. Thus, Nelson concluded that the appropriate exurban density along the exurban-farmland boundary should be at least 20 acres; anything less can have undesirable effects on the market for farmland.

Farmland and Farming

As research progressed on plan implementation and its effects on land value, other researchers examined its effects on the number of farms, the quantity of farmland, and farm productivity. This line of research inferred various impacts of the farmland preservation program from the census of agriculture.

The research was begun by Furuseth (1980, 1981), who compared census data from 1974 and 1978, the census period that immediately followed the passage of Senate Bills 100 and 101. Furuseth found that the quantity of land in agricultural production over the four-year period had increased, even though the state's population had grown rapidly. Furuseth also found growth in the number of farm operators and the value of farm capital investments; and he found that the average age of farm operators had declined. Furuseth interpreted these findings as evidence that Oregon's farmland preservation program had beneficially affected the farm economy.

Nelson (1983) sharply criticized Furuseth's interpretations, however. Nelson argued that the observed trends in number of farms, quantity of farmland, value of farm investment, and age of farm operators were actually national trends. He noted that the growth in average farm value and farm investment was more rapid in the rest of the country than in Oregon. Nelson said that the data from Oregon closely resembled data from Washington State, which had an agricultural sector similar to Oregon's but which had no state land use program. Finally, he noted that the average farm size in Oregon fell more rapidly in Oregon than it did in Washington or the rest of the nation. Since Furuseth did not compare Oregon to other parts of the U.S., Nelson suggested, Furuseth had provided inconclusive evidence that the farmland preservation program had favorably influenced the farm economy.

Further discussion on the effectiveness of Oregon's farmland preservation program followed the publication of the 1982 census of agriculture. Daniels and Nelson (1986) compared data from 1978 and 1982 for Oregon, Washington, and the U.S. on number of farms, acres of farmland, and percentage of total farms in commercial use. They found that, between 1978 and 1982, the number of farms rose 20 percent in Oregon and 16 percent in Washington, and fell 0.1 percent in the nation (excluding Oregon). Compared to the rest of the nation, both Oregon and Washington added more farms that are smaller than 50 acres in size and lost more farms that are larger than 500 acres. Total acres in farm use fell 1.7 percent in Oregon, 1.5 percent in Washington, and 3 percent in the nation. The ratio of acres used for commercial farming (defined as farms reporting more than $10,000 in annual sales) to total farm acres increased 0.3 percent in Oregon, 0.1 percent in Washington, and 0.6 percent in the nation.

Table 27. Determinants of Rural Land Value, Washington County, 1983 to 1986[a]

| Variable | Regression coefficient, price per acre[b] (Beta)[c] [t][p] | |
	Whole sample (N = 150)	Exurban sample (N = 109)
Intercept	6.238	6.267
Location in greenbelt zone	−0.255 (−0.150) [2.886]***	—— —— ——
Parcel size, in acres	−0.433 (−0.686) [12.247]***	0.503 (−0.746) [11.347]***
Distance from Portland CBD, in 100-foot units	−0.281 (−0.090) [1.523]*	−0.316 (−0.101) [1.467]*
Distance from UGB, in 100-foot units	−0.042 (−0.053) [0.893]ns	0.020 (0.027) [0.395]ns
Month of sale (no. of months after 9/83)	−0.139 (−0.152) [3.157]***	−0.129 (−0.141) [2.631]***
Soil quality (pasture-raising potential, in half-ton units, and proxy for septic suitability)	0.446 (0.126) [4.408]***	0.450 (0.144) [2.424]***
Percentage of land in 100-year floodplain	−0.029 (−0.237) [4.161]***	−0.023 (−0.189) [2.570]***

[a]Dependent variable is log of land value per acre.
[b]Unstandardized regression coefficient.
[c]Standardized regression coefficient.
* $p < 0.10$, one-tailed test.
*** $p < 0.01$, one-tailed test.
ns p not significant.
SOURCE: Nelson 1988

Continued on next page

Table 27. Continued

| Variable | Regression coefficient, price per acre[b] (Beta)[c] [t][p] | |
	Whole sample (N = 150)	Exurban sample (N = 109)
View potential (percentage of parcel with > 25% slope)	0.011 (0.074) [1.272]ns	0.012 (0.089) [1.335]*
Waterfront location	−0.248 (−0.074) [1.427]*	−0.327 (−0.095) [1.615]*
Adjusted R^2	0.682	0.700
Degrees of freedom	9; 140	8; 100
F	36.521	32.470

Based on these data, Daniels and Nelson concluded that Oregon's farmland program appears to have been successful at protecting farmland from conversion to urban use. They cautioned, however, that Oregon's program may at the same time contribute to the growth of hobby farms, which could cause a loss of productivity in commercial farms.

Recently, Nelson (1992) reexamined Oregon's farm economy using the 1982 and 1987 census of agriculture. The basis of his examination is presented in tables 30 to 33. From table 30, Nelson surmised that Oregon's farm vitality indicators compare favorably to those for Washington and the U.S. Compared to Washington and to the rest of the nation, Oregon lost slightly fewer farms, retained considerably more farmland, increased average farm size, and increased the value of total sales per farm.

As shown in table 31, Oregon lost more farms less than 10 acres in size than both Washington and the rest of the nation, but lost fewer farms larger than 10 acres in size. Oregon gained more farms larger than 500 acres in size, while Washington and the rest of the nation lost farms of similar size. While recognizing that it is not possible to tell whether small farms had merged into larger farms, Nelson concluded from these data that Oregon's farm preservation policies do not encourage proliferation of small farms and that the policies preserve, if not encourage, large farms.

Table 28. Determinants of Rural Land Value by Proximity to 5- and 10- Acre Exurban Districts, Washington County, 1983 to 1986

Variable	Regression coefficient, price per acre	
	Coefficient $(t)^p$	Standard error
Intercept	−2,107.047	
Parcel size, in acres	3.271 (−1.678)*	0.656
Distance from Portland CBD, in 100-foot units	−1.715 (−0.955)ns	1.797
Distance from UGB, in 100-foot units	−3.522 (−3.526)*	0.999
Month of sale (no. of months after 9/83)	−18.035 (4.985)*	10.487
Soil Quality (pasture-raising potential, in half-ton units, a proxy for septic suitability	220.689 (2.124)*	103.884
Distance from Washington Square, in 100-foot units	2.259 (−1.533)*	1.474
Distance from nearest 5- or 10-acre district	−0.063 (−2.049)*	0.031
R^2	0.730	
Standard error of estimate	384.331	
F	5.410	
N	22	

* $p < 0.10$, one-tailed test.
ns p not significant.
SOURCE: Nelson 1988

While the total number of small farms in Oregon fell, the number of small commercial farms increased, far more than in Washington or in the rest of the nation. As shown in table 32, Oregon lost fewer commercial farms than Washington or the rest of the nation. Acres in commercial farms, however, fell in Oregon and rose both in Washington and nation-

Table 29. Determinants of Rural Land Value by Proximity to 20-Acre Exurban Districts, Washington County, 1983 to 1986

Variable	Regression coefficient, price per acre	
	Coefficient $(t)^p$	Standard error
Intercept	−1,001.842	
Parcel size, in acres	2.591 (−1.748)*	0.248
Distance from Portland CBD, in 100-foot units	−3.518 (−2.990)*	1.177
Distance from UGB, in 100-foot units	−4.386 (−3.775)*	1.162
Month of sale (no. of months after 9/83)	−12.938 (10.467)*	11.864
Soil quality (pasture-raising potential, in half-ton units, a proxy for septic suitability)	172.460 (3.670)*	46.997
Distance from Washington Square, in 100-foot units	3.417 (−2.990)*	1.098
Distance from nearest 20-acre district	0.099 (2.612)*	0.038
R^2	0.913	
Standard error of estimate	274.767	
F	16.415	
N	19	

* $p < 0.10$, one-tailed test.
ns p not significant.
SOURCE: Nelson 1988

ally. These results, Nelson concluded, may reflect Oregon's performance standards for home construction in EFU zones. Specifically, suggested Nelson, if many commercial farms between 50 and 499 acres had been divided into smaller farms, and if to obtain approval for division they were required to remain in commercial production, then Oregon's performance standards may have contributed to the rise in the number of small

Table 30. Farm Vitality Indicators, Oregon, Washington, and U.S., 1982 to 1987

Indicator	Oregon			Washington			U.S.[a]		
	1982	1987	Percentage change	1982	1987	Percentage change	1982	1987	Percentage change
No. of farms	34,087	32,014	−6.08	36,087	33,559	−7.01	2,207,037	2,055,745	−6.85
Acres used for farming, in thousands	17,740	17,809	0.39	16,470	16,116	−2.15	996,724	946,662	−5.02
Average farm size, in acres	520.43	556.29	6.89	456.40	480.23	5.22	451.61	460.50	1.97
Acres of harvested cropland, in thousands	3,306	2,833	−14.31	5,279	4,597	−12.92	326,306	282,224	−13.51
Acres of irrigated farmland, in thousands	1,808	1,648	−8.85	1,638	1,519	−7.26	49,002	46,386	−5.34
Nominal value per farm, $	371,644	299,755	−19.34	423,352	355,976	−15.91	345,869	289,387	−16.33
Nominal value per acre, $	705	542	−23.12	933	739	−20.79	784	627	−20.03
Value of sales per farm, $	48,129	57,664	19.81	78,469	87,000	10.87	58,858	65,165	10.72
No. of fulltime operators	15,542	15,359	−1.18	17,968	17,654	−1.75	1,234,787	1,138,179	−7.82
No. of parttime operators	18,545	16,655	−10.19	18,112	15,905	−12.19	1,006,189	949,580	−5.63
Average age of operator	50.4	52.7	4.56	50.1	51.6	2.99	50.5	52	2.97

[a]Figures adjusted to exclude Oregon.

SOURCES: USDA 1982; USDA 1987

Table 31. Distribution of Farms by Size, Oregon, Washington, and U.S., 1982 to 1987

Size, in Acres	Oregon			Washington			U.S.[a]		
	1982	1987	Percentage change	1982	1987	Percentage change	1982	1987	Percentage change
					No. of farms				
1–9	5,987	5,476	-8.54	6,425	6,040	-5.99	181,712	177,781	-2.16
10–49	12,415	11,448	-7.79	12,717	11,362	-10.66	436,886	400,989	-8.22
50–179	7,662	7,219	-5.78	7,755	7,216	-6.95	704,039	637,630	-9.43
180–499	3,906	3,617	-7.40	4,035	3,796	-5.92	522,660	474,677	-9.18
500+	4,117	4,254	3.33	5,155	5,145	-0.19	361,740	364,668	0.81
TOTAL	34,087	32,014	-6.08	36,087	33,559	-7.01	2,207,037	2,055,745	-6.85
					No. of acres, in thousands				
All sizes combined	17,740	17,809	0.39	16,470	16,116	-2.15	996,724	946,662	-5.02

[a]Figures adjusted to exclude Oregon.

Sources: USDA 1982; USDA 1987

Table 32.   Distribution of Commercial Farms by Size, Oregon, Washington, and U.S., 1982 to 1987[a]

Size, in acres	Oregon			Washington			U.S.[b]		
	1982	1987	Percentage change	1982	1987	Percentage change	1982	1987	Percentage change
				No. of farms					
1–9	476	634	33.19	864	994	15.05	40,128	44,008	9.67
10–49	1,767	1,891	7.02	3,100	3,072	–0.90	75,528	71,574	–5.24
50–179	3,156	3,010	–4.63	3,832	3,697	–3.52	284,171	241,058	–15.17
180–499	2,706	2,479	–8.39	2,982	2,760	–7.44	398,585	353,971	–11.19
500+	3,658	3,694	0.98	4,843	4,764	–1.63	334,083	340,948	2.05
TOTAL	11,763	11,708	–0.47	15,621	15,287	–2.14	1,132,495	1,051,559	–7.15
				No. of acres, in thousands					
All sizes combined	15,488	15,441	–0.30	13,017	13,766	5.75	795,792	813,580	2.24

[a]Farms reporting $10,000 or more in annual sales, not adjusted for current dollars.
[b]Figures adjusted to exclude Oregon.

Sources: USDA 1982; USDA 1987

commercial farms. To explore this issue further, Nelson examined data for the Willamette Valley, where the pressures for hobby farms and farmland subdivision are great.

Table 33 shows that the number of farms in the Willamette Valley fell by more than 1,000 between 1982 and 1987, while the amount of farmland acreage remained nearly the same, falling by slightly more than one-half of one percent over the period. These data, Nelson suggested, offer evidence of the conclusion made by Daniels and Nelson (1986) that state preservation policies had been helping to stabilize the farmland base in the Willamette Valley since 1978.

Nelson found that the number of commercial farms in the valley rose by nearly 18 percent and that acreage in commercial farms rose by 12 percent, or nearly 150,000 acres. The largest share of commercial farm increases occurred in the 1–9-acre category while the largest amount of farm acreage gained was in the 500+-acre category. From these data Nelson surmised that, in the valley, farmland owners are either taking land out of production or making their holdings commercially productive, either on their own or by merging with other owners by sale, rental, or other agreement.

While noting that census information does not permit adjustments for inflation, Nelson reported that commercial farm production rose to $909 million in 1987 from $619 million in 1982, or nearly 50 percent—an increase that far exceeded inflation during the period. Average income among commercial farms rose to $196,000 in 1987 from $157,000 in 1982, or by nearly 25 percent. As a result, Nelson concluded that hobby farms and commercial farms in Oregon generally, and in the Willamette Valley especially, gained in economic vitality after full implementation of farmland preservation policies. Contrary to concerns raised in literature that the rise of hobby farms would reduce commercial farming productivity, Nelson concluded, many hobby farmers had become viable commercial farming operators in their own right, contributing significantly to the Oregon farm economy.[7]

DISCUSSION

Oregon's farmland preservation program incorporates a variety of policy instruments and serves policy objectives that include preserving farmland and farm productivity. The program began in earnest with the enactment of Senate Bills 100 and 101, which integrated urban growth boundaries,

Table 33. Distribution of Farms in Willamette Valley[a], 1982 to 1987

Size, in acres	1982	1987	Percentage change
	No. of farms		
1–49	10,986	9,900	−9.89
1–9	3,721	3,256	−12.50
10–49	7,265	6,644	−8.55
50–499	5,076	4,674	−7.92
50–179	3,579	3,301	−7.77
180–499	1,497	1,373	−8.28
500+	764	791	3.53
TOTAL	16,826	15,365	−8.68
	No. of acres		
1–49	189,129	174,745	−7.61
1–9	18,913	16,315	−13.74
10–49	170,216	158,430	−6.92
50–499	770,045	714,556	−7.21
50–179	330,064	309,182	−6.33
180–499	439,981	405,374	−7.87
500+	860,640	917,912	6.65
TOTAL	1,819,814	1,807,213	−0.69
	No. of commercial farms		
1–49	1,157	1,490	28.78
1–9	242	391	61.57
10–49	915	1,099	20.11
50–499	2,133	2,248	5.39
50–179	1,323	1,233	−6.80
180–499	810	1,015	25.31
500+	644	900	39.75
TOTAL	3,934	4,638	17.90
TOTAL commercial farm acreage	1,184,739	1,326,453	11.96

[a]Benton, Clackamas, Lane, Linn, Marion, Multnomah, Polk, Washington, and Yamhill Counties.

SOURCES: USDA 1982; USDA 1987

exclusive farmland zoning, farm tax deferral, and right-to-farm laws into a comprehensive land use program. While these statutes established the foundations of the program, the program continues to evolve in both the substance and the implementation of farmland policy.

Research by DLCD and 1000 Friends showed that county governments approve a large proportion of applications for dwellings and land partitions in EFU zones. Research also showed that not all of these dwellings and partitions occur on land ostensibly used for farming. These findings have led some to conclude that local implementation does not work. But the research results are neither conclusive nor surprising. Data on rates of approvals for farm dwellings and partitions provide no information on rates of approvals that would have occurred without a state preservation program or on applications that were never submitted because of the program. Further, the state farmland program was created out of dissatisfaction with local programs; thus dissatisfaction with local implementation of state farmland programs is to be expected. Such dissatisfaction can only be eliminated by replacing local implementation by state implementation—a change that has been proposed, with little political support. Perhaps what the research by 1000 Friends and DLCD makes most clear is that the threat to Oregon's farmland comes far less from urban development than from exurban development.

During the acknowledgment period, the demand for exurban development was met through the exception process. Households wanting land for hobby farms or ranchettes could purchase land already committed to non-farm use. But meeting this demand through the exception process caused several problems. First, exurban development may have taken more land than necessary. Exurban households desiring 1- and 2-acre lots found themselves in 5- to 10-acre minimum lot zones. As a result more land was taken out of productive farming than was necessary to meet the demand for exurban residents. Second, the demand for future exurban land remains unattended, which may create additional development pressures on the most productive farmlands. Finally, haphazardly located exurban developments may have negative impacts on neighboring land values in EFU zones, causing spillover effects and land speculation.

Research by Nelson showed that land zoned for exurban use at less than 20 units per acre caused speculation on land in bordering EFU zones, and that land zoned for exurban use at greater than 20 units per acre imposed spillover effects on land in bordering EFU zones. Based on these findings, and recognizing the need to accommodate future demands for exurban development, Nelson (1990b) proposed a regional landscape in which small exurban-acreage tracts (1 to 2 acres) are provided within UGBs, large exurban-acreage tracts surround UGBs, and even larger EFU-acreage tracts surround exurban zones—perhaps with isolated areas of marginally productive land with relaxed EFU restrictions.

While Nelson's findings concerning spillover effects between EFU and exurban zoning must be interpreted with caution, his proposed planning scheme reflects the growing recognition that blanket EFU zoning of farmland outside UGBs does not work. Growing political support for secondary land designations outside UGBs recognizes both the demand for hobby farms and ranchettes and the limited suitability of some farmland for commercial use. Such recognition is driving the push for a secondary land designation. Pease (1990) and his colleagues developed new criteria for secondary lands based on soil quality, tract size, density patterns, block size and past commercial use. These criteria offer promise for resolving technical problems in identifying secondary lands. Although both technical and political problems with secondary land proposals remain, LCDC expects some sort of tiered standard for regulating farmland in the near future (Oregon DLCD 1991a).

Despite the proliferation of hobby farms, there is considerable evidence that the Oregon farm economy is in relatively good health. The rate of farmland conversion to urban use has slowed dramatically, commercial farming is up, as are farm sales and farm income. Given the cyclical variability and unique composition of the Oregon agricultural economy, it is impossible to attribute these trends exclusively to Oregon's farmland preservation policies. Regardless of its cause, however, a most interesting recent trend is the growing productivity (measured in gross revenue) of small farms.

Research by Daniels and Nelson demonstrated that the number of hobby farms, defined as farms earning less than $10,000 in annual gross sales, grew more rapidly in Oregon from 1978 to 1982 than in any other state. These findings raised concerns that hobby farming would sap the productivity of farmland in Oregon. Recent trends reported by Nelson, however, demonstrate that commercial farming in Oregon grew more rapidly in Oregon than in Washington and the rest of the nation from 1982 to 1987, especially in the 1- to 9-acre farm category. These findings suggest that small farms can contribute significantly to the Oregon farm economy.

Nelson's findings have significant implications for the administration of agricultural zoning. If small farms can indeed contribute to the farm economy, then minimum lot requirements may protect farmland and open space while diminishing farm productivity. That is, minimum lot requirements may force commercial farms to be larger than necessary and may force hobby farms to occupy more farmland than desired. In the absence of conclusive information about scale economies in farming in all combinations of farm products, climates, soils, and terrains, performance zoning may serve as a better policy instrument for enhancing farm productivity in agricultural zones. Performance zoning may be better able to address the unique requirements of diverse farming operations and provide an incentive for maintaining productivity on hobby farms.

As the evidence of county administration indicates, however, performance zoning is only likely to succeed with clear and objective standards of farm performance. Recent evidence from Polk County suggests that a tiered system based on owner occupation, gross farm sales, and farm-specific contributions to the agricultural sector offers a promising mechanism for establishing appropriate farm-size standards in EFU zones (Pease 1991). Such quantifiable standards help remove much of the remaining conflict currently involved in rural land use decision making and enhance the overall effectiveness of Oregon's farmland preservation program.

LESSONS FROM OREGON

Farmland preservation policies have been adopted by many state and local governments throughout the United States. Policy instruments used in Oregon—urban growth boundaries, agricultural zoning, farm tax deferral, and right-to-farm laws—are not unique. What is unique is that local governments in Oregon are required to integrate these instruments through comprehensive land use planning. Specifically, all land outside urban growth boundaries in Oregon must be zoned for resource use, unless excepted through a rigorous process; all land in EFU zones qualifies for farm tax deferral; and all land in EFU zones is protected by right-to-farm laws. Through this integrated approach Oregon seeks to preserve both farmland and the productivity of the farm economy.

Although mandated and structured by specific statewide goals and guidelines, Oregon's program is implemented by local governments. Local implementation enables local governments to consider their unique soil, climate, and farm practices in local land use decisions. But local implementation represents both the boon and the bane of Oregon's program. The available research suggests that local governments have been less than zealous in protecting farmland from land division and rural residential development, and that considerable state oversight and administrative guidelines are needed if local governments are expected to implement state policies.

In spite of concerns about local implementation, there is evidence that Oregon's farmland and farm economy remain in good health, perhaps in part as a result of farmland preservation. Through the acknowledgment process, over 16 million acres have been zoned for exclusive farm use. Since the acknowledgment period, farmland has been disappearing at a much slower rate than in previous years and also at a slower rate than in other parts of the nation. Farm productivity is up. And the number of commercial farms has risen in several farm-size categories, but especially in small farm-size categories.

The productivity of small farms raises doubts about minimum lot requirements as an instrument to enhance the productivity of farms. Not only is it difficult to establish appropriate minimum lot sizes for effective farming, but minimum area restrictions can result in excessive land being devoted, ostensibly, to rural residential use. Performance zoning appears better suited for addressing the unique requirements of farmers in a diverse agricultural region. But local administration of performance zoning also requires specific standards for measuring farm performance. Such standards involve complex technical and political issues and are thus extremely difficult to develop. In short, minimum lot requirements and performance zoning both have limitations as farmland preservation instruments. State-imposed minimum lot requirements may preserve too much farmland; locally administered performance standards may preserve too little.

Finally, it is clear that agricultural zoning affects land value. In a manner consistent with economic theory, EFU zoning transfers speculative land values from EFU zones to exurban and urban zones. Thus, EFU zoning may reduce the impermanence syndrome and encourage farmers to invest in farm capital.

In spite of considerable evidence of impacts, however, Oregon's farm preservation program remains in flux. Blanket EFU zoning of farmland outside UGBs has not withstood political pressure for more regulatory flexibility. Uncertainty remains concerning secondary lands and exurban development. Oregon's future farmland program will likely, however, include lower development standards in nonexclusive farm use zones, higher performance standards in exclusive farm use zones, and greater state oversight of local controls in all farm use zones.

Notes

1. Conversely, some argue that too little farmland is converted to urban use as a result of farm price supports and subsidies (Rose 1984).
2. For a comprehensive review, see Nelson (1990b).
3. The test requiring compelling reasons and facts was difficult to meet for two reasons. First, it required local governments to provide supporting data, which many were unprepared to present. Second, some compared the burden of the test to the burden of "reasonable doubt" in a capital crime (Nelson 1992).
4. The acknowledgment process was also accelerated by legislation imposing new deadlines, by changes in the composition of LCDC, and by political pressure from Governor Atiyeh's office.
5. The impacts of UGBs are discussed in chapter 2.
6. In fact, some exurban residents have mobilized to oppose further exurban development in adjacent EFU zones.
7. The degree of significance is, of course, debatable. As in most rank-size distributions, the largest proportion of farm sales comes from the largest farm-size groupings.

6

Land Use Planning and
Economic Development

I N THE U.S. BEFORE 1970 most economic development programs were
initiated and sponsored by the federal government (James 1984). But
as the industrial base of the economy changed across sectors and across
regions, and as federal programs and responsibilities devolved to the states,
states assumed an increasingly prominent role in economic development
(Eisinger 1988). Led by Massachusetts, Tennessee, Michigan, and California, states in the 1970s began developing programs designed to recruit
industry and subsidize capital investment (Fosler 1988); these programs
featured venture capital funds, revolving loans, industrial revenue bonds,
and marketing programs to attract tourists and new firms (Matz and Ledebur
1986). By 1980, nearly every state offered financial incentives to relocating
or expanding firms and touted its exceptional quality of life to tourists and
potential residents.

Disillusioned with the recruitment results of the 1970s, states entered a
"third wave" of economic development programming in the mid-1980s
(Ross and Friedman 1990). According to Ross and Friedman, states in this
wave reached beyond industrial recruitment and initiated programs designed to foster entrepreneurship, incubate new firms, support research and
development, educate workers, and more. Implementing these new programs, however, required new economic development institutions, institutions capable of more than marketing and recruitment. Many of these new
institutions featured public-private partnerships, multiagency task forces,
and intergovernmental commissions (Clarke 1986). Few, however, were

designed to coordinate economic development efforts between state and local governments.

As state governments established new economic development programs and agencies, local governments also took new initiatives. Similar to state governments, local governments throughout the 1970s offered tax abatements and interest subsidies to attract new firms and capital. In the 1980s, however, many local governments recognized the potential of land use controls as economic development instruments. By influencing the supply of land, the location of transportation networks, the provision of infrastructure, and the quality of the environment, land use regulations could perhaps influence economic decision making and thus the performance of local economies. Land use plans consequently became viewed as policy instruments for economic development (Sharpe 1990, chapter 10).

Even as the potential for using land use planning and regulation as instruments of economic development became recognized, many local governments did not have economic development or land use plans. And since many economic development programs offered by state governments required participation by local governments, many local governments were unprepared to participate. In Oregon, however, the state had since 1973 required all local governments to prepare comprehensive plans in conformance with state-prescribed goals and guidelines. As a result, Oregon had in place an institution for integrating local land use planning with state programs for economic development.

The relationship between Oregon's statewide land use program and Oregon's economy, however, has been controversial and misunderstood. It remains so today. Where land use planning in Oregon was once widely criticized for increasing the depth of the 1981 recession, today it is hailed as a major factor in the state's economic recovery. While both views have merit, one thing is clear: the economic development goal of Oregon's land use program, once largely ignored, became perhaps the most prominent land use goal of the 1980s.

Unfortunately few studies have explored the relationship between land use planning and economic development, in Oregon or anywhere else. The reasons are twofold. First, land use plans have only recently included substantive economic components. And since it takes considerable time for economic policies to have measurable impacts on economic outcomes, there have been few opportunities to conduct meaningful policy analyses. Second, land use plans have the potential to influence economic performance in a variety of ways, none of which is easy to isolate. Therefore, the influence of land use planning on economic performance must be inferred from studies that focus on employment, factor prices, and the policy implementation process (Hatry et al. 1989).

Although there has been little research on the relationship between land use planning and economic development in Oregon, an exploration of the relationship is critical. Planning remains perceived, by some in Oregon and by many elsewhere, as detrimental to economic development. And because Oregon has the longest experience with state land use planning, it offers perhaps the best opportunity to validate or refute this view. Further, due to the cyclical sensitivity of the Oregon economy, the economy itself has perhaps had as great—if not a greater—impact on the land use program as the land use program has had on the economy. A thorough understanding of Oregon's land use program alone is therefore not possible without examining the relationship between the planning program and the state's economy. Finally, Oregon's land use program provides the state with a unique instrument for implementing state economic development policies. Thus, an exploration of the economic impacts of state land use planning in Oregon provides insights into the efficacy of a relatively new instrument for economic development.

To examine the relationship between planning and economic development in Oregon, this chapter begins by presenting Goal 9—Oregon's original economic development goal. Goal 9 in its original form shaped the relationship between planning and economic development until 1981. The chapter then examines the impact of the 1981 recession on the Oregon economy; this examination provides the context for the mid-recession debate over the future of the state land use program. Next, the chapter describes the outcome of that debate: a new economic development goal. The chapter concludes with an evaluation of the new economic development goal and the prospects for pursuing economic development through land use planning.

PLANNING AND ECONOMIC DEVELOPMENT IN OREGON BEFORE 1982

Although economic development was one of the original 14 goals adopted by LCDC in 1974, the subject attracted little attention through most of the 1970s. Much of the attention economic development did receive was negative. Lack of interest in the subject is evident in the language of the original Goal 9, in the scrutiny given the goal during the acknowledgment process, and in the plans submitted by local governments.

Goal 9: Economy of the State

The original Goal 9, "To diversify and improve the economy of the state," read as follows:

> Both state and federal economic plans and policies shall be coordinated by the state with local and regional needs. Plans and policies shall contribute to a stable and healthy economy in all regions of the state. Plans shall be based on inventories of areas suitable for increased economic growth and activity after taking into consideration the health of the current economic base; materials and energy availability; labor market factors; transportation; current market forces; availability of renewable and non-renewable resources; availability of land; and pollution control requirements.
>
> Economic growth and activity in accordance with such plans shall be encouraged in areas that have underutilized human and natural resource capabilities and want increased growth and activity. Alternative sites suitable for economic growth and expansion shall be designated in such plans. (Oregon LCDC 1975)

Although Goal 9 in its original form advanced the goal of economic development, it defined the term quite broadly. The goal expressed a desire for stability and diversity, and for growth only in those areas with underutilized resources and a desire for economic growth. In the guidelines interpreting the goal, desired growth was defined as changes "consistent with the availability of long-term human and natural resources," a statement that implied a natural limit to economic growth. In essence, the goal reflected the prevailing view of the relationship between economic development and land use planning: comprehensive plans had to address economic issues, but plans were not considered significant instruments for economic development.

Implementing Goal 9

Consistent with the limited goal of land use planning toward economic development, and consistent with the limits-to-growth attitude of the late 1970s, Goal 9 received little scrutiny in the acknowledgment process. Comprehensive plans had to address the spatial needs of economic activity, which meant local governments were required to zone land for industrial and commercial use, but much greater scrutiny was given to resource conservation, housing, and urban growth containment—at least until the 1981 recession.

Lack of interest on the part of local governments toward economic growth contributed to the neglect of economic development in local comprehensive plans. This lack of interest stemmed in part from the unique structure of Oregon's property tax system (Weber 1989). Local governments in most states pursue economic growth because growth contributes to the local tax base. That is, in most states, the tax rate is fixed, and tax revenues rise when new development is added to the tax base. In Oregon, property tax revenues are fixed (except for a 6 percent annual increase). Therefore, in Oregon, increases in the tax base result in lower property tax rates rather than in greater property tax revenues. The only way that property tax revenues in Oregon can rise (above the 6 percent statutory allowance) is if the voters approve a higher tax levy. As a result there is little incentive for local governments to pursue economic development.[1] To a certain extent, then, economic development represents just another locally undesirable land use (Popper 1981b), contributing more to public costs than to public revenues.

As described later, state interest in economic development changed markedly during the 1981 recession. After 1981, Oregon modified state policy toward economic development and required local governments to do the same. But the state's acquired desire for economic growth must be understood in the context of its recent economic history.

A RECENT HISTORY OF THE OREGON ECONOMY

The Oregon economy has always suffered from business cycles. Since becoming a state in 1859, Oregon has depended heavily on lumber and wood products for its economic base. Cycles in the Oregon economy closely followed cycles in the national housing market. Postwar recessions thus came and went, but most recessions were shallow and short-lived, at least until the early 1980s.

1981 Recession

The 1981 recession ravaged the Oregon economy. Unemployment in the state exceeded 9 percent in late 1980, reached 12 percent in 1983, and stayed above 9 percent until early 1985 (table 34). As jobs left the state, people followed. From 1982 to 1983, nearly 65,000 people moved out; another 30,000 left in 1986, resulting in an unprecedented net loss of population. Comparing these figures with those from the late 1970s, when an average 40,000 moved to

Table 34. Oregon Population Migration, Employment, and Income, 1970 to 1990

Year	Population, in thousands[a]	Net migration[b]	Employment, in thousands[a]	Unemployment rate[a]	Per capita personal income, $[c]	Percentage of U.S. per capita income[c]
1970	2,092	22,633	803	7.1	3,889	96.0
1971	2,130	19,167	835	7.6	4,149	96.6
1972	2,167	25,300	894	6.8	4,558	97.7
1973	2,218	40,100	939	6.2	5,066	97.8
1974	2,272	43,400	939	7.5	5,619	99.5
1975	2,326	41,600	929	10.6	6,053	99.7
1976	2,387	46,900	966	9.6	6,769	101.8
1977	2,452	48,900	1,047	7.3	7,413	101.6
1978	2,522	52,850	1,124	6.0	8,297	102.0
1979	2,584	42,700	1,134	6.8	9,176	101.6
1980	2,640	33,806	1,188	8.3	9,866	99.5
1981	2,661	429	1,205	9.9	10,448	95.4
1982	2,656	−25,250	1,171	11.5	10,589	92.2
1983	2,635	−39,535	1,196	10.8	11,281	93.2
1984	2,660	8,100	1,210	9.4	12,069	92.0
1985	2,676	50	1,200	8.8	12,641	91.0
1986	2,662	−30,250	1,245	8.5	13,128	89.9
1987	2,690	13,600	1,301	6.2	13,851	89.8
1988	2,741	36,550	1,343	5.8	14,883	90.2
1989	2,791	34,050	1,391	5.7	16,009	91.0
1990	2,847	38,921	1,409	5.5	17,156	91.8

[a]SOURCES: OEDD 1985; OEDD 1991.
[b]SOURCE: Center for Population Research and Census 1992.
[c]SOURCE: U.S. Dept. of Commerce, Bureau of Economic Analysis 1991.

Oregon each year, it is no surprise that the focus of state planning changed from growth management to economic development, or why the sign at the California border which once read "Welcome to Oregon, enjoy your visit," now simply says "Welcome to Oregon."

After 1986, the Oregon economy again grew rapidly. Unemployment fell below the national average in 1987, and employment levels reached an all-time high in 1989. But by some measures, the Oregon economy never fully recovered. Per capita income, which was above the national average in 1979, fell 9 percent below the national average in 1981 and has remained below ever since. The Oregon economy did recover from the 1981 recession, but the recovery left incomes well below the national average.

Structural Economic Change

Oregon's long-term economic decline reflects the structure of the Oregon economy. Similar to much of the rest of the nation, the Oregon economy underwent significant and permanent structural change in the 1980s. Production in the state's largest basic industry—forest products—set new records in 1986 and 1987, surpassing old records set in 1979 (Hibbard 1989). But these new production records were set with fewer mills and fewer mill workers (figure 12). In 1989, there were 25 percent fewer mills and 33 percent fewer mill workers than there were in 1979. High real interest rates in the early 1980s not only depressed the demand for wood products but, by increasing the value of the dollar, placed Oregon mills at a competitive disadvantage against Canadian mills. In response, the forest-products industry retooled and implemented less labor-intensive technologies. Efficiency increased; wages fell. Driven by technological change in lumber and wood processing, Oregon's average hourly wage, in constant dollars, has fallen every year since 1978. As a result, fewer are now employed in wood-products industries, and those who still are earn less (Hibbard 1989).

The long-term prospects for the forest-products industry in Oregon are not good. As old-growth timber stands disappear, the forest-products industry continues to move south—to Georgia, Alabama, and Louisiana. And with the spotted owl on the endangered species list, many of the remaining stands of old-growth timber on public lands must be preserved.[2] With little doubt, Oregon will not be able to rely on the lumber- and wood-products industry as its future economic base.

As employment in the wood-products industry declined, however, employment in high-technology industries increased (figure 13). Tektronics,

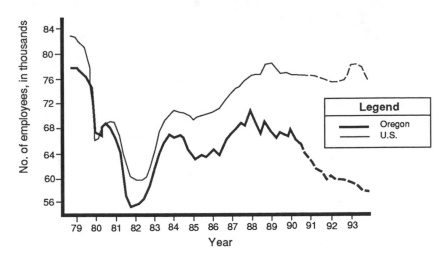

SOURCE: Oregon Executive Department 1990

Figure 12.   Oregon Employment in Lumber and Wood Products, 1979 to 1993

currently Oregon's largest employer, has been producing electrical equipment in the state since 1946. Following Tektronics' lead, several silicone valley firms opened new productions facilities in the Portland metropolitan area in the 1970s and 1980s. From 1977 to 1987, employment in the electric and electronics industry grew at a rate 2.5 times the national average (OEDD 1988).

More recently, however, employment in the state's high-tech industry has also fluctuated significantly. From 1982 to 1987, it fell more than 10 percent. Tektronics restructured, laying off many middle-management employees. Overseas competition escalated, leaving the future of the high-tech industry highly uncertain. Since 1987, however, Oregon employment in high tech once again increased and is projected to do so into the distant future.

Although high tech is replacing wood products as the dominant industry in the manufacturing sector (table 35), the primary structural shift has occurred between the manufacturing and the service sector (table 36). Where manufacturing employment fell from 35.1 percent to 21.5 percent of total

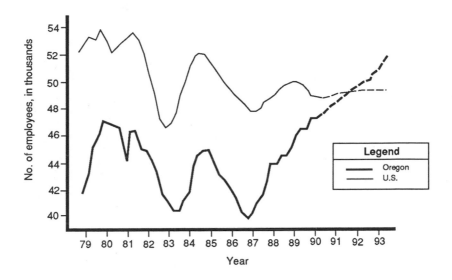

SOURCE: Oregon Executive Department 1990

Figure 13.   Oregon Employment in High Technology, 1979 to 1993

employment in the period from 1959 to 1989, employment in services increased from 15.8 percent to 28.9 percent. Much of the increase in services took place in business and health services (Whitelaw and Niemi 1989).

Unbalanced Urban-Rural Growth

The impacts of structural change in Oregon's economy, though pervasive, vary significantly across the state. Today, many speak of two Oregons: one in the metropolitan areas of the western valleys and the other in the rural areas that comprise the rest of the state (Hibbard 1989). As the Oregon economy changed from a resource to a service base, "metro" Oregon prospered while the "other" Oregon stagnated. In 1988, unemployment ranged from 4.6 percent in the Portland metropolitan area to 12 percent in Hood River County, a rural county; per capita income similarly ranged from approximately $13,500 in metropolitan Portland to approximately $9,000 in eastern Oregon (Oregon Department of Human Resources 1989). Thus,

**Table 35. Oregon Manufacturing Employment by Subsector,
1959 to 1989**

Subsector	Percentage			
	1959	1969	1979	1989
Lumber and wood	53	42	33	30
Printing	4	4	5	8
Paper	6	5	4	4
Food and kindred	12	10	9	9
Transportation equipment	3	7	5	5
High tech	5	11	22	22
Metals	7	9	12	11
Other	10	12	10	11
TOTAL	100	100	100	100

SOURCE: U.S. Dept. of Commerce 1991

as the state lags others in economic fortune, the "other" Oregon lags metropolitan Oregon, placing large segments of the state at a dual disadvantage.

In sum, the Oregon economy differs dramatically in 1991 from 1973,
when the state planning program began. The state's basic industries suffered severely during the 1981 recession. And the long-term prospects for
the forest-products industry are mixed at best. Meanwhile, the structure of
the Oregon economy changed from dependence on natural resources to
dependence on human resources.[3] This transition left incomes well below
the national average, and incomes in rural areas of the state well below the
state average. These economic conditions produced a mandate for policies
to reverse the decline and to distribute economic growth more evenly
around the state.

THE MID-RECESSION DEBATE

The dismal performance of the Oregon economy during the early 1980s
had significant and lasting impact on the focus of state land use planning.
When the unemployment rate reached 12 percent in 1982, many were
convinced that state land use planning contributed to the loss of jobs and

Table 36.   Oregon Employment by Sector, 1959 to 1989

Sector	Percentage			
	1959	1969	1979	1989
Agricultural services	0.4	0.5	0.9	1.0
Mining	0.4	0.3	0.2	0.2
Construction	5.9	5.6	6.5	4.5
Manufacturing	**35.1**	**32.0**	**26.4**	**21.5**
Transportation and public utilities	8.8	7.5	6.3	6.4
Wholesale trade	8.8	8.6	7.8	7.5
Retail trade	20.4	20.8	23.2	23.5
Finance, insurance, and real estate	4.8	6.3	7.1	6.5
Services	**15.4**	**18.4**	**21.6**	**28.9**
TOTAL	100.0	100.0	100.0	100.0

SOURCE: U.S. Dept. of Commerce 1991

the inability to attract new jobs. After all, the state planning program was created largely to manage growth, and it appeared that growth had been managed to death. Antiplanning sentiment was widespread. A *Wall Street Journal* editorial, published just prior to the 1982 initiative to end state planning, expressed a commonly held view:

> Complaints in Oregon about the special severity of the recession there prompted the writer of a UPI dispatch to recall the days not so long ago when the state was at the forefront of the limits to growth movement. It was then that former Governor Tom McCall said that the rest of the nation was welcome to visit Oregon but not to live there. Tight land use planning that is locking up land so that no one could use it was one of the policy spinoffs. Now, however, double-digit unemployment is causing Oregonians to have doubts. Next week they'll vote on a ballot proposition to discontinue state land use planning and return to local zoning. We'll learn, at least for one state, how serious unemployment concerns really are. (*Wall Street Journal* 1982)

Although there had been two previous initiatives to end state planning in 1976 and 1978, at issue in 1982 was whether state land use planning in Oregon inhibited or fostered economic growth. Not much else mattered.

Opponents of state planning argued that land use planning restricted the supply of industrial land, raised industrial land prices, and constrained industrial development (OEDD 1982). Supporters argued just the opposite: that planning increased the supply of industrial land, lowered industrial land costs, and stimulated industrial development (Richmond 1984).

Planning and Industrial Land Supplies

Evidence on both sides of this issue, though somewhat anecdotal, was provided by 1000 Friends of Oregon, which in 1981 adopted economic development as a priority issue. One Thousand Friends found that local governments poorly addressed economic development in their comprehensive plans (1000 Friends 1982b). For example, the organization found that the city of Salem had needed to plan for 1,386 acres of buildable industrial land but had zoned only 802 acres for industrial use. Out of 16,400 acres zoned for industrial use in the Portland metropolitan area, 1000 Friends found that 4,100 acres were located in a 100-year floodplain; only 4,200 had sewer or water service within 1,000 feet; and 9,200 acres needed major transportation improvements. According to 1000 Friends, the city of Klamath Falls allowed art galleries, recreation centers, and day care facilities in industrial zones. Thus, concluded 1000 Friends, there was little evidence that local governments had zoned adequate land for industrial use, provided services to land in industrial zones, or prevented incompatible land use in and near industrial zones.

While documenting the shortcomings of local comprehensive plans, 1000 Friends also sought to demonstrate that state review of local plans would help overcome these shortcomings. Towards that end, 1000 Friends examined industrial land supplies in ten metropolitan areas before (in 1975) and after (in 1982) LCDC acknowledgment review (1000 Friends 1982e). The results of the study are presented in table 37. According to the study, LCDC review resulted in a 79 percent increase in land zoned for industrial use, amounting to over 12,000 acres. Further, 1000 Friends found substantial improvements in the quality of industrial land, which they measured in terms of the size of land parcels, the compatibility of adjoining land uses, the absence of natural hazards (such as steep slopes or floodplains), and the availability of urban services. These findings were documented on a case-by-case basis in various communities. As a result of LCDC review, many local governments set aside large parcels for specific industrial uses, limited partitions of industrial lands, and designed new industrial districts to meet

Table 37. Vacant Industrial Land, Selected Areas in Oregon, 1975/76 to 1990

| Urban area | Acres of land zoned for industry | | | | Population |
	Before LCDC review (1975/76)	After LCDC review (1982)	Change	Percentage change	
Multnomah County[a,b]	4,683	7,049	2,366	51	545,486
Clackamas County[b]	2,267	4,084	1,817	80	246,100
Eugene/Springfield UGB[b]	2,220	3,605	1,385	62	193,500
Washington County[c]	1,377	2,493	1,116	81	142,282
Salem UGB[b]	362	2,951	2,588	715	138,700
Corvallis/Philomath UGBs	748	1,170	422	56	48,300
Medford UGB	1,635	1,339	−296	−18	45,873
Bend/Redmond UGBs[b]	715	2,134	1,419	198	41,000
Klamath Falls UGB	613	2,000	1,387	226	36,498
Albany/Millersburg UGBs	1,374	1,757	383	18	34,745
TOTAL	15,964	28,581	12,587	79	1,472,484

[a]Within Portland Metro UGB.
[b]Plan was acknowledged at time of study.
[c]Within Portland Metro UGB, unincorporated areas only.

Source: 1000 Friends 1982e

the needs of specific industries, such as high-tech firms (Richmond 1984). Thus, according to 1000 Friends, state review of local comprehensive plans increased not only the quantity, but also the quality, of industrial land supplies in Oregon.

A 1981 report of the Society of Industrial Realtors (published in 1000 Friends 1982c) provided evidence supporting the conclusions of 1000 Friends. In average sales price of prime industrial land, the report showed, Portland ranked among the lowest of all western cities in the U.S. (table 38).

Planning and Payroll Growth

Five years after 1000 Friends explored the influence of plan acknowledgment on industrial land supplies, Knaap (1988) explored its influence on payroll growth. Using payroll data from all 36 Oregon counties from 1978 to 1986, Knaap examined the relationship between payroll growth in each of nine industries (defined by single-digit standard industrial classifications (SIC)) and the extent of plan acknowledgment in each county. Knaap's regression model is presented in the box insert.

Because payroll data were available only at the county level, and because every county contained several jurisdictions with acknowledged plans, Knaap constructed two variables to measure the extent of plan acknowledgment in each county. These variables index the extent of plan acknowledgment in each county in each year by a number between 0 and 1, depending on

Table 38. Industrial Land Price in Selected Western Cities, 1980

	Average price per square foot, $	
City	2- to 5-acre parcels	>10-acre parcels
Seattle	3.50	3.00
Oakland	3.00	2.25
Phoenix	2.75	2.10
Denver	2.15	1.90
Portland	2.25	1.10

SOURCE: 1000 Friends 1982c

Regression Model of Impact of Acknowledgment on Payroll Growth

The regression equation in the analysis by Knaap (1987) can be expressed as follows:

Payroll change in County *J*, in Industry *I*, from year *A*
   to year *B* =
Constant for Industry *I* +
Total payroll change in County *J*, from year *A* to year *B* +
Total payroll change in Industry *I* from year *A* to year *B* +
Percentage of plans acknowledged in County *J*, in year *A*,
   weighted by population +
Percentage of plans acknowledged in County *J*, in year *A*,
   weighted by land area +
a Stochastic error.

Where, Counties   = 36,
          Industries = 9, and
          Years   = 1978 to 1986 (8 inclusive time periods).

Total observations = 288, i.e., those industries in which payroll data for all 36 counties for all 8 time periods were available.

SOURCE OF DATA: Oregon Department of Labor 1979 to 1986

the populations and sizes of jurisdictions that have acknowledged plans within the county.

Percentage acknowledged–population measures the percentage of the county's total population living in jurisdictions with acknowledged plans. For example, if in 1978 Jurisdiction 1 was the only jurisdiction in County A with an acknowledged plan, and Jurisdiction 1 had 100,000 residents and County A had 200,000, then Knaap assigned 0.5 for Percentage acknowledged–population for County A in 1978. This system places greater weight on jurisdictions with large populations.

Percentage acknowledged–land measures the percentage of the county's total land area included in jurisdictions with acknowledged plans. For example, if in 1978 Jurisdiction 1 was the only one in County A with an acknowledged plan, and Jurisdiction 1 is 100 acres in size and County A is 1,000 acres, then Knaap assigned 0.1 for Percentage acknowledged–land for County A in 1978. This system places greater weight on jurisdictions that are large in area.

Percentage acknowledged–land is a good measure of the land use constraints faced by land-intensive industries, such as agriculture and mining. Percentage acknowledged–population is a good measure of the land use constraints faced by industries that are largely urban, such as retailing, wholesaling, and services.

Knaap included two other independent variables in the analysis. Total county payroll measures the sum of the payrolls in all industries in the county. Total industry payroll measures the sum of the payrolls of all counties in the particular industry. To focus the analysis on changes in industry payrolls, the dependent variables and these independent variables were all "first-differenced" to measure changes from year to year.[4] Knaap's regressions, then, measure the influence of plan acknowledgment on payroll growth in each industry, after adjusting for fluctuations specific to the industry and for fluctuations specific to the county. Knaap's results are reported in table 39.

The regressions were able to explain approximately one-tenth to one-half of the year-to-year variation in payroll growth in Oregon counties. The poorest fit of the regression model was for the mining industry, which Knaap attributed to the relatively small changes in mining payrolls and the insensitivity of mining to local economic conditions. The best fit of the regression model was for the finance, insurance, and real estate industry. Most of the explanatory power for this industry came from the variable, Total county payroll, which Knaap attributed to the market orientation of this sector. That is, payrolls in these industries, according to Knaap, are highly sensitive to local economic conditions. As expected, payroll growth in most industries was found to be positively related to growth in both total industry payrolls and total county payrolls.

Percentage acknowledged–land, the land-weighted variable, was insignificant for every industry. Since this measured the percentage of the county land area with plan acknowledgment, Knaap did not expect the variable to explain payroll variation in urban industries. But Percentage acknowledged–land was also insignificantly related to payroll growth in resource-intensive industries, such as mining and agriculture, forestry, and fishing. From these results, Knaap concluded that state acknowledgment of local comprehensive plans did not affect the payrolls of resource-based industries during the study period.

Percentage acknowledged–population, the population-weighted variable, was insignificant for every industry but two: services, and transportation and public utilities. The relationship between Percentage acknowledged–

population and payroll growth in these industries was positive. Although Knaap expected one spuriously significant correlation out of 10 analyses, using a 90 percent confidence interval, he offered reasons for interpreting the positive influence of plan acknowledgment on payroll growth in these industries as meaningful. First, transportation and public utilities are capital-intensive industries; thus growth reflects long-term decisions; and long-term decisions are more easily made in certain regulatory environments. The positive relationship between plan acknowledgment and payroll growth in the transporation and public utilities industry therefore supports the proposition that acknowledged plans can foster economic development by enhancing certainty in the regulatory environment. Services, on the other hand, are labor-intensive and also are perhaps the most amenity-sensitive industry. The positive relationship between plan acknowledgment and payrolls in services, therefore, supports the proposition that plan acknowledgment can stimulate economic development by securing an environment favorable to amenity-based industries.

Knaap concludes that land use planning can perhaps serve to foster economic development. Since plan acknowledgment was found to be positively related to payroll growth in services, plan acknowledgment can perhaps foster economic growth in the service industries—if acknowledgment promotes the preservation of environmental amenities. And since plan acknowledgment was found to be positively related to payroll growth in transportation and public utilities, it can perhaps foster economic growth in capital-intensive industries—if acknowledgment increases certainty in the regulatory environment.

Although Knaap's results are plausible and consistent with expectations, they must be interpreted with caution. First, the land use variables are at best a crude measure of the influence of land use planning. The weighting schemes used to generate the land use variables are highly imprecise and poorly suited to capture effects that accrue over time. Second, the variable, Total county payroll, while useful in capturing county-specific variation in payroll growth, may also capture some of the influence of plan acknowledgment—if plan acknowledgment uniformly influences all industries in a given county. Finally, since Knaap's data come exclusively from Oregon, his results are unable to capture the influence state planning may have had on payroll growth in Oregon relative to other states.

In sum, Knaap's results offer limited empirical support for the argument that plan acknowledgment can stimulate economic development by enhancing the quality of the urban environment and by removing uncertainty

Table 39.   Determinants of Payroll Growth in Oregon, 1978 to 1986

Variable	Regression coefficient $(t)^p$			
	Agriculture, forestry, and fishing ($N = 267$; $R^2 = 0.10$)	Mining ($N = 243$; $R^2 = 0.04$)	Construction ($N = 274$; $R^2 = 0.23$)	Manufacturing ($N = 253$; $R^2 = 0.37$)
Intercept	7.04×10^4 $(0.46)^{ns}$	4.44×10^4 $(0.65)^{ns}$	2.79×10^5 $(0.43)^{ns}$	8.12×10^5 $(0.49)^{ns}$
Percentage acknowledged—population	-2.69×10^5 $(0.96)^{ns}$	4.31×10^4 $(0.24)^{ns}$	1.13×10^6 $(0.64)^{ns}$	-6.11×10^5 $(0.15)^{ns}$
Percentage acknowledged—land	3.29×10^5 $(1.03)^{ns}$	4.63×10^5 $(0.23)^{ns}$	-2.74×10^6 $(1.38)^{ns}$	-4.45×10^6 $(0.97)^{ns}$
Total county payroll	3.16×10^{-3} $(3.93)^{**}$	1.67×10^{-5} $(0.01)^{ns}$	1.29×10^{-2} $(3.89)^{**}$	0.12 $(10.35)^{**}$
Total industry payroll	1.80×10^{-2} $(3.29)^{**}$	2.67×10^{-2} $(2.81)^{**}$	2.71×10^{-2} $(7.55)^{**}$	2.33×10^{-2} $(4.73)^{**}$

*$p < 0.10$, one-tailed test.
**$p < 0.05$, one-tailed test.
ns p not significant.
SOURCE: Knaap 1988

in the regulatory environment. Knaap's results provide no evidence, however, that planning in Oregon was the cause of slow economic growth during the acknowledgment period. For most industries in Oregon, plan acknowledgment had no significant impact on payroll growth, after adjusting for industry- and county-specific economic effects.

PLANNING AND ECONOMIC DEVELOPMENT IN OREGON AFTER 1982

Lacking information on the influence of land use planning on economic development, prior to the 1983 legislative session, Governor Atiyeh appointed a 12-member task force to study the impact of land use planning

	Regression coefficient $(t)^p$			
Transportation and public utilities ($N = 281$; $R^2 = 0.44$)	Wholesale trade ($N = 283$; $R^2 = 0.37$)	Retail ($N = 288$; $R^2 = 0.46$)	Finance, insurance, and real estate ($N = 287$; $R^2 = 0.47$)	Services ($N = 287$; $R^2 = 0.43$)
-5.22×10^5 $(0.55)^{ns}$	1.06×10^5 $(0.13)^{ns}$	-9.17×10^6 $(2.40)^{**}$	-4.38×10^5 $(0.53)^{ns}$	5.17×10^6 $(1.49)^{ns}$
2.70×10^6 $(2.00)^{**}$	4.80×10^4 $(0.03)^{ns}$	-1.01×10^7 $(1.02)^{ns}$	2.03×10^6 $(1.43)^{ns}$	4.93×10^6 $(1.61)^{*}$
-2.43×10^6 $(1.51)^{ns}$	-9.62×10^5 $(0.48)^{ns}$	9.44×10^6 $(0.81)^{ns}$	-1.36×10^6 $(0.85)^{ns}$	-2.66×10^6 $(0.77)^{ns}$
5.45×10^{-2} $(14.13)^{**}$	6.24×10^{-2} $(12.34)^{**}$	0.43 $(15.00)^{**}$	6.19×10^{-2} $(15.38)^{**}$	0.14 $(16.35)^{**}$
1.89×10^{-2} $(1.81)^{*}$	1.18×10^{-2} $(1.28)^{ns}$	2.31×10^{-2} $(2.64)^{**}$	1.23×10^{-2} $(1.15)^{ns}$	-1.23×10^{-2} $(0.77)^{ns}$

on the Oregon economy. Specifically, Atiyeh charged the task force with answering the following question: How does Oregon's land use program impact economic development? The task force submitted its findings in September 1982. In general, the report was favorable to the planning program: it offered no verifiable evidence of a firm choosing not to locate in Oregon due to obstacles presented by state land use planning. The task force also found, however, that Goal 9 had not served effectively to develop the Oregon economy.

Changing the Focus of Planning

The task force made specific recommendations to enable state land use planning to serve better as an economic development instrument. Specifically, the task force recommended:

1. Shortening the appeals process
2. Facilitating the acknowledgment process by allowing acknowledgment for "substantial compliance"
3. Replacing the Land Use Board of Appeals (LUBA) with a new land use court

4. Requiring all plans to be submitted by January 1, 1984, and
5. Encouraging all local governments to place more emphasis on economic development and public facilities planning.

Except for eliminating LUBA, all these recommendations were adopted by the 1983 legislature (BGRS 1984).

The 1983 legislature enacted changes in the land use statutes with the intent "not to prohibit, deter, delay, or increase the cost of appropriate development, but to *enhance economic development* and opportunity for the benefit of all citizens" (ORS 197.707 to 197.717, emphasis added). This new legislation changed dramatically the relationship between land use planning and economic development. Specifically, it defined economic development as vital to the welfare of the people of Oregon. It required LCDC to adopt new goals or rules, requiring that local comprehensive plans meet these standards:

- Include an analysis of local economic patterns as they relate to state and national economic trends
- Contain specific policies designed to foster economic development
- Provide at least an adequate supply of industrial and commercial land
- Provide for compatible land usage near commercial and industrial sites
- Prepare and adopt public facility plans for areas within urban growth boundaries
- Provide for reasonable opportunities for residential and industrial development outside urban growth boundaries, and
- Complete the above by the first periodic review of each local plan.

Further, the legislation required the Oregon Economic Development Department (OEDD) to provide local governments with information on state and national economic trends and to assist local governments in planning and zoning for industrial and commercial land uses, developing public facility plans, and streamlining local permit procedures.

New Goal 9: Economic Development

To meet these legislative requirements, LCDC adopted in 1986 an extensive set of administrative rules for implementing Goal 9. To maintain consistency between the goal and its new administrative rules, Goal 9 was rewritten in 1988 and is now entitled Economic Development, "To provide adequate opportunities throughout the state for a variety of economic activities vital to the health, welfare, and prosperity of Oregon's citizens."

Comprehensive plans and policies shall contribute to a stable and healthy economy in all regions of the state. Plans shall be based on inventories of areas suitable for increased economic growth and activity after taking into consideration the health of the current economic base; materials and energy availability; labor market factors; *educational and technical training programs; availability of key public facilities; necessary support facilities; current market forces; location relative to markets;* transportation, current market forces; availability of renewable and non-renewable resources; availability of land; and pollution control requirements.

Comprehensive plans for urban areas shall:

1. *Include an analysis of the community's economic patterns, potentialities, strengths, and deficiencies as they relate to state and national trends;*
2. *Contain policies concerning the economic development opportunities in the community;*
3. *Provide for at least an adequate supply of sites of suitable sizes, types, locations, and service levels for a variety of industrial and commercial uses consistent with plan policies;*
4. *Limit uses on or near sites zoned for specific industrial and commercial uses to those which are compatible with proposed uses.*

In accordance with ORS 197.180 and Goal 2, state agencies that issue permits affecting land use shall identify in their coordination programs how they will coordinate permit issuance with other state agencies, cities and counties. (LCDC 1990, italic indicates new language)

The new Goal 9 represents a significant change in the economic intent of land use planning in Oregon. Where the old version sought to accommodate economic development, the new version seeks to foster economic development through comprehensive land use planning—a novel approach to economic development at the state level. Further, to assist local governments in fostering economic development though comprehensive planning, all state agencies that issue permits are required to coordinate their activities with local comprehensive plans.

In accordance with the administrative rules, the OEDD in 1986 produced an extensive volume of information to assist local governments in revising comprehensive plans (OEDD 1986). This volume contains an analysis of short- and long-term state and national economic trends; a business growth-and-decline study; a growth-industries report; a growth industries profile, which lists the 25 highest-ranked growth industries; a growth-industries survey, which identifies location factors, site requirements and marketing techniques for attracting growth industries; and a local development program guide, which provides instructions for local governments on how to interpret information and utilize information for economic planning. For better or for worse, LCDC now requires, and OEDD now facilitates, state-of-the-art economic development planning by local governments.

In essence, Goal 9 promulgates a 3-part and -party development strategy. The OEDD must analyze the state economy and assist local governments with targeting specific industries; local governments must meet the land and public service needs of targeted industries through comprehensive land use planning; and all other state agencies must issue permits in local jurisdictions in accordance with local comprehensive land use plans. As a result, land use planning since 1986 has played a central role in Oregon's economic development strategy.

Local Government Response

To assess the implementation of Oregon's new development strategy, the Bureau of Governmental Research and Service (BGRS) (1989) conducted a survey of cities, counties, and councils of government. The survey asked local governments to identify economic development activities pursued at the local level. According to the BGRS, the response rate to the survey (80 percent) indicated a strong local interest in economic development.

A large set of questions in the BGRS survey addressed "land use planning in local economic development." In response to these questions, local officials expressed belief that land use planning is an effective instrument for economic development, second only to providing infrastructure. Many local officials also indicated that they used comprehensive planning as a tool for economic development.

Two-thirds of the survey respondents had used comprehensive planning, zoning, or land management to promote new business formation, recruit established businesses, or retain existing businesses. Nearly one-third of all cities and two-thirds of all counties had eliminated public hearing requirements to streamline the building permit review process. Similar percentages of local governments had streamlined site design reviews or development permit standards to foster economic development. One-half of all cities and three-fourths of all counties had amended zoning standards or procedures to foster economic development, largely by allowing industrial or commercial uses in more areas. Finally, one-half of all cities and three-fourths of all counties had altered land management practices to encourage economic development. Most had inventoried industrial and commercial land and had listed industrial land on OEDD's inventory of industrial property.

From these responses the BGRS concluded that comprehensive planning had become a widely used instrument for economic development in Oregon communities. And, according to the BGRS, the use of comprehensive planning for economic development is certain to increase as more local governments come up for periodic review.

DISCUSSION

The evidence reviewed above suggests that the relationship between land use planning and economic development changed over the last two decades. Whereas comprehensive plans largely ignored economic development in the 1970s, they play a central role in linking state and local development strategies in the 1990s. Quite clearly, the objectives of planning related to economic development in Oregon have changed, but there is little evidence that the influence of planning on economic development has also changed.

The efficacy of Oregon's integrated development strategy rests on critical yet uncertain assumptions. Oregon's approach assumes that targeting is an effective economic development strategy. While it is certainly more preferable to attract growing than declining industries, tomorrow's growth industries may differ markedly from the growth industries of today. Thus the efficacy of targeting based on historical data remains highly in doubt (Vaughn and Pollard 1986). Further, the planning approach assumes that the land and service needs of targeted industries can be foreseen. However, different firms in the same industry may have different locational requirements. Production-oriented high-tech firms, for example, may require low-cost land, while development-oriented high-tech firms may require proximity to universities. Thus, identifying the local requirements of targeted industries is difficult at best. Finally, the Oregon strategy assumes that land has magnetism—that firms and jobs can be attracted by land and public services. Since there are relatively few firms looking for new locations at any given time, and since most jobs are created by the birth and expansion of in-state firms, there is considerable doubt that a land-based development strategy will have much success at the state level (Niemi 1984).

Furthermore, Goal 9 may still focus too narrowly on industrial development. All the available evidence indicates that Oregon's economic growth is occurring in services (especially business services), and that service industries are attracted to high-quality environments. Although other goals address natural resources, transportation, and recreation, the relationship between these goals and economic development could be made more direct. Further, although urban growth boundaries were designed to conserve resource lands and manage urban growth, compact urban growth may foster agglomerative economies in Oregon cities.[5] Thus economic development could perhaps be more closely linked to urban containment. Finally, the 278 comprehensive plans contain a wealth of information on public services, transportation, employment, population, and urban growth; yet there have been no attempts to standardize this information for use in economic development planning. Perhaps such use of planning data will usher in the fourth wave of economic development.

Comprehensive planning, of course, is but part of Oregon's larger economic development program. *Oregon Shines: An Economic Development Strategy for the Pacific Century* (OEDD 1989) outlines Oregon's comprehensive economic development strategy for the future. The strategy entails three key strategic initiatives: a superior work force, an attractive quality of life, and an international frame of mind. In brief, the strategy involves changing the economic base in Oregon from natural resources to human resources. To assure progress toward implementing that strategy, the state established a progress board to assess strategy implementation periodically and to make appropriate recommendations (Oregon Progress Board 1990). Comprehensive planning will not likely play a leading role in restructuring Oregon's economy, but comprehensive planning may play an important role in coordinating economic development.

LESSONS FROM OREGON

The relationship between Oregon's land use program and economy remains highly controversial and uncertain. What is certain is that the relationship has changed. Where the economic goal of the land use program was once largely ignored, it now represents a fundamental component of state industrial policy. The reasons for the change in emphasis are also quite clear. The Oregon economy suffered severely during the 1981 recession, which permanently weakened the state's traditional employment base. Income levels, even after the 1981 recession, remain well below the national average. Oregon, once the vanguard of no-growth economic policies, now has an integrated strategy to promote economic growth. Changes in Goal 9 of the statewide land use program reflect this change of strategy.

The lessons provided by Oregon's experience are interesting if less than complete (Sullivan et al. 1984). First, there is no evidence that state oversight of land use planning is detrimental to economic growth. In fact the available evidence, though preliminary, suggests just the opposite. While industrial land may serve as a poor magnet for industrial development, there is evidence that maintaining a high-quality environment may stimulate amenity-based economic growth and that increasing certainty in the regulatory environment may stimulate capital-intensive growth. Certainty regarding these positive effects, however, awaits further empirical support.

The Oregon experience demonstrates with certainty that, through mandated comprehensive planning consistent with statewide planning goals, the state is able to force local governments to plan for economic development. This is no small feat. A recent survey in Illinois, which has no state planning program, found that over 18 percent of cities with populations less than 25,000 had made no economic development efforts whatsoever; 21 percent never prepared an economic development plan—in spite of many state incentives to do so. Oregon doesn't rely on incentives. In Oregon, every city greater than 2,500 in population will plan for economic development by the date of its first periodic review. Every city will have analyzed the local economy; every city will have adopted an economic development plan; every city will have inventoried industrial and commercial land; and every city will have streamlined local permit procedures.

Although the efficacy of stimulating economic development through comprehensive land use planning remains in doubt, there is little doubt that through comprehensive planning, state agencies and local governments in Oregon can offer better-integrated economic development programs than most other states. What is more, Oregon cities will plan for economic development even though such planning provides local governments with few fiscal benefits.

Notes

1. Oregon recently passed a sweeping property tax limitation measure. The measure may stimulate substantive changes in the structure of Oregon's property tax system. See Oregon DLCD (1991c).
2. At this writing the spotted owl controversy remains unresolved.
3. As suggested by Bill Fischel in his review of the manuscript, the change in economic base from natural resources to human resources in part represents a change in economic base from one type of natural

resource to another. Labor responds to amenities with a willingness to work for lower nominal wages, which in turn makes amenity-rich areas attractive to industry. This effect may account for part of Oregon's income loss, if industries discovered that labor is willing to move to, or remain in, Oregon for low wages.

4. "First-differenced" means that the dependent variable was specified as the change in payroll from one year to the next.

5. Agglomeration economies are defined as the economic advantage of a firm locating near other firms in the same industry, near firms in complementary industries, or near both. By fostering compact urban growth, UGBs may foster agglomeration economies.

7

Statewide Planning and
Land Use Politics

THE OREGON LAND USE program is often described as innovative and pioneering—perhaps for two reasons. First, Oregon was one of the first states to retract from local governments, in whole or in part, the authority to plan and regulate land use, thus establishing a state role in land use control. Second, as the previous chapters describe, Oregon's program embraced many unique approaches to contemporary land use issues, including urban growth management, public services, affordable housing, economic development, and resource conservation. Previous chapters, however, began with the state land use program as a given, offering little explanation of how or why it developed at all. These, of course, are two of the most important and intriguing questions about any program described as innovative and pioneering.

The short answer to these questions is politics. Land use programs, as well as all other state activities, reflect political, economic, and social forces in the body politic. These forces generate the momentum for reform and shape the procedures and instruments of change. These are not new insights. Researchers across the country for some time have based their work on these simple premises. Paradigms, of course, vary. Some scholars take a structural view, arguing that state land use policies reflect the social, spatial, and economic organization of the state (Knaap 1987b). Others take an institutional view, saying that policies reflect the outcome of institutional processes and pluralist politics (Rosenbaum 1976, Nourse 1977, Popper 1981a). Still others take a Marxist view, arguing that state land use policies reflect the struggle among social classes (Heiman 1988, Plotkin 1987).

Such diversity of paradigmatic perspectives notwithstanding, land use politics is played on two primary levels that are visible for analysis: the popular level and the interest-group level. Politics at the popular level reflects the interests and actions of the population at large. Popular politics helps explain why particular land use policies are adopted at particular locations at particular points in time. Politics at the interest-group level reflects the interests and actions of interest groups. Interest-group politics helps explain why land use policies take particular forms and result in particular outcomes. The Oregon land use program has been analyzed at both of these levels.

POPULAR POLITICS AND LAND USE

The popular approach to land use politics presumes that the adoption and sustenance of land use policy is influenced by the interests of the local population. The approach has been used to explain why some communities or states adopt growth controls as a principal objective of land use policy and others do not. Not surprisingly, most of the research on growth controls analyzed the experience of California and Florida, two of the fastest-growing states in recent years. Using survey methods, researchers examined whether support for controlling growth in these states is correlated with residents' income, occupation, education, place of residence, and other characteristics. The evidence is now extensive and provides fairly conclusive results.[1]

Because much of the research was performed by sociologists, research in the popular politics arena focused ostensibly on a single issue: Is the movement to control growth divided by social class? That is, do land use policies that control growth serve exclusively, or primarily, the interests of the upper class? The overwhelming answer to this question has been no. In fact, the evidence has been so overwhelming that in 1983 a leading researcher in the field called for a moratorium on studies showing that support for growth management is not divided by class (Gottdiener 1983).

In rejecting the class-based theory of growth politics, the empirical evidence has not rejected the hypothesis that support for growth management is divided by social strata. On the contrary, the evidence strongly suggests that support for growth management is correlated with the income, occupation, education, gender, location, and home ownership status of the population. Instead, the evidence refutes class-based theories of growth politics because the social divisions that stratify support for growth management are only weakly correlated with the social divisions that have traditionally stratified class.[2]

An alternative to the class-based theory, based on public-opinion theory, was offered by deHaven-Smith (1987). This theory suggests that public support for land use and other policies is divided not by social divisions that define class, but instead by narrow issues that confront individuals personally every day. Based on this theory, for example, support for health policy comes from individuals who are sick or old, support for environmental regulation comes from individuals who live in degraded environments, and support for growth management comes from individuals who suffer ill consequences from rapid urban growth. For the most part, the evidence from both Florida and California is consistent with this theory (deHaven-Smith 1987, 1991; Deakin 1989).

POPULAR POLITICS IN OREGON

The available evidence from Oregon is largely consistent with evidence from other states, although the methodologies and interpretations vary. Researchers in both California and Florida analyzed the results of surveys, while work in Oregon focused on the results of binding referenda, specifically, statewide referenda to end state land use planning. In keeping with the populist tradition of the state, all four referenda to end statewide planning (1970, 1976, 1978, 1982) were launched by initiative petition. On three other occasions (1973, 1984, 1986), initiative petitions fell short of the number of signatures necessary to place the issue on the ballot. This history suggests, at a minimum, that state planning is important to the Oregon public, that the public is divided on land use issues, and that statewide planning requires sustained popular support.

Using referenda as the basis for research has both strengths and weaknesses. The strengths are threefold. First, referenda results are binding, which eliminates the possibility that respondents are engaging in strategic behavior.[3] Second, referenda focus on concrete policy issues rather than on hypothetical questions; for example, voters respond to a question on ending statewide land use planning rather than to a generic question concerning support for controlling growth. Finally, referenda reflect only the views of those who vote; this limits the sample—by definition—to those whose views are politically influential.

Weaknesses of using referenda as the basis for research arise because individual votes are confidential; information is unavailable on individual voters. Sample units in studies based on referenda are therefore limited to voting precincts or higher geographic aggregations of votes and populations. As discussed below, this weakness makes it difficult to interpret such studies.

1976 Referendum

An early study of the popular support for land use planning in Oregon was conducted by Medler and Mushketel (1979) in 1976—just two years after the program began. The 1976 referendum failed 57 percent to 43 percent. Medler and Mushketel analyzed the referendum results at the county, city, and voting-precinct levels. They also analyzed the results of a survey administered in the city of Eugene. Using covariance analysis, they tested four hypotheses, which can be paraphrased as follows:

1. Support for state planning is positively related to income
2. Support for state planning is positively related to housing value
3. Support for state planning is positively related to economic growth, and
4. Support for state planning is negatively related to the rate of unemployment and to the level of employment in the forest-products industry.

Medler and Mushketel found evidence to support each of their hypotheses at both the city and county levels. Cities and counties with high incomes, high housing values, and high growth rates were more supportive of state planning than were counties with high rates of unemployment and large numbers of forest-products workers.

At the individual level, however, their results provided evidence that is contrary to hypothesis 1, insufficient to support hypotheses 2 and 3, and unable to test hypothesis 4. That is, in Eugene, Medler and Mushketel found high-income residents less supportive of controlling growth than low-income residents; and Eugene homeowners and long-time residents were no more supportive of controlling growth than renters and newcomers. Based on these results, Medler and Mushketel concluded:

> Interpreting the observed aggregate relations as a set of contextual effects still brings us to the conclusion that the issue of land use planning is, in essence, a class conflict. Though there is little evidence of conflicting views between groups within communi-

ties, the data do indicate conflicting views between aggregate units. Simply put, the better off counties and cities favor land use planning while the less well off reject it. (349)

Medler and Mushketel's results and interpretations invite two questions: How should observers interpret the contradiction between the aggregate- and the individual-level results? And, does this evidence confirm the hypothesis that support for planning is divided by social class?

In response to these questions, Medler and Mushketel describe their results as illustrating potential "ecological fallacy," or distortions due to aggregation. Ecological fallacy occurs when researchers assume that the results of aggregate analyses also hold true at the individual level. This occurs, for example, if researchers find support for state planning in high-income cities and conclude that support for state planning therefore comes from high-income individuals. To avoid an ecologically fallacious interpretation, Medler and Mushketel accept at face value both that higher-income cities and counties are more supportive of state planning and that, within cities and counties, high-income individuals are less supportive than low-income individuals.

These contradictory results, however, leave the social-class hypothesis open to interpretation. In fact, Medler and Mushketel admit:

> However it is important to note that we are accepting, in effect, the hypothesis [social class] for the wrong reason. This hypothesis was derived from a literature that focused on the individual calculus of self-interest and personal utility, which, when formulated as aggregate behavior, suggested that support for planning would be a middle-class phenomenon. At three levels of aggregation, the available data confirm the aggregate form of the hypothesis. However, the limited individual data available suggest that the wealthiest individuals are the most hostile to controlling growth, while education seems to have no discernible effect. Overall, it appears that social class, as a contextual variable, is a relevant variable for explaining the vote on Measure 10 [the measure to repeal state planning]. (346)

In sum, Medler and Mushketel's results confirm the theory that support for state planning is divided by social class only if social class is defined at the community level. That is, judging by Medler and Mushketel's results, state planning is supported by upper-class communities, not upper-class individuals.

1982 Referendum

Two referenda later, Knaap (1987a, 1987b) reexamined popular support for state land use planning. In 1978, a referendum to end state planning was rejected 61 percent to 39 percent and was defeated in 31 of 36 counties. In 1982, a similar referendum failed by only 55 percent to 45 percent and was defeated in only 15 of 36 counties. The counties favoring repeal in 1982 contained over two-thirds of the state's land area, but the counties rejecting repeal contained over two-thirds of the state population. The margin of majority in both supporting and opposing counties, however, was small.

The 1982 referendum was held under much different circumstances than the referendum in 1976. In 1976, the state planning effort had just begun, and the state was continuing to grow rapidly. By 1982, the planning effort was well underway, and the Oregon economy was deep in recession. The state unemployment rate stood at 11.5 percent, causing 25,000 people to move out. Such dismal conditions quite clearly threatened the survival of the state land use program.

Like Medler and Mushketel, Knaap analyzed the results of the 1982 referendum at different levels of aggregation. Also like them, he found that support for state planning was positively related to income at the more aggregated level and negatively related to income at the less aggregated level. Unlike Medler and Mushketel, who used correlation analysis, however, Knaap analyzed the voting results using regression analysis. Also unlike them, he interpreted his results as rejecting the social-class hypothesis.

Following the public-opinion theory discussed above, Knaap (1987a) argued that support for state planning in Oregon was based on a specific set of subissues that directly affects individuals. These issues Knaap labeled home rule, urban growth management, economic development, and housing. According to Knaap, the home rule issue divided popular support by geographic location. That is, residents of the Willamette Valley supported state planning as a means of overcoming problems of coordination among Willamette Valley governments, while residents of nonvalley counties viewed state planning as usurping home rule powers. Support for urban growth management, Knaap suggested, divided urban residents from rural residents. Where urban residents stood to benefit from lower public service costs and protected open space, rural residents stood to lose rights to develop their land.

Support for economic development, Knaap argued, divided individuals employed in resource-based occupations from individuals employed in amenity-based occupations.[4] Farm and forest land conservation, for example, threatened the jobs of those in resource-based occupations, while it posed no threat to those employed in service occupations. Finally, the housing issue, according to Knaap, divided homeowners from renters. Because state planning serves to mitigate exclusionary zoning and diminishes real property rights, renters support state planning more than homeowners.

Knaap found evidence to support each of these hypotheses at both the county and the census-tract levels. Support for state planning was greater among valley residents than among nonvalley residents, greater among urban residents than rural residents, greater among service-based employees than resource-based employees, and greater among renters than owner-occupants. Since these divisions define individual self-interests better than they define social class, Knaap argued, the findings support the theories based on self-interest better than they support those based on social class. Regardless of social class, Knaap concluded, individuals supported state planning if they viewed components of the program as serving their personal interests.

Because Knaap found income positively related to support for planning at the county level and negatively related at the census-tract level, he also had to confront the question of ecological fallacy. As opposed to Medler and Mushketel, however, Knaap discounted the aggregate results and emphasized the census-tract-level results. His logic was as follows. Income variation across counties largely reflects differences in cost-of-living rather than differences in real income. Therefore, Knaap adjusted the county income data using land value data (as a proxy for differences in the cost-of-living). After this adjustment, he found no relationship between adjusted income and support for planning at the county level. As a result, he accepted the negative relationship between income and support for planning at the census level as a better indicator of the true relationship.

In sum, both Knaap and Medler and Mushketel found the support for state land use planning, as measured by the results of referenda to end state planning, significantly related to socioeconomic characteristics of the population. At the county level, both found the support for state planning positively related to income and negatively related to employment in resource-based industries. At the census level (Knaap) and at the individual level (Medler and Mushketel) both found the support for state planning negatively related to income. Medler and Mushketel interpreted their results as supporting hypotheses based on social class; Knaap interpreted his results as supporting hypotheses based on individual self-interest. The question of class thus remains unresolved. The class issue aside, however, the consistency of results between Medler and Mushketel's study in 1976 and Knaap's study in 1982 suggests that the divisions in popular support for state planning remained fairly consistent over the six-year period—in spite of dramatic changes in economic conditions (Knaap 1989a).

INTEREST-GROUP POLITICS
AND LAND USE

The other level at which politics bears on land use policy is at the level of interest groups. Interest-group politics, of course, is not independent of popular politics. Interest groups represent concentrated, organized interests of the general population—or channels through which specific popular interests are expressed. Interest-group positions on state planning are fairly predictable. According to Nourse (1977, 32), "Land owners, developers, apartment renters, commercial and industrial interests and minorities have all lost from [local land use planning]. On the other hand, conservationists and ecologists have lost in situations in which the developers have had a freer reign. All these groups have supported shifting land use control to the state and regional level.

While the birth and general thrust of state land use policies represent the outcome of a widespread popular movement for land use reform (Gottdiener 1983), it is in the legislature, in government agencies, and in the courts where policies and plans become substantive and influential instruments. These institutions are the battlegrounds of interest groups. Understanding how a popular movement for land use reform becomes transformed into specific land use plans and policies, therefore, requires analysis of interest-group politics.

In his prize-winning reflection on the centralization of land use policy in the United States,[5] Popper (1988) describes two divergent perspectives—conservative and liberal—on the politics of interest groups in state planning issues. According to Popper, conservatives, led primarily by developers and local officials, oppose state planning out of fear of repressive government intervention. Liberals, which include environmentalists, land use attorneys, and progressive businesspersons, support state planning to overcome problems of coordination, exclusion, and fragmentation inherent in local land planning. After reviewing the effects of several state land use programs, Popper concludes the following:

> Centralized land use planning did not collapse from insufficiency, as the liberals maintain. Nor did it collapse from overextension, as the conservatives argue. Instead, it did not collapse at all: it continues to expand, but more slowly than liberals hope and conservatives fear. Its fortunes ebb and flow, depending mainly on the politics of

the individual states, federal agencies, or land use fields that apply it; but on the whole it is quietly thriving. (1988, 296)

In short, Popper believes the politics of state planning have not been one-sided; some have gained and some have lost, depending on the outcome of interest-group politics. Understanding who gains and who loses, then, requires state-specific research into interest-group politics.

An early penetrating look at this issue was provided by Godwin and Shepard (1975), who drew upon evidence from Florida, Vermont, and Oregon. Godwin and Shepard base their analysis on the typology of regulatory systems pioneered by Lowi (1964) and extended by Salisbury and Heintz (1970). The typology classifies regulatory policies into four categories: distributive, self-regulatory, redistributive, and regulatory. In brief, distributive policies draw resources from the general public and distribute them to selected groups; self-regulatory policies draw power from the general public and distribute this power to selected groups; redistributive policies draw resources from specific groups and redistribute these resources to other specific groups; and regulatory policies take powers from disparate individuals and groups and redistribute these powers to a centralized authority. Godwin and Shepard suggest that redistributive and regulatory policies are difficult to enact because they explicitly identify winners and losers. For this reason, they argue, state land use policies, when enacted, are largely self-regulatory.

Next, Godwin and Shepard describe regulatory politics as a politics of pluralism—politics dominated by organized interest groups. According to Godwin and Shepard three interest groups dominate state land use politics. Group A includes developers, land speculators, builders, mortgage financiers, etc., who prefer local, if any, control over land use. Group B includes highly organized groups interested in preserving environmental quality; these groups prefer planning at the state level or higher. Group C includes an amorphous coalition of homeowners and neighborhood groups who prefer decentralized planning to preserve the character of their social environment. According to Godwin and Shepard, these three interest groups share similar upper-class origins but disagree over which elements of the status quo should receive the greatest protection. As a result, state land use policies tend to lack substance, provide benefits for each of the three active interest groups, and harm those not sufficiently organized to participate in interest-group politics, largely the poor. Based on this logic, Godwin and Shepard formulate six specific hypotheses about the development and internal dynamics of statewide land use programs:

1. (Procedural focus): State land use policies will deal mainly with procedural rather than allocative outcomes
2. (Inconsistent objectives): To the extent that state land use policies do include statements of goals, the goals will incorporate the interests of all three of the Issue Publics (interest groups) without attempting to solve inconsistencies among competing objectives
3. (Decentralized start): The procedural elements of initial state land use legislation will be more self-regulatory (decentralized) than regulatory (centralized) in form
4. (Increasing centralization): As state land use policies develop and change over time, they will shift from the hypothesized initial condition of self-regulatory (more decentralized) policy toward regulatory (more centralized) policy
5. (Concentrated benefits): The allocations involved in state land use policies will be distributive in form, and
6. (Lower social justice): The level of social justice will be decreased in our society if statewide land use policies and politics continue on their present course.

INTEREST-GROUP POLITICS IN OREGON

In reviewing the experience of state land use planning in Oregon, Knaap (1989a) examined the validity of each of the six hypotheses offered by Godwin and Shepard. Knaap found evidence to support some but not all of them. According to Knaap, the hypotheses of Godwin and Shepard are based on a consistent pattern of interest-group coalitions; but as predicted by Nourse (1977), interest-group coalitions change. In fact, while the extent and division of popular support for planning has remained fairly constant in Oregon over the last 15 years, perhaps the most interesting feature of land use politics in the state has been the changing posture of participating interest groups.

If interest-group coalitions vary, it is necessary to examine interest-group politics at various stages of the planning process. In the following pages, then, interest group politics in Oregon is explored at three distinct stages in the land use planning program: the adoption stage, the acknowledgment stage, and the postacknowledgment stage. As appropriate, the discussion addresses the six hypotheses of Godwin and Shepard.

The Politics of Adoption

Charles Little (1974) was the first to analyze the passage of Senate Bill 100: Oregon's pioneering statute. Little's chronicle focuses largely on the players involved and the roles they had, rather than on the interests they represented. Although more descriptive than analytical, Little provides three valuable insights. First, although there may appear to be a public mandate for land use reform, the passage of legislation altering fundamental property rights is not easy. Inertia favors the status quo. Second, political divisions on land use issues—at least in Oregon—are nonpartisan. As Little documents, legislative votes on Senate Bill 100 were closely aligned with the geographic origin of the legislator, not with the legislator's political party. Finally, as Little describes in detail, inertia can be overcome, but only with considerable effort on the part of dedicated individuals. While personalities are not the foundation of interest-group politics, it is difficult, as Little makes clear, to overestimate the influence of Senator Hector McPherson as the instigator of land use reform, of Governor Tom McCall as the figurehead of Oregon's land ethic, and of L.B. Day as a master of political compromise (Zachary 1978).

Though interest groups were behind the scenes when the legislators cast their ballots on Senate Bill 100, the groups played a leading role in drafting the legislation. As described in detail by Little (1974), DeGrove (1984), and Leonard (1983), the original draft of Senate Bill 100 would have greatly expanded state land use authority—via state-level permit authority, state-controlled areas of critical concern, and regional land use councils—enough to draw overwhelming interest-group opposition. Facing certain defeat in the Senate Environmental and Land Use Committee, Senate Bill 100 was referred to an ad hoc committee, whose mission was to produce a bill that could be passed by the committee and the entire legislature. Members of the ad hoc committee represented cities, counties, business and industry, homebuilders, and environmentalists.

At this point in the adoption process, the politics of interest groups became most pronounced. Conflict and compromise among interest groups occurred as predicted by Godwin and Shepard. As a result, the bill that came out of committee, and subsequently was passed by the legislature, provided evidence to support each of the first three hypotheses of Godwin and Shepard. The bill established a novel procedure for meeting state land use objectives through a state-level review process; but the bill itself contained no formulas, quantitative guidelines, or other substantive components (Hypothesis 1: procedural focus). The bill required local governments to formulate comprehensive plans, which established a decentralized form of planning (Hypothesis 2: initial decentralization). And, the goals of the bill obviously conflict: farm and forest land must be preserved without harming the economy; urban growth must be contained without increasing housing prices, and transportation must be facilitated while conserving energy (Hypothesis 3: conflicting objectives).

Thus, despite the public mandate for action, the influence of interest groups in the legislature severely limited the extent of state intervention. In order not to antagonize powerful interest groups, the Oregon land use act became void of substance, preserving much of the discretion of local governments and establishing only minimal guidelines for state land use policy. In the end, the bill contained something for everyone, except perhaps for those who felt it had been lobbied to death (DeGrove 1984).

The Politics of Acknowledgment

Though perhaps it was necessary to have made such changes for Senate Bill 100 to pass through the legislature, the ambiguity of the bill left much to be settled. Urban growth boundaries had to be drawn, but nobody knew where. Farmland had to be protected, but nobody knew how. The economy had to be developed, but nobody knew when. And housing had to be provided, but nobody knew for whom. Answering these questions became the responsibility of the newly created Land Conservation and Development Commission (LCDC) and its administrative arm, the Department of Land Conservation and Development (DLCD) (also see chapter 2).

After many public hearings throughout the state, LCDC adopted 14 goals and guidelines for local governments to follow in preparing comprehensive plans. Five more goals were added later. Compliance with each of the goals is mandatory, and LCDC was provided with administrative procedures for assuring that local comprehensive plans were consistent with the goals (see DeGrove 1984, Liberty 1989b, and Rohse 1987 for more details on administrative and legal procedures). But the goals, like the legislation that led to their adoption, were vague and contradictory.

Lacking specificity when adopted, the goals became more clearly defined through the acknowledgment process. As the previous chapters make clear, the acknowledgment process had substantive impacts on the content of local comprehensive plans. Through acknowledgment review, urban growth boundaries were tightened; more land was reserved for exclusive farm use;

residential areas were zoned for higher density; and more land in urban areas was zoned for industrial use. As predicted by Godwin and Shepard, the process of planning became highly centralized during the acknowledgment period (Hypothesis 4: increasing centralization).

As land use planning became increasingly centralized in the acknowledgment process, however, state policies became more firm and specific through precedent-setting LCDC decisions, administrative rules, and case law. Specific decisions, furthermore, resulted in winners *and* losers—contrary to Godwin and Shepard's hypothesis suggesting that state land use policies are distributive (Hypothesis 5: concentrated benefits).

In instances where farmland holders received farm tax deferrals, where cities received grants for preparing land use plans, and where developers were permitted to develop at high densities inside growth boundaries in exchange for development bans outside growth boundaries, Hypothesis 5 held: state land use planning provided benefits for particular groups at the expense of the general public. But cases of direct conflicts among interest groups forced LCDC (or LUBA, the state land use court) to identify distinct winners and losers. Clearly, suburban interests lost, for example, when the DLCD decided to prohibit exclusionary zoning and facilitate high-density housing (Leonard 1983, 113); city governments lost when the DLCD decided to restrict urban growth boundaries in favor of farmland and forest land preservation (Leonard 1983, 101); and the forest-products industry lost on decisions to limit uses on forest lands (DeGrove 1984, 280). On various occasions, then, a compromise simply could not be bought with general tax dollars. Thus, as decisions affecting competing interest groups had to be made, the allocations involved became more redistributive than distributive.

When the land use program became more redistributive (having to identify both winners and losers), interest-group alignments changed. The environmentalist groups remained strongly supportive of state planning, and the support of the League of Cities had been bought by intergovernmental grants. County governments (especially rural county governments), once strongly supportive of state planning, became increasingly antagonistic (DeGrove 1984, 277–8). Then, in 1975, a powerful new interest group entered the fray. With the aid of then–Governor Tom McCall, 1000 Friends of Oregon formed as an independent "watchdog" organization to give "the people of Oregon a powerful tool to help America's leading state land use program succeed" (1000 Friends 1982d). The organization began as a small group of land use attorneys but has since broadened its membership and become an extremely influential player in the design and implementation of Oregon's land use laws.

This unique interest group has been active in offering testimony and taking administrative and judicial appeals to further its causes. At first, 1000 Friends focused primarily on resource conservation and environmental protection; later it took on other causes, such as affordable housing and economic development. As a result, the base of support for 1000 Friends—and for the entire land use program—broadened considerably. After supporting the losing side on the 1976 referendum to repeal state land use statutes, and after viewing the effectiveness with which 1000 Friends could influence state policy to further its causes, the development groups found that state land use planning could serve their interests (Hales 1991). Now, 1000 Friends has on its board of directors representatives of business, industry, and home builders. Armed with this new political and financial support, 1000 Friends pressed at length for implementation of the housing goal. Thus in 1982, due largely to the ability to make the program work in its favor, the development lobby joined the environmental lobby in support of state participation in land use planning (Knaap 1987b).

In retrospect, the interest-group politics of state planning in Oregon began as predicted by Godwin and Shepard; but as the program changed, so did the positions of interest groups. Groups that once opposed state intervention in land use planning found it advantageous once they saw the process as regulatory politics. Other groups found that a vaguely defined decentralized planning system can develop into a sharply defined centralized planning system, one that can severely harm proprietary interests.

The Politics of Postacknowledgment

By 1986 all local comprehensive plans had been acknowledged by LCDC and a number of the goals and guidelines had been codified into statutes and administrative law. At this time the postacknowledgment period began. In this continuing period, DLCD is required to review plan amendments, coordinate the programs of state agencies, review every plan in four- to seven-year cycles, staff the Joint Legislative Committee on Land Use, and convert LCDC policies into administrative rules. Although the role of DLCD remains important, the key role in the postacknowledgment period is played by local governments, who must implement their comprehensive plans.

They do this by administering building permits, zoning, road and public facility construction, subdivision regulations, and other implementing ordinances. Comprehensive plans acknowledged by LCDC have the force of state law, and LCDC retains authority to issue enforcement orders. The agency also has automatic standing in appeals to the LUBA (Liberty 1989b). But the upper hand in the postacknowledgment stage clearly returns to local governments. Whereas the burden of proof that comprehensive plans comply with state goals and guidelines rests with local governments in the acknowledgment stage, the burden of proof that plan implementation does not comply with comprehensive plans (and thus state goals and guidelines) rests with DLCD in the postacknowledgment stage.

This shift in the relative burden of proof during the postacknowledgment period shifts the arena of interest-group politics from the state capital back to city halls and county seats. And the change in venue changes the influence of interest groups. Local land use control favors local developers and local landowners (Babcock 1966, Davis 1963, Fischel 1985) and frustrates environmentalists, such as 1000 Friends (Liberty 1989b).

The shift of burdens in the postacknowledgment period has also raised concerns about the vigor with which local governments will implement acknowledged land use plans. Robert Liberty of 1000 Friends, for example, characterized local governments in the postacknowledgment stage as "guardian foxes," and described local implementation as a fundamental flaw in the Oregon land use program (Liberty 1988). This "flaw" (from the perspective of a state-level interest group) reflects neither a lack of popular support for state planning nor a lack of interest-group participation in planning at the state level. Instead the "flaw" illustrates the friction between the politics of planning at the state level and the politics of implementation at the local level (Knaap forthcoming).

DISCUSSION

Comparing the evidence on popular politics to the evidence on interest-group politics offers some interesting insights. While divisions in the popular support for state planning remained fairly constant from 1976 to 1982, divisions in interest-group support—and the focus of planning—changed considerably over the same period. Whereas the popular support for state planning remained divided by geographic region, urban-rural location, occupation, and ownership status, the focus of planning changed from resource conservation and urban growth management to economic development and affordable housing, largely in response to changes in the Oregon economy and to changes in the relative influence of interest groups.

This suggests that the general thrust of state planning is determined by the general population but that specific policy issues are resolved by competition among interest groups.

The 19 goals of the program, for example, which were determined through a long process of legislative debate, public hearings, and citizen participation, have rarely changed. Administrative rules sharpening the goals into substantive land use instruments, however, were established through interest-group conflict during the acknowledgment process. As a result, only those goals arousing the interests of powerful interest groups or agencies—e.g., Goals 3 (Agricultural Land), 4 (Forest Lands), 5 (Open Spaces, Scenic and Historic Areas, and Natural Resources), 10 (Housing), 14 (Urbanization), 16, 17, and 18 (relating to the coastal resources)—strongly influenced the plans of local governments. Other goals—e.g., Goals 8 (Recreational Needs), 12 (Transportation), and 13 (Energy Conservation)—have had little impact (Liberty 1989b). The housing goal (Goal 10) in particular received little attention until it became a priority of 1000 Friends and the development lobby.

The developer's conversion and subsequent crusade for state planning (Hales 1991) provides an important lesson on state land use politics: The winners in state land use planning are those able to influence state legislatures, agencies, commissions, and courts. This lesson explains the success of environmentalists (in protecting environmentally sensitive areas), conservationists (in protecting farmland and forest land), and industrialists (in fostering economic development). Meanwhile, those less able to influence state-level institutions—who instead fought to destroy these same institutions in the legislature, through referenda, and by the courts—ended up losers. These groups included county governments (on maintaining local control), farmers (on developing farmland), and exclusionists (on zoning out the poor). Why some interest groups were better able to influence policy at the state level remains unclear; but it is clear that interest groups successful at land use politics at the state level were not necessarily the same interest groups successful at land use politics at the local level (Knaap 1989a).

Based on the influence of interest groups, Godwin and Shepard's final hypothesis suggests that state land use policies will ultimately hurt those who are too disorganized to participate in state land use politics—largely the poor—and, as a result, the overall level of social justice will be reduced (Hypothesis 6: lower social justice). In essence, Godwin and Shepherd's social-justice theory represents an interest-group version of the social-class theory. There are two reasons to doubt the interest-group version of the social-class theory along with the popular version.

First, the poor are not the only group that has been ineffective at state land use politics. The farmers, homeowners, and the forest-products industries have scored few victories at the state level. Thus the social-justice hypothesis overstates the influence of some interest groups in state land use politics. Second, state land use planning, as practiced in Oregon, remains a state *and* a local affair. Although planning did become centralized during the acknowledgment stage, plan implementation became decentralized once again in the postacknowledgment stage—a stage that favors local interest groups. Thus the social-justice hypothesis also overstates the influence of state-level interest groups in land use control—at least in Oregon.

The evidence suggests that different interest groups are successful at influencing land use policy at different levels of government. Resource-based industries and neighborhood groups are more effective at the local level; service-based industries and environmentalists are more effective at the state level. Developers, thus far, appear remarkably effective at both levels of government.

But before dismissing state land use planning as the triumph of developers, it is important to remember that even the developers made significant concessions, especially regarding urban growth boundaries. As a result, state participation in land use planning can best be summarized not as the victory of one particular interest group, but instead as another venue for political struggle between interest groups. As such, the social-justice hypothesis remains highly in doubt. Based on outcomes, it is not clear that the influence of state-wide planning—even when it favors developers—has always been detrimental to the poor.[6] Based on process, it is even less clear that a new venue for interest-group conflict will necessarily reduce social justice.

LESSONS FROM OREGON

Where previous chapters provided policy analysis, this chapter analyzed policy making. It examined how state land use policies were established through the political expression of the general population and through political conflict between special interests. The chapter drew upon a large volume of literature, focused on both Oregon and other parts of the nation, rich both in theory and in empirical analysis.

Analysis of popular politics around the nation focused primarily on the issue of class. Do land use policies, as they serve to manage urban growth and conserve environmental quality, further the interests of the upper class? The evidence from Oregon cannot resolve this controversy. Support for state land use planning in Oregon is distinctly divided by social strata: support for state planning is stronger in high-income, urban areas of the Willamette Valley. But within cities in the Willamette Valley, support for state planning is not stronger among high-income than among low-income residents. Whether these findings confirm the hypotheses that support for state planning comes from the upper class is largely a matter of interpretation.

Evidence from referenda to end state land use planning in Oregon, however, provides less ambiguous insights. First, support for state planning is clearly divided by geography: Willamette Valley residents support state planning, while nonvalley residents do not. Second, support for state planning divides urban residents from rural residents: urban residents support it, while rural residents do not. Finally, support for state planning is divided by occupation; service-based employees support state planning while resource-based employees do not. Although the Willamette Valley is contained within Oregon, most states have geographic regions with distinct political cultures; most states contain both urban and rural populations, and most states have both service- and resource-based employees. Therefore, the support for state planning in other states is likely to be similarly divided by region, urbanization, and occupation (Fischel 1979, Bollens 1989).

Perhaps more important than identifying social divisions over state planning, the Oregon referenda and analyses thereof provide insights into the focus and policy direction of state-level planning programs. Since support for state planning comes primarily from urban, service-based workers in metropolitan areas, by implication, politically viable state planning programs must contain elements that elicit the support of those constituencies. Thus successful state planning initiatives are likely to contain objectives that include urban growth management, environmental preservation, and urban economic development, although conflicting goals may acquire lip service at the adoption stage. Finally, the diminishing interest in initiative petitions and referenda to end state planning over time supports Popper's proposition that state planning, once institutionalized, becomes as difficult to end as it is to begin (Popper 1988). State planning, with time, becomes part of the status quo and should thus be considered a long-term endeavor.

Even with widespread popular support for planning, the Oregon experience suggests, state planning goals must be sufficiently vague to pass through the legislature. To prevent drawing the opposition of influential interest groups, state planning programs can identify winners and losers only after the programs are politically entrenched. But by then it is too late. After the passage of state land use statutes, even if the statutes specify procedure without specifying substance, land use politics has been moved to a new level. Once so moved, the politics of land use changes significantly.

Although popular politics determines the general parameters for the adoption and sustenance of state planning programs, interest-group politics sharpens popular parameters into policy instruments. Following adoption, the process of establishing state land use policy becomes centralized. In Oregon, state land use policy was formulated through the process of acknowledging local land use plans. The Land Conservation and Development Commission had to determine whether local plans conformed to state land use goals. But participants in the process of establishing substantive criteria for evaluating local plans included, among others, the Oregon Planning Council (which represents business), the Oregon Homebuilders Association, and, perhaps most influentially, 1000 Friends of Oregon. These interest groups played central roles in establishing Oregon's land use policies.

Seemingly as important as the interest groups that helped establish land use policy in Oregon were those who did not. Almost conspicuous by their absence were the homeowners associations, the farmers groups, and the small wood-lot owners. In light of their absence during the acknowledgment process, it is no surprise that the burden of state planning in Oregon has fallen largely upon these groups. The message to interest groups is thus quite clear: those interest groups effective at influencing state-level decisions will benefit from state planning; those that cannot, will not. What is more, interest groups that are effective at the state level are not necessarily the same as those that are effective at the local level.

The homeowners and neighborhood associations provide perhaps the best example of interest groups that were influential at the local level but less influential at the state level. At the local level, homeowner groups and neighborhood associations are extremely effective at excluding undesirable land uses—including low-income housing and industrial development. Local planning thus serves NIMBY (not-in-my-backyard) interests quite well. But because undesirable land uses wind up in somebody's backyard, NIMBY interests are much more difficult to mobilize at the state level. At the local level, it's we against them; at the state level, its we against us.

The evidence from Oregon reveals that state land use planning and regulation involve political conflict—conflict at both the popular and the interest-group levels. The outcome of such conflict, once set in motion by the general population, depends on the relative power of the groups involved. When conflict takes place at the state level, the battle favors interest groups with a statewide base of support. When conflict takes place at the local level, the battle favors interest groups with a local base of support. And when the program involves conflict in both arenas, winning requires political support at both levels.

Notes

1. See Deakin (1989) for a recent review.
2. Although support for growth management appears strongly divided by social strata—e.g., urban v. rural, young v. old, high income v. low income, professionals v. farmers—these strata tend to cross the social characteristics that have traditionally defined class—e.g., capitalist v. labor.
3. Strategic behavior occurs when a survey respondent gives false or exaggerated answers to influence the outcome of the survey.
4. Resource-based occupations are defined as those dependent on resource extraction and development, e.g., farmers, miners, developers, and workers in wood-products industries. Amenity-based employees are defined as those attracted to high-quality environments, e.g., teachers, lawyers, and engineers. See Knaap (1987b).
5. Popper won the prize for the best paper in Volume 54 of the *Journal of the American Planning Association.*
6. Some argue that benefits to developers trickle down to the poor in the form of lower housing prices and rents. See Hales (1991).

8

Lessons on Statewide Land Use Planning from Oregon

S TATE LAND USE PLANNING is a multidimensional, intertemporal, and intergovernmental process; it requires balancing goals, sequencing actions, and coordinating government agencies. As a result, the social environment in which planning takes place, the government agencies participating in the planning process, and the instruments used for plan implementation influence the efficacy of planning (Mazmanian and Sabatier 1983), where efficacy is defined as the ability of planning to achieve its intended goals. Previous chapters described Oregon's land use program, explored the impacts of the program on specific land use issues, and analyzed the influence on the program of popular and interest-group politics. This chapter collects information from the previous chapters to extract from the Oregon experience general policy lessons on state land use planning.

While Oregon's experience with state land use planning offers an interesting case study, it is hazardous to draw general policy lessons from the experience of one state—indeed a unique state. Oregon's dependence on forestry, its scenic beauty, its environmental ethic, and its populist government are well known. The state's land use program reflects these and other unique social and environmental characteristics.

Still, there are similarities between social forces operating in Oregon and social forces operating in other states—forces that may lead to similar land use policies. Further, there are structural features of Oregon's state land use program that, if duplicated, may lead to similar land use outcomes. Finally, the land use issues addressed by the Oregon program are issues currently faced by many other states. Thus, at the risk of overgeneralizing, the following sections examine the influence of social context on the development and focus of state planning, the influence of state institutions on the process of planning, and the influence of the program's structure on plan implementation. These are followed by a review of the influence of state planning on specific land use issues.

CONTEXTUAL FOUNDATIONS
FOR LAND USE REFORM

State land use planning represents substantive reform of long-held land use relationships. In state land use programs, the power to control land use, once delegated exclusively to local governments, is retracted in part by state government. Such substantive land use reforms never occur in a social vacuum; instead they reflect social pressure for policy change.[1]

As described in chapter 1, the history of land use planning in Oregon can be viewed in four stages. In stage one the state enabled cities and counties to engage in zoning and land use planning, largely to manage the rapid growth of cities. In stage two the state required local governments to plan, as many local governments—especially county governments—had declined the opportunity. In stage three the state preempted local planning in areas of statewide interest—specifically along the Pacific coast and Willamette River shorelines. And in stage four the state required local plans to meet statewide goals and guidelines, to assure that local plans served statewide land use interests.

While the development of Oregon's land use program would appear to reflect logical administrative responses to state-specific land use issues, there were in fact larger forces at work. The growth of cities in the Willamette Valley, which spurred the enabling legislation, stemmed largely from the postwar industrialization of the Oregon economy. Similarly, continuing industrialization and its impact on Oregon's coastline created a need for planning and regulation beyond the capabilities of local governments. Rapid population growth fueled by the northwestern migration of the 1960s and 1970s caused urban areas to grow beyond the control of urban governments. Finally, the decentralization of the state's largest metropolitan area, the Portland area, created suburban jurisdictions with land use interests that were hostile to the interests of the state at large. In sum, Oregon's land use problems reflected manifestations of national social and economic trends.

Oregon's approach to solving its land use problems also reflected national trends. The transformation of the state's economy in the postwar period created a population of Oregonians less economically dependent on natural resources and better able to "afford" growth controls and environmental regulations than they were before. Further, postindustrialization concentrated the Oregon population in the Willamette Valley and created a balance of power in which ostensibly valley-oriented problems could elicit statewide land use reform. The declining dependence of the state economy on resource extraction and the concentration of population in a single geographic region thus fostered political momentum for a statewide response. Had Oregon's population remained economically dependent on farming and forestry, more evenly dispersed geographically, or regionally polarized, the scope of statewide planning would likely have been much more limited and might have included regional hierarchies in land use authority.

The Oregon land use program was conceived during the height of the first national environmental movement. In the early 1970s Congress passed the Clean Air Act, the Clean Water Act, the National Environmental Policy Act, the Coastal Zone Management Act, and nearly passed a National Land Use Act. California, Washington, and Idaho—all neighbors of Oregon—adopted limited versions of state land use programs. And Oregon passed its famous bottle, beaches, and billboards bills. Although Oregon's land use program remains widely viewed as pioneering and innovative, it occurred during a policy cycle that included a wide range of environmental reforms in Oregon, other western states, and the nation (Rosenbaum 1976).

Understanding the social context of the time helps explain why Oregon adopted a statewide land use program in the early 1970s and why the program focused initially on resource conservation and growth management. It also explains why the focus of the program changed markedly from resource conservation and growth management to economic development and urban service provision in the recessionary 1980s. Finally, social context helps assess the prospects for a similar approach to land use reform in other states. For example, in light of the recent resurgence of urban growth and popular environmentalism in the eastern U.S., it is not surprising to witness there a second wave of interest in state land use programs.

PROGRAM EVOLUTION THROUGH
STATE GOVERNANCE

Although social forces generate the thrust and direction of land use reform, land use programs evolve through the process of state governance. Specifically, land use laws are made by the state legislature, enforced by the state executive, and interpreted by the state courts. As the Oregon experience illustrates, actions taken by these institutions shape the influence of state land use programs.

Legislative Oversight

According to Hedrick and Zeigler (1987), Oregon has a weak legislature. Legislators meet only once every two years, have little staff support, and are poorly paid. Interest groups dominate political parties in state-level politics. But even under these circumstances, the legislature repeatedly and significantly influenced the development of Oregon's land use program—in both intended and perhaps unintended ways.

As discussed in chapter 7, the legislative process had considerable influence on the content of Senate Bill 100. The legislature passed Senate Bill 100 only after removing provisions for state permitting authority, state-controlled areas of critical concern, and regional planning councils. Due to the weakness of Oregon's political parties, the legislative vote on Senate Bill 100 split along geographic—not party—lines. After passing Senate Bill 100 into law, the legislature did not leave the program to develop on its own; instead the legislature remained active in shaping state land use policy.

Since passing Senate Bill 100, the legislature initiated several major reforms in the land use program. The 1977 legislature repealed LCDC's authority to enact and enforce its own plan for recalcitrant local governments and authorized LCDC to adopt enforcement orders; the 1979 legislature created the Land Use Board of Appeals; the 1981 and 1983 legislatures established and revised the postacknowledgment review process; the 1983 legislature required LCDC to place more emphasis on economic development and public facilities; the 1985 legislature required LCDC to study means for designating secondary farmland; the 1987 legislature created the Ocean Resources Planning Program and removed from counties control over forest practices; and the 1989 legislature appropriated funds to LCDC to study the effectiveness of urban growth management and farmland preservation. In short, the legislature altered some aspect of the land use program in every legislative session.

To monitor the program between legislative sessions, the legislature created a permanent Joint Legislative Committee on Land Use. Proposals for land use legislation, including funding proposals, often originated from this committee. The legislature appropriated an average of $3.6 million for land use planning, approximately 56 percent of which went to local governments for preparing plans and for plan implementation. The legislature never attached strings to appropriations to achieve specific policy objectives or to accelerate the planning process (DeGrove 1984). Less than half of total appropriations went to DLCD for staffing reviews, for monitoring land use trends, and for research (Oregon DLCD 1991b). This pattern of appropriation sharply curtailed the influence of LCDC and served to maintain local control over local land use. (The box insert offers a comparative perspective on LCDC funding.)

Executive Administration

Although Oregon is also believed to have a weak state executive (Hedrick and Zeigler 1987), it is difficult to overestimate the influence of the governor and executive administration on statewide planning. Governor Tom McCall, famous for his speeches welcoming out-of-state visitors as long as they did not stay, is appropriately recognized as the father of Oregon's land use program. McCall used his charisma and his office to promote statewide land use planning. After his two terms as governor, he formed 1000 Friends of Oregon, which continues as a powerful influence on planning long after his death.

Doing More with Less

Despite the scope of its mission, DLCD remains one of the smallest agencies in state government. Its 1991 staff of 42 was smaller than the staff of several city and county planning departments. The chart illustrates how DLCD's budget compares to other state agency budgets in Oregon.

State agency budgets for 1989 - 91, in $ million

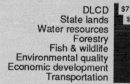

DLCD	$7
State lands	$29
Water resources	$71
Forestry	$103
Fish & wildlife	$135
Environmental quality	$175
Economic development	$228
Transportation	$1,085

SOURCE: Oregon DLCD 1991b

Governor Victor Atiyeh, who as a legislator cast the deciding vote bringing Senate Bill 100 out of legislative committee, provided critical executive support for planning during the difficult 1981 economic recession. Although a continuing supporter of state land use planning, Atiyeh used his influence to alter the focus of state planning from resource conservation to economic development during his terms in office. Governor Neil Goldschmidt, after serving as Secretary of Transportation in the Carter administration, integrated land use planning in his comprehensive development strategy for the state. Barbara Roberts, Oregon's governor since 1991, strongly supports statewide planning and has called for greater control over urban growth management.

Perhaps the governors' most influential actions, however, have been their appointments to LCDC. As described in previous chapters, the substantive elements of Oregon's land use policies were formed primarily through decisions by LCDC, a commission which has been generally supportive of state land use planning (DeGrove 1984). Over the years the need for direct executive oversight has diminished, but through appointments to LCDC, the thrust of the program continues to reflect the influence of the governor.

The program has also been strengthened by the skill and dedication of staff of DLCD, although views on their efficacy vary (DeGrove 1984, Liberty 1989b). With limited resources, DLCD staff has not only reviewed all the local comprehensive plans, but also has promulgated administrative rules that transformed vague goals into substantive policies and regulations.

Judicial Interpretation

As described in chapter 1, the Oregon supreme court played a major role in affirming and shaping state land use planning. In matters of process, the court ruled that zoning decisions represent quasi-judicial decisions, which apply general policy to specific persons or property, thus guaranteeing individuals certain procedural rights (Fasano v. Washington County). The supreme court also ruled that comprehensive plans serve as the general policy statement to which local zoning and land use decisions must conform (Baker v. Milwaukie). On many occasions the supreme court affirmed the constitutionality of state land use planning in general. Through these landmark decisions, the court provided critical judicial support for statewide planning.

The Oregon courts, however, contributed more than just support for the planning process. Often instigated by 1000 Friends of Oregon, Oregon courts established important and influential legal precedents. The courts ruled, for example, that agricultural land goals dominate housing goals outside urban growth boundaries (UGBs) *(Peterson v. City of Klamath Falls)*, that zoning urban land for low-density use can violate state housing goals *(Seaman et al. v. City of Durham)*, and that the capacity of public services can be considered in making changes to land use plans or regulations *(Dickas v. City of Beaverton)*. By interpreting state land use goals, these decisions established substantive elements of state land use policy.

The structure as well as the decisions of the Oregon courts supported statewide planning. The creation of LUBA in 1979 increased the efficacy of the land use program in several ways.

First, it greatly simplified the appeals process, removing confusion over questions concerning standing and judicial process. Second, it created an entire judiciary specializing in land use law, increasing both the quality and consistency of judicial decision making (Liberty 1989b). Finally, it accelerated and reduced the costs of land use appeals. Laws governing LUBA require that decisions on appeals be made within three months.

In sum, Oregon's land use program continues to be shaped by the state legislature, the state executive, and the state courts—government institutions that, in states without state land use programs, have considerably less influence on land use. Although indirectly influenced by popular opinion, interest groups, and at times the federal government,[2] the Oregon land use program clearly reflects the structure and composition of the state's governing institutions. It is impossible, of course, to predict how institutions of state government would influence state land use programs in other states, but the Oregon experience suggests that they will indeed be influential long after the program has been adopted.

OPPORTUNITIES AND CONSTRAINTS OF PROGRAM STRUCTURE

State land use planning is a process through which land use plans are made, implemented, and enforced. Although the process continues to evolve through legislative initiative, executive administration, and judicial interpretation, some elements of the planning process remain unchanged and represent the essential structure of Oregon's land use program. These elements include mandatory statewide planning goals, intergovernmental planning, and local implementation.

Statewide Goals

Although statewide planning was adopted in large to manage urban growth, protect the environment, and conserve natural resources, the planning program includes 19 varied and often conflicting goals. The expression of multiple goals serves several purposes. The goals establish the scope of state interests in land use planning, they help generate political support for state planning, and they serve as a legally binding framework for guiding the planning process.

The goals of state planning, like those of local planning, are inherently multifaceted. The pursuit of growth management alone requires difficult balancing between providing urban services, supporting housing construction, protecting farmland, and more. Sometimes the goals conflict. But planning, by definition, requires a priori decision making in pursuit of multiple, sometimes competing, goals. Further, contradiction in the goals allows state and local planners to balance one goal against another and to emphasize different goals at different points in time. In Oregon's cyclically sensitive economy, for example, this allows LCDC to alternate its focus between conservation and development over the course of the business cycle.

The expression of many goals also facilitates the consensus-building process. Political support for state planning is critical at all stages of the process. Particularly important consensus-building goals include citizen participation (Goal 1), economic development (Goal 9), and housing (Goal 10). The citizen participation goal helps establish popular legitimacy, just as it does at the local level. The economic development goal, and in particular the housing goal, help defuse opposition by industry and development groups. To aid in building consensus, however, the goals cannot be too specific. By leaving the goals relatively vague, the legislature avoids identifying winners and losers and thus avoids engendering the opposition of powerful interest groups.

Finally, the statewide planning goals serve as a legally binding framework for guiding the planning process—as a type of planning constitution. As a constitutional framework, the goals serve three purposes. Before acknowledgment of a comprehensive plan, they serve as the legal basis for challenging local land use decisions. During acknowledgment, they serve as a checklist for determining whether local plans comply with state land use goals. After acknowledgment, they serve as a basis for reviewing plan amendments. As a legally binding constitutional framework, the statewide planning goals have become increasingly specific and influential over the course of the planning process.

Multiple statewide planning goals thus serve important functions in state land use programs. In essence, the statewide goals offer an opportunity to articulate a comprehensive vision for land use in the state. Giving inadequate care to how the goals are worded and how they will be received by interest groups, however, imposes constraints on achieving that vision.

Intergovernmental Planning

In Oregon, the LCDC sets state planning goals, promulgates rules to pursue them, and determines whether local plans are consistent with those rules. Local governments prepare plans and revise them until they meet LCDC approval. Planning is thus an intergovernmental process. Intergovernmental planning as practiced in Oregon facilitates three types of coordination: coordination among local governments, coordination among agencies in state government, and coordination between state agencies and local governments.

At the local level, governments must coordinate their plans with each other. Every local plan must be formally coordinated with both regional and other nearby local governments. Failure to have an affected local government "sign-off" means that a local plan is not yet ready for LCDC acknowledgment or periodic review. Often disputes among local governments are settled either by regional planning agencies (where they exist) or with help from LCDC. Requirements for local coordination force local governments to settle disputes—regarding urban growth management and urban service provision, for example—that would otherwise remain unresolved or require costly litigation.

At the state level, a variety of agencies affect land use. State agencies construct highways, airports, and parks; they also protect fish and wildlife, environmental quality, and public health. State agencies participate in planning by offering comments during the acknowledgment process. In addition, Oregon state law requires all state agencies with programs that affect land use to carry out such programs in compliance with Oregon's planning goals and in a manner comparible with all state-approved local comprehensive plans. To meet this requirement state agencies must develop coordination programs and submit them to LCDC for review and certification. By coordinating with local plans and LCDC, then, state agencies coordinate with each other. For example, highway investments by the Department of

Transportation and economic development grants from the Economic Development Department must be compatible with local comprehensive plans. As a result, the local plan serves as a vehicle for assuring that investments by these state agencies do not conflict with each other. Similarly, local plans serve to mitigate conflicts over timber cutting between the Department of Fish and Wildlife and the Department of Forestry.

Finally, and perhaps foremost, state and local planning serves to assure that local plans conform to state land use goals and administrative rules—primarily through acknowledgment and periodic reviews. At these stages, local governments prepare plans that reflect local geography, demographics, resource productivity, development trends, and visions of the future. LCDC then reviews the plans based on recommendations from DLCD staff, many of whom specialize in specific land use goals—sometimes only one. As a result, local planners focus on local conditions and DLCD staff focuses on state requirements. But this functional separation of focus and expertise causes friction between local governments and DLCD, friction that impedes the planning process.

To overcome this problem, DLCD has staffed several regional offices to decentralize some of the plan review functions. The regional offices assume a mediation role between DLCD and local planners. Indeed, many potentially explosive confrontations between local governments and DLCD central staff (located in Salem) are defused and successfully settled by regional DLCD representatives. Thus some decentralization of state activities can serve to facilitate the planning process, especially in a planning program with only a two-level planning hierarchy.

Another source of conflict is the difference in interests between state and local planners. Many local governments promote urban expansion; LCDC promotes urban containment. Many local governments discourage certain types of housing development; LCDC encourages variety in housing development. Many local governments favor farmland development; LCDC favors farmland preservation. Political conflict over these and other issues inhibits and prolongs the planning process. But political conflict is inherent in intergovernmental planning. Indeed, the difference in interests between state and local governments is the major reason for adopting a state land use program.

Because of inherent conflicts between state and local governments, statewide planning requires an enforcement mechanism. In Oregon, local governments that refuse to prepare and maintain plans consistent with statewide planning goals face state-imposed development moratoria, loss of state transfer funds, and the prospect of having LCDC order their planning departments to prepare appropriate plans. LCDC rarely, however, exercises these powers (Liberty 1989b). In the first decade, LCDC issued only about a dozen enforcement orders (BGRS 1984).[3] Thus, the threat of enforcement action—only occasionally carried out—appears sufficient to precipitate local action.

On more than one occasion, however, it was LCDC that was forced to compromise its position, occasionally under pressure from the governor or from state legislators. Persistent political challenge in the legislature and at the polls never succeeded in eliminating the state's role in land use planning, but such challenges did keep LCDC from dominating the planning process.

In spite of inherent conflicts, intergovernmental planning can work well. As evidence of success, LCDC has never asserted control over areas of state concern, although it has the authority to do so. Instead, LCDC requires local governments to regulate developments that affect coastal, mountain, and other sensitive lands in accordance with state goals. These environmentally sensitive areas are managed by local governments to the satisfaction of LCDC through state-level acknowledgment and review. In Oregon, then, intergovernmental planning has replaced state planning in areas of statewide concern.

In sum, state and local intergovernmental planning offers an opportunity to coordinate the actions of disparate state and local agencies. As the process is structured in Oregon, such coordination is accomplished primarily by LCDC and primarily at three points in the planning process: during plan acknowledgment, during periodic plan reviews, and during certification of state agency coordination plans. Oregon's planning structure thus offers an opportunity for considerable intergovernmental coordination among numerous and varied state and local agencies. But the opportunities are constrained by the lack of an explicit hierarchy of authority and by the limits through which LCDC can coordinate such a large number of autonomous agencies.

Local Implementation

Whereas land use planning in Oregon is an intergovernmental process, plan implementation remains largely a local process. Implementation takes place as local governments construct roads, extend sewers, approve subdivisions, enforce zoning ordinances, and grant building permits. Local implementation serves to maintain local control of land use decision making, but it also enables local governments to subvert—at least partially—state interests in land use planning.[4]

LCDC has essentially three mechanisms for maintaining state interests in land use decision making after plan acknowledgment. It can appeal a local land use decision to the LUBA. It reviews amendments to local plans and, if necessary, appeals the amendment to LUBA. Finally, it reviews all local plans on a periodic basis to assure that they remain consistent with state land use goals. But LCDC does not issue permits, enforce zoning ordinances, or initiate infrastructure development. Thus it does not participate as closely in plan implementation as it does in plan preparation.

The difference in the degree to which LCDC participates in planning and plan implementation creates friction. As discussed above, local interests differ from state interests. And as discussed in chapter 7, local politics differs from state politics because a different set of actors participates in land use politics at the local level than at the state level. Finally, plan implementation involves decision making from a different temporal perspective than plan preparation. A decision to designate an area for industrial use, for example, is different from a decision to grant a building permit for a chemical plant—even if the building permit is consistent with the planned use designation. Whereas a decision to designate land for industrial use involves an abstract, uncertain, and future event, a decision to grant a building permit authorizes a specific plant, with certain specifications, for immediate construction.

Land use in Oregon therefore differs—and will likely continue to differ—systematically from land use planning. Oregon planning law, which requires land use decisions to conform with comprehensive land use plans, constrains the ability of local governments to make decisions capriciously. But the structure of Oregon's planning program, which allows LCDC to monitor planning much more closely than plan implementation, exacerbates inconsistency between land use and land use plans.

In sum, multiple statewide planning goals, a state and local planning structure, and local implementation represent the fundamental elements of Oregon's statewide planning program. Multiple statewide planning goals establish the scope of state land use interests and thus the scope of state influence in land use planning. An intergovernmental planning structure helps coordinate the plans of disparate state and local agencies. Local implementation serves to maintain local control over land use decision making. But because the state participates less in plan implementation than in plan formulation, state interests are less effectively expressed in land use than in land use plans.

PROGRAM IMPACTS IN SPECIFIC POLICY DOMAINS

Social context, state government institutions, and program structure each shape the way that state planning influences land use decision making. But as previous chapters make clear, the influence differs from issue to issue both because of the uniqueness of the various issues and because they call for the use of different policy instruments.

Urban Growth Management

A major goal of the Oregon land use program is to improve the urbanization process. Local land use planning was sufficiently comprehensive neither in scope nor in strength to manage the process of urbanization in Oregon in the late 1960s and early 1970s. To manage urban growth, Goal 14 required local governments to establish UGBs around all urban areas in the state. UGBs as growth management instruments have had measurable but qualified success.

By establishing UGBs, urban growth in Oregon appears to have been spatially constrained. Local governments have not extended urban services beyond the limits of UGBs, urban-density development has not been allowed without urban services outside UGBs, and UGBs have been amended only on rare occasions. As a result of urban geographic containment, farmland and forest land have suffered less pressure from urban encroachment.

As the centerpiece of Oregon's state land use program, UGBs also force urban governments to coordinate their planning efforts. Designating areas for future urban growth facilitates coordination between city and county governments over urban service extension and precipitates annexation agreements between city governments. UGBs also appear to affect land values soon after they are established, perhaps providing information about future urban development that could enhance efficiency in the urban development process. These well-established effects of UGBs demonstrate that state land use planning can significantly affect land use and land development when the state imposes on local governments a policy instrument that is unequivocal and easily monitored.

Despite the demonstrated influence of UGBs, however, lingering problems in the urban development process remain. First, UGBs leak. Although they succeed in containing high-density development, development at low densities continues outside of UGBs. More than 700,000 acres of land outside UGBs—designated exception areas—have become havens for exurban development. These exception areas, so designated because of their precommitment to urban use or limited usefulness for forestry or farming, are designated neither for urban nor for resource use. As a result, these areas represent potential threats to neighboring farmers and to future urban development. The state has yet to determine how best to manage these areas.

A related problem concerns the long-term management of UGBs. Most UGBs were drawn to accommodate urban growth until approximately the year 2000. What to do after that date remains in many communities unresolved. At present it appears that many existing UGBs will remain in force until land within them is nearly exhausted or until pressure for amendment rises with rising land prices.[5] Then UGBs can be extended through the periodic review process. But if UGB expansion occurs through an incremental process, important virtues of the UGB will be lost.

If expanded through an incremental process, UGBs will lose their ability to designate future developable land. They will lose much of their ability to coordinate urban growth between urban governments and to guide the extension of urban services. They will also lose their ability to provide landowners and developers with information concerning the future location of urban development—information that in the early 1980s was capitalized into land value. Urban development, as in other states, will occur on a piecemeal basis; but unlike other states, urban development will require double approval—first by local governments, then by LCDC. Statewide planning will thus serve less to facilitate land use planning and more to facilitate land use regulation (Fischel 1988a).

Housing

The housing goal is a critical aspect of Oregon's land use program, not only because everybody needs a home but also because the housing industry is highly influential in state policy making. Local planning was clearly unable to address the land use elements of the housing problem. In fact, a national consensus is forming that local planning and regulation contribute more to the cause than to the solution to affordable housing (Fischel 1989). In Oregon, however, statewide planning has helped to overcome regulatory obstacles to affordable housing.

The state housing goal is to provide for the housing needs of all Oregon residents. The combined efforts of housing interest groups, LCDC, the legislature, and the Oregon courts resulted in an extensive set of laws, administrative rules, and judicial interpretations designed to implement the goal. State law now requires that comprehensive plans by local governments in the Portland metropolitan area meet minimum density requirements, facilitate the construction of multiple-family, manufactured, or government-supported housing, and contain clear and consistent development approval standards. LCDC has also assured, through the review process, that all local plans and zoning ordinances comply with these rules.

This extensive reform in planning for residential development, furthermore, has been accomplished without adversely affecting housing prices. The median housing price in the Portland metropolitan area is nearly equal to median housing prices across the nation and it is much below the median housing prices of other western cities. Housing prices in the remainder of the state are lower than in Portland. Thus state land use planning and urban growth management in Oregon have clearly not fulfilled widely held expectations for housing cost escalation. The primary reason for Oregon's relatively low housing prices, however, is also quite clear: in the 1980s, there was little growth to manage.

Although research has shown that land prices inside the Portland- and Salem-area UGBs are higher than land prices outside them, the influence of planning and zoning on aggregate land and housing values throughout the state remains uncertain. There is little evidence that UGBs have constrained the supply of developable land or the supply of housing. There is evidence, however, that state requirements for higher-density zoning have increased the potential supply of housing inside UGBs. There is also evidence that state requirements for streamlining the development process have reduced the costs of housing development (Hales 1991). Thus it is quite possible, contrary to national consensus, that by forcing local governments to accommodate higher-density housing, streamline the permitting process, and remove vague and discretionary development conditions, growth management in Oregon has resulted in lower rather than higher housing prices. More research is necessary, however, before such conclusions are confirmed.

Despite circumstantial evidence suggesting favorable impacts on aggregate housing prices, however, there is little evidence that state planning in Oregon has resulted in more affordable housing or in higher-density development. Multiple-family housing starts in recent years are up; but over the past five years, multiple-family housing starts are no higher and affordability indexes are no lower in Portland than in other western metropolitan areas. Therefore, although state planning appears not to have contributed to housing problems, there is not yet strong evidence that it has contributed much to housing solutions.

While state participation in planning has changed the content of local land use plans and zoning ordinances, the state has not imposed on local governments a policy instrument that effectively makes housing more dense and affordable. Instead it has only forced local governments to remove local land use constraints to density and affordability. But this will not overcome fundamental market contradictions between housing affordability and compact urban growth. Low-cost housing requires low-cost land and rapid extension of urban services which, if provided, lead to increased housing consumption and low-density growth. But even if land and urban services were free, new housing would still remain beyond the financial reach of many low-income households. Conversely, compact urban growth, in a competitive housing market, requires high land and housing prices, which encourages developers to use less land and residents to consume less housing. But intentionally inflated land and housing prices are politically unacceptable.

The state land use program in Oregon has reduced local constraints to multiple-family, low-income housing. The program may also have contributed to lower aggregate housing prices. But the program cannot foster compact urban growth and low-cost housing without more extensive intervention in the housing market, intervention such as minimum-density zoning, publicly financed housing, or in-kind transfers to the poor. It remains to be seen whether the coalition that intervened to make low-cost housing possible will intervene to make low-cost housing available.

Urban Service Provision

Before 1973, urban services were poorly planned by local governments. Urban services were provided by numerous cities, counties, and special districts, often without coordination. In fact, the provision of urban services by one jurisdiction often undermined the planning efforts of another. This situation fostered leapfrog development and precluded capturing economies of scope and scale. The urban service goal was designed to capture these economies. The goal has been achieved, in part, through institutional reform.

This goal and its recent amendments will improve planning for urban services.[6] By the time the plan of every city greater than 2,500 in population comes up for periodic review, the city must have prepared a public facility plan addressing water, sewer, and transportation services for all land within the UGB. The public facility plan will include an inventory of public facilities, a list of significant public facility projects, rough cost estimates, policy statements identifying the agency responsible for providing facilities, and a discussion of the mechanism for funding each public facility. When all subject cities have completed their plans, development within UGBs should take place according to a carefully planned schedule of public service extension.

Under the new rules governing public facilities, developers need demonstrate only extant or expected water, sewer, drainage, and street capacity. Such practices are not unusual. But in a recent case *(Dickas v. Washington County)*, LUBA accepted the argument that school capacity did not exist to accommodate students from the proposed development. LUBA rejected the school district's evidence that it would have adequate capacity by the time it was needed. Such action moves Oregon toward the concurrency doctrine used in Florida, where all facilities and services must exist or be planned for installation prior to development.

Until all public facilities are in place, therefore, development must wait. But here lies the dilemma. Although local governments in the near future will have prepared extensive public facility plans, public facility construction, and hence urban development, must await financing. And since local governments in Oregon are severely limited in their ability to generate tax revenues, such funds remain scarce. Therefore, urbanization within UGBs is unlikely to change substantially without a better means of addressing problems in public service finance. As with the housing issue, Oregon still lacks a policy instrument capable of addressing this fundamental obstacle to providing sufficient urban services.

Unlike providing affordable housing, however, providing urban services does not inherently conflict with urban growth management, and providing urban services is not opposed by any powerful interest groups. Instead the planning structure is already in place for creating new regional-scale provider organizations, organizations better able to capture economies of scale in public service management and finance. The structure also exists for better coordinating local service providers with state funding agencies. Although the state's general fiscal health remains a continuing obstacle to resolving problems in facility finance, the land use program offers considerable promise for improving urban services management through intergovernmental cooperation and institutional reform.

Farmland Protection

Another key goal of Oregon's statewide planning program is farmland preservation. Farming contributes substantially to the Oregon economy and embodies the cultural identity of the state. Under local planning farmland suffered the classic problems of a common-access resource, especially in the Willamette Valley. From the local perspective, farmland was plentiful and ripe for urban development; from the state perspective, farmland was rapidly consumed by urban growth. Given the overwhelming majority of urban residents in the Willamette Valley, a consensus quickly formed that the state needed to act to protect farmland. With consensus support, farmland has been protected, but no consensus has formed on how to protect farming.

The Oregon planning program embraces a number of techniques for farmland preservation: exclusive farm use (EFU) zoning, urban growth boundaries, farm use tax deferral, and right-to-farm laws. Through these instruments, all urban land is contained within UGBs and all rural land is designated for exclusive farm use, exclusive forest use, or as "exception" land. Within EFU zones, homebuilding and land subdivision are prohibited except when it can be proven that they would improve farm productivity. Development on exception lands is restricted to large-acreage minimum lot sizes and a variety of other restrictions designed to prevent conflicts with nearby farming or forestry operations.

The available evidence suggests that Oregon's farmland protection programs have been influential. Not only has the program preserved large blocks of rural land for farm use, but it appears that farm productivity in Oregon has increased relative to national trends, especially in the Willamette Valley. Between 1982 and 1987, farms in the valley increased in average size and productivity per acre, contrary to national and regional trends. In addition, many small farms in the Willamette Valley have become commercially viable, at least by some measures of viability. These trends reflect poorly on minimum lot zoning as a farmland policy instrument if productivity of farms is the real policy objective.

Further, evidence from the land market suggests that EFU zoning influences land value and land speculation. Studies suggest that speculative value has been removed from land in EFU zones and that farmland value in them has not been diminished by proximity to exception lands. Thus landowners in EFU zones are likely to make long-term investment decisions that will maintain the infrastructure necessary for productive farm activity.

Difficult problems in rural land management, however, remain. To augment minimum lot zoning, most Willamette Valley governments adopted performance standards for making decisions on land development and land divisions in EFU zones. But even with such standards, it is difficult to distinguish between a small farm and a large homesite. More work on designing performance standards is currently underway.

But even as performance standards are improved, the land use program will have difficulty enhancing farm productivity. Local governments have been less than zealous in their efforts to prevent farmland development and division. Thus LCDC, perhaps with support from 1000 Friends or other statewide conservation groups, must monitor rural land use decision making. Further, there is no assurance that landowners who satisfy certain performance standards will continue to maintain them. And the first LCDC decision to revoke the right of landowners to live in their farmhouse because they no longer choose to farm would be the decision ending all public support for state land use planning.

Overall, then, Oregon's land use planning program has successfully protected farmland from urban development; however, it has not protected it from rural development. On this issue, state policy makers continue to face limitations imposed by local implementation, by minimum lot and performance zoning, and by a lack of clear consensus concerning which activities are threats to farmland.

Economic Development

Historically, Oregonians have never had great interest in economic development. Reasons for this include the state's pioneer culture, which favors wooded isolation over urban diversity; the sensitivity of the Willamette Valley to population pressure; and Oregon's system of local public finance, which little rewards municipalities for accommodating economic growth. Of course, attitudes changed during the 1981 recession, when unemployment peaked at 12 percent and relative per capita income began a precipitous decline. Since then, land use planning has become an instrument for economic development.

Oregon's current planning approach to economic development is two-fold: stop planning from becoming an impediment to economic development, and integrate land use planning into an overall strategy for economic development. The second approach is made possible by the coordinating function LCDC plays between state agencies that affect economic development and land use. The first approach reflects the widely held perception that state land use planning inhibits economic growth. The evidence to support this claim, however, ranges from anecdotal to nonexistent. Research on these issues found that planning had no impact on economic development, at worst, and that, at best, it fosters economic development by increasing certainty in the regulatory environment, by enhancing environmental quality, and by lowering industrial land costs. Relatively obscure evidence, however, is less influential than widely held myths. Thus in 1983 the legislature mandated specific changes in planning requirements to foster economic growth.

To facilitate economic growth local governments were required to analyze the local economy, identify industrial targets, conduct industrial land inventories, plan to service industrial lands, and accelerate the development approval process. In short, local governments were to adopt a land-based strategy for economic development. The efficacy of the strategy, however, remains highly uncertain and requires overcoming formidable obstacles. Many local governments lack the expertise to produce sound economic development plans; infrastructure is difficult for local governments to finance; and the state lacks resources to examine the quality of industrial lands.

Finally, the aggressiveness with which the state now uses land use planning for economic development runs counter to many of the original motivations for state participation in planning: to promote resource conservation, to manage urban growth, and to promote citizen participation. Encouraging economic development in rural areas, expanding UGBs to provide more industrial land, and eliminating public hearings to expedite the approval process shift the focus of the state planning agency sharply from land conservation to land development.[7]

The role of economic development in Oregon's land use program reflects Oregon's changing attitudes and socioeconomic conditions. Since the early 1960s, Oregon has discouraged growth when it arrived and chased it when it left. The role of economic development in the future will thus likely depend on the future fortunes of the Oregon economy. State land use planning will never play a leading role in economic development, but the Oregon experience suggests that it can play a supporting role.

CONCLUDING COMMENTS

State participation in land use planning represents the most recent, though perhaps not the last, stage in the evolution of planning in Oregon. State planning evolved out of discontent with the ability of local planning to address the consequences of rapid population growth—discontent by the general population, powerful interest groups, the state legislature, and a highly popular governor. To address the problems of rapid population growth—urban sprawl, costly housing, inadequate public services, and resource depletion—Oregon launched a planning program that returned substantial control over land use planning from local governments to the state government. Under the statewide planning program, local comprehensive plans had to serve multiple state land use goals. Through actions taken by the legislature, the LCDC, and the Oregon judiciary, vague and conflicting goals were sharpened into an extensive set of land use statutes, administrative rules, and judicial interpretations.

There is considerable evidence that actions taken in Oregon to resolve multiple and complex land use issues substantially changed the content of local comprehensive plans. As a result, planning policies and procedures crafted in Oregon have been widely acclaimed and emulated in a growing number of states. Unfortunately, there is considerably less evidence that state-acknowledged but locally implemented land use plans have come close to resolving the issues that such planning was designed to address.

One reason for this shortage of evidence is rooted in LCDC's initial failure to set fundamental mapping, recordkeeping, and terminology standards, making it difficult to compare and coordinate comprehensive plans. Zoning definitions in one city differ from those in another, even in the same metropolitan area. Map scales also differ from city to city. There is no state requirement to computerize land use maps, to record annexations, to monitor development, to document land use decisions, or to monitor buildable land supply.

A second reason is political. Since the planning goals conflict, evidence that state planning furthers one goal provides information—which LCDC will ultimately have to justify—that state planning impedes another. In part because the survival of LCDC and DLCD has been threatened nearly every two years, the state planning agency and commission have only recently begun seeking to evaluate their own effectiveness.

A third reason is financial. Throughout much of the history of Oregon's planning program, the state has suffered considerable fiscal stress. Thus funding for a sound monitoring and research program had to compete with maintaining the program itself. Not surprisingly, monitoring and research lost—despite potentially high benefit-cost ratios.

A fourth reason is methodological. As mentioned in chapter 1, an ideal research design requires a comparison of land use in Oregon with state land use planning to land use in Oregon without state land use planning. Unfortunately, no such comparison is possible.

The lack of information for assessing the impacts of Oregon's land use program offers an important lesson for other states now embarking on a similar planning endeavor. Strategies for monitoring and evaluation should be adopted as an integral part of the program. Program evaluation would be much easier and would yield many more definitive conclusions if information on land use, urban development, housing price, public facilities, farmland productivity, economic development, and public opinion were maintained expressly for the purpose of evaluation.

The information that is available has been provided by students and faculty of Oregon's universities, by 1000 Friends of Oregon, and by studies recently funded by DLCD. The information suggests that support for state land use planning by the general population and interest groups is systematically divided but not by class. Urban growth boundaries can spatially constrain urban growth and influence land value through development expectations. State planning clearly alters land use plans and zoning ordinances but less clearly alters housing price, housing density, and housing mix. Urban services are more efficiently provided by a centralized agency, at least in the Portland metropolitan area. Farmland is protected from urban but not rural development. And state land use planning is not detrimental to economic development.

In sum, state land use planning in Oregon has overcome many of the limitations of local land use planning. Through the institutions of state government, the process has been opened to a wide range of citizens and organizations. And by enfranchising a wider citizenry, the process of planning has been able to balance urban growth against farmland preservation, economic development against affordable housing, and public services against private property rights. It is reasonable to expect that improvements in process will eventually lead to improvements in outcome. But only in those cases where the state has mandated and monitored binding policy instruments—such as urban growth boundaries and exclusive farm use zoning—is there yet clear evidence that statewide land use planning has affected land use.

Notes

1. This section draws extensively from Knaap (1987b).
2. Federal influence comes through funding for Oregon's coastal zone management program, administered by LCDC.
3. There have been at least five enforcement orders issued since 1989.
4. See Reagan (1987) for more on intergovernmental implementation.
5. In theory, all land within a UGB would never become completely exhausted, even with a permanently fixed UGB. Instead, land holders would always keep some land off the market to capture rising scarcity rents. See Hotelling (1931).
6. At this writing not all local governments have been reviewed for compliance with the state's new requirements for public facility planning.
7. The conflict between conservation and development has diminished in recent years as the Oregon economy has become more dependent on tourism and other amenity-based industries. See chapter 6.

References

Babcock, R. 1966. *The zoning game: municipal practices and policies.* Madison: Univ. of Wisconsin Press.

Babcock, R., and F. Bosselman. 1973. *Exclusionary zoning: Land use and housing in the 1970's.* New York: Praeger.

Beaton, C. R. 1982. An examination of relationships between land use planning and housing costs in Oregon, 1970–1980. Willamette University.

Beaton, C. R., J. S. Hanson, and T. H. Hibbard. 1977. *The Salem area urban growth boundary: Evaluation of policy impacts and recommendations for the future.* Salem, OR: Mid-Willamette Valley Council of Governments.

Beaton, C. R., and T. Hibbard. 1991. *Task one: Status of the land resource base—Literature review and analysis.* Salem, OR: Oregon Department of Conservation and Development.

Berry, D. 1976. Idling of farmland in the Philadelphia region, 1930–1970. University of Massachusetts at Amherst Regional Science Research Institute, discussion paper series (88).

————. 1978. Effects of urbanization on agricultural activities. *Growth and Change* 9(3): 2–8.

Berry, D., E. Leonardo, and K. Bieri. 1976. The farmer's response to urbanization. University of Massachusetts at Amherst Regional Science Research Institute, discussion paper series (92).

Black, T., and F. Dunau. 1981. *The effect of regulation on residential land prices.* Washington, DC: Urban Land Institute.

Boehm, T., and J. McKenzie. 1981. *The investment demand for housing.* Washington, DC: Office of Policy and Economic Research.

Bolen, R. 1979. *Building moratoriums—Impacts and alternatives.* Portland, OR: Home Builders Association of Metropolitan Portland.

Bollens, J. C., and H. J. Schmandt. 1982. *The metropolis.* New York: Harper and Row.

Bollens, S. 1989. Constituencies for limitation and regionalism approaches to growth management. Paper presented at the meetings of the Association of Collegiate Schools of Planning, Portland, OR.

Bosselman, F., and D. Callies. 1971. *The quiet revolution in land use control.* Washington, DC: Council on Environmental Quality, U.S. GPO.

Bureau of Governmental Research and Service. 1984. Guide to local planning and development. Eugene, OR.

———. 1989. Local economic development in Oregon. Eugene, OR.

Capozza, D., and R. Helsley. 1989. The fundamentals of land prices and urban growth. *Journal of Urban Economics* 26(3): 295–306.

Center for Population Research and Census. 1992. *Oregon population: Components of change, 1960–1991.* Portland State University School of Urban and Public Affairs.

Center for Urban Studies at Portland State University, and Regional Financial Advisors, Inc. 1990. *Local government infrastructure funding in Oregon.* Salem, OR: Land Conservation and Development Commission.

Christensen, K. S., M. Smith-Heimer, and A. Pumuk. 1988. *Local government response to severe reductions in federal funding for low-income housing.* Berkeley, CA: Institute for Urban and Regional Development.

Clarke, M. K. 1986. *Revitalizing state economies.* Washington, DC: Center for Policy Research and Analysis of the National Governors' Association.

Cornelius, J. C. 1989. Oregon's agricultural sector. In *Oregon policy choices,* ed. L. McCann, 155–90. Eugene, OR: Bureau of Governmental Research and Service.

Correll, M. R., J. H. Lillydahl, and L. D. Singell. 1978. The effects of green belts on residential property values. *Land Economics* 54(2): 207–17.

Courant, P. N. 1976. On the effect of fiscal zoning on land and housing values. *Journal of Urban Economics* 3(1): 88–94.

Currier, B. A. 1978. An analysis of differential taxation as a method of maintaining agricultural and open space land uses. *University of Florida Law Review* 30(5): 821–42.

Daniels, T. L. 1986. Hobby farming in America. *Journal of Rural Studies* 2(1): 31–40.

———. 1990. Policies to preserve prime farmland in the USA. *Journal of Rural Studies* 6(3): 331–36.

Daniels, T. L., and A. C. Nelson. 1986. Is Oregon's farmland preservation program working? *Journal of the American Planning Association* 52(1): 22–32.

Davis, O. 1963. Economic elements of municipal zoning decisions. *Land Economics* 39(4): 375–86.

Deakin, E. 1989. Growth controls and growth management: A summary and review of the empirical research. In *Understanding growth management: Critical issues and a research agenda,* ed. D. Brower, D. Godschalk, and D. Porter. Washington, DC: The Urban Institute.

DeGrove, J. M. 1984. *Land, growth, and politics.* Chicago: Planners Press.

DeGrove, J. M., and N. E. Stroud. 1980. *Oregon's state urban strategy.* Washington, DC: Department of Housing and Urban Development, U.S. GPO.

deHaven-Smith, L. 1987. *Environmental publics: Public opinion on environmental protection and growth management.* Cambridge, MA: Lincoln Institute of Land Policy.

———. 1991. *Environmental concern in Florida and the nation.* Gainesville: Univ. of Florida Press.

Downing, P. B. 1973. User charges and the development of urban land. *National Tax Journal* 37(4): 631–37.

Eber, R. 1984. Oregon's agricultural land protection program. In *Protecting farmlands,* ed. F. Steiner and J. Theilacker. Westport, CT: AVI Publishing Co.

ECO Northwest, Brown and Caldwell Consulting Engineers, and Government Finance Associates. 1989. *An assessment of funding for sewerage and drinking water facilities in the state of Oregon.* Portland, OR: Department of Environmental Quality and Department of Human Resources, Health Division.

ECO Northwest and David J. Newton Associates. 1991. *Urban growth management study: Case study report*. Salem, OR: Department of Land Conservation and Development.

Eisinger, P. K. 1988. *The rise of the entrepreneurial state: State and local economic development policy in the United States*. Madison: Univ. of Wisconsin Press.

Ellickson, R. 1982. The irony of "inclusionary" zoning. In *Resolving the housing crisis*, ed. M. Bruce. Cambridge, MA: Ballinger.

Fischel, W. 1979. Determinants of voting on environmental quality. *Journal of Environmental Economics and Management* 6(2): 107–18.

———. 1985. *The economics of zoning laws: A property rights approach to American land use controls*. Baltimore: Johns Hopkins Univ. Press.

———. 1988a. Centralized control. *Journal of the American Planning Association* 55(2): 205–6.

———. 1988b. Do growth controls matter? A review of empirical evidence on the effectiveness and efficiency of local government land use regulation. Lincoln Institute of Land Policy.

———. 1989. What do economists know about growth controls? A research review. In *Understanding growth management*, ed. D. Brower, D. Godshalk, and D. Porter. Washington, DC: Urban Land Institute.

Fosler, R. S. 1988. *The new economic role of American states*. New York: Oxford Univ. Press.

Frank, J. E. 1989. *The costs of alternative development patterns: A review of the literature*. Washington, DC: Urban Land Institute.

Fulton, W. 1989. Two states find a way to keep the peace. *Planning* 55(10): 16–17.

Furuseth, O. J. 1980. The Oregon agricultural protection program. *Natural Resources Journal* 20: 603–14.

———. 1981. Update on Oregon's agricultural protection program. *Natural Resources Journal* 24(1): 57–70.

Godwin, K., and B. Shepard. 1975. State land use policies. *Environmental Law* 5(3): 703–26.

Goldberg, M., and P. Chinloy. 1984. *Urban land economics*. New York: Wiley.

Gordon, R. 1981. *Macroeconomics*. 2nd ed. Boston: Little, Brown & Co.

Gottdiener, M. 1983. Some theoretical issues in growth control analysis. *Urban Affairs Quarterly* 18(4): 565–69.

Governor's Task Force on Land Use in Oregon. 1982. *Report to Governor Victor Atiyeh.* Salem, OR: State Capitol.

Gustafson, G. C., T. L. Daniels, and R. P. Shirack. 1982. The Oregon land use act. *Journal of the American Planning Association* 48(3): 365–73.

Hagman, D. C., and J. Juergensmeyer. 1986. *Urban planning and land development control law.* St. Paul, MN: West.

Hales, C. 1991. Higher density + certainty = affordable housing for Portland, Oregon. *Urban Land* 50(9): 12–15.

Halprin, Lawrence and Associates. 1972. *Willamette Valley: Choices for the future.* Salem, OR: State Executive Department.

Hatry, H. P., M. Fall, T. O. Singer, and E. B. Liner. 1989. *Monitoring the outcomes of economic development programs.* Washington, DC: The Urban Institute.

Hedrick, W., and L. H. Zeigler. 1987. Oregon: The politics of power. In *Interest group politics in the American West,* ed. R. Hrebenar and C. Thomas. Salt Lake City: Univ. of Utah Press.

Heiman, M. 1988. *The quiet evolution: Power, planning, and profits in New York State.* New York: Praeger.

Hibbard, M. 1989. Small towns and communities in the other Oregon. In *Oregon policy choices,* ed. L. McCann. Eugene, OR: Bureau of Governmental Research and Service.

Hotelling, H. 1931. The economics of exhaustible resources. *Journal of Political Economy* 39(2): 137–75.

James, F. 1984. Urban economic development: A zero-sum game? In *Urban economic development,* ed. R. Bingham and J. Blair. Beverly Hills: Sage Publications.

Johnson, M. B., ed. 1982. *Resolving the housing crises: government policy, decontrol and the public interest.* San Francisco: Pacific Institute for Public Policy Research.

Joint Center for Housing Studies. 1989. *The state of the nation's housing.* Cambridge, MA: Joint Center for Housing Studies.

Kamara, S. G. 1984. Fringe area growth in metropolitan Portland. Ph.D. diss., Portland State University.

———. 1987. Effect of local variations in public services on housing production at the fringe of a growth-controlled multi-county metropolitan area. *Urban Studies* 24(2): 109–117.

Keene, J. C., D. Berry, R. Coughlin, J. Farnham, E. Kelly, T. Plant, and A. L. Henry. 1975. *Untaxing open space.* Washington, DC: Council on Environmental Quality.

Knaap, G. J. 1981. *The price effects of an urban growth boundary.* Portland, OR: Metropolitan Service District and Western Interstate Commission for Higher Education.

———. 1982. The price effects of an urban growth boundary: A test for the effects of timing. Ph.D. diss., University of Oregon.

———. 1985. The price effects of an urban growth boundary in metropolitan Portland, Oregon. *Land Economics* 61(1): 26–35.

———. 1987a. Self-interest and voter support for Oregon's land use controls. *Journal of the American Planning Association* 53(1): 92–97.

———. 1987b. Social organization, profit cycles, and statewide land use controls in Oregon. *Journal of Applied Behavioral Science* 23(3): 371–86.

———. 1988. Land use controls and economic development: An exploratory analysis. University of Wisconsin-Green Bay.

———. 1989a. The political economy of growth management. *Review of Regional Studies* 19(1): 1–7.

———. 1989b. State land use control and inclusionary housing: Evidence from Oregon. Paper presented at meetings of the Association of the Collegiate Schools of Planning, Portland, Oregon.

———. 1990. State land use planning and inclusionary zoning. *Journal of Planning Education and Research* 10(1): 39–46.

———. Forthcoming. Land use politics in Oregon. In *Planning the Oregon way: A twenty-year evaluation,* ed. C. Abbot, S. Adler, and D. Howe. Corvallis, OR: Oregon State Univ. Press.

Lapping, M. B., and J. F. FitzSimmons. 1982. Beyond the land issue. *GeoJournal* 6(6): 519–24.

Lapping, M. B., G. E. Penfold, and S. MacPherson. 1983. Right to farm laws. *Journal of Soil and Water Conservation* 38(6): 465–67.

Lapping, M. B., and N. R. Leutwiler. 1987. Agriculture in conflict: Right-to-farm laws and the pari-urban milieu for farming. In *Sustaining agri-*

culture in cities, ed. W. Lockeretz. Ankeny, IA: Soil and Water Conservation Society of America.

Leonard, J. 1983. *Managing Oregon's growth: The politics of development planning.* Washington, DC: The Conservation Foundation.

Leutwiler, N. R. 1986. Farmland preservation laws: What do they do? Can they be justified? Master's thesis, University of Colorado at Denver.

Lewis, S. 1989. Border wars. *Planning* 55(10): 8–13.

Liberty, R. L. 1988. The Oregon planning experience: Repeating the success and avoiding the mistakes. Paper presented at the Conference on the Chesapeake Bay Critical Area Protection Program.

————. 1989a. *Annotated abstract of studies analyzing county administration of Oregon's statewide planning conservation goals.* Portland, OR: 1000 Friends of Oregon.

————. 1989b. *An overview of the Oregon planning program.* Paper presented at the Lincoln Institute of Land Policy, Cambridge, MA (December).

Little, C. E. 1974. *The new Oregon trail: An account of the passage of state land-use legislation in Oregon.* Washington, DC: The Conservation Foundation.

Lim, G. C. 1983. *Regional planning.* Totowa, NJ: Rowman & Allanheld.

Listokin, D. 1976. *Fair share housing allocation.* New Brunswick, NJ: Center for Urban Policy Research.

Lowi, T. 1964. *The end of liberalism: Ideology, policy, and the crisis of public authority.* New York: Norton.

Mallach, A. 1984. *Inclusionary housing programs: Policies and practices.* New Brunswick, NJ: Rutgers Univ. Press.

Matz, D., and L. Ledebur. 1986. The state role in economic development. In *Financing economic development in the 1980s: Issues and trends,* ed. N. Walzer and D. L. Chicoine. New York: Praeger.

Mazmanian, D., and P. Sabatier. 1983. *Implementation and public policy.* Glenview, IL: Scott Foresman.

Medler, J., and A. Mushketel. 1979. Urban-rural class conflict in Oregon land-use planning. *Western Political Quarterly* 32(3): 338–49.

Mercer, L. J., and W. D. Morgan. 1982. An estimate of residential growth controls' impact on house prices. In *Resolving the housing crisis,* ed. M. Bruce. Cambridge, MA: Ballinger.

Metropolitan Service District. 1979. *Urban growth boundary findings*. Portland, OR.

―――. Undated. *Comments on UGB study*. Portland, OR.

Mills E. S., and B. Hamilton. 1987. *Urban economics*. Glenview, IL: Scott Foresman.

Morgan, T. 1984a. Exclusionary zoning. *Environmental Law* 14: 779–829.

―――. 1984b. The Oregon approach to exclusionary zoning law and the Happy Valley cases. *Land Use and Zoning Digest* 3(2): 6–8.

National Association of Realtors. 1991. *Homes sales yearbook, 1990*. Washington, DC: U.S. GPO.

Nelson, A. C. 1983. Comment. *Natural Resources Journal* 23(1): 1–5.

―――. 1984. *Evaluating urban containment programs*. Portland, OR: Portland State University, Center for Urban Studies.

―――. 1985a. Demand, segmentation, and timing effects of an urban containment program on urban fringe land values. *Urban Studies* 22(3): 439–443.

―――. 1985b. A unifying overview of greenbelt influences on regional land values. *Growth and Change* 16(2): 43–48.

―――. 1986a. Towards a theory of the American rural residential land market. *Journal of Rural Studies* 2(4): 309–19.

―――. 1986b. Using land markets to evaluate urban containment programs. *Journal of the American Planning Association* 52(2): 156–171.

―――. 1987. The effect of a regional sewer service on land values, growth patterns, and regional fiscal structure within a metropolitan area. *Urban Resources* 4(2): 15–18.

―――. 1988. An empirical note on how regional urban containment policy influences an interaction between greenbelt and exurban land markets. *Journal of the American Planning Association* 52(2): 178–84.

―――. 1989. Appropriate boundary effects of regional urban containment policy. Paper presented at the meetings of the Association of Collegiate Schools of Planning, Portland, OR.

―――. 1990a. The analytic basis for farmland preservation. *Journal of Rural Studies* 6(3): 337–46.

————. 1990b. Economic critique of prime farmland preservation policies in the United States. *Journal of Rural Studies* 6(2): 119–142.

————. Forthcoming. Preserving prime farmland in the face of urbanization. *Journal of the American Planning Association.*

Nelson, A. C., and G. J. Knaap. 1987. A theoretical and empirical argument for centralized regional sewer planning. *Journal of the American Planning Association* 53(4): 479–86.

Nelson, A. C., and J. R. Recht. 1988. Inducing the residential land market to grow timber in an antiquated rural subdivision. *Journal of the American Planning Association* 54(3): 529–36.

Nicholson, W. 1990. *Intermediate microeconomics.* 5th ed. Chicago: Dryden Press.

Niemi, E. G. 1984. Oregon's land use program and industrial development. *Environmental Law* 14(4): 707–11.

Nourse, H. 1977. *The political economy of land use regulation.*

Ohls, J. C., R. C. Weisberg, and M. White. 1974. The effect of zoning on land value. *Journal of Urban Economics* 1(1): 428–44.

1000 Friends of Oregon. 1982a. The impact of Oregon's land use planning program on housing opportunities in the Portland metropolitan region. Portland, OR.

————. 1982b. Making land use planning part of the solution to Oregon's economic recovery: A two year plan. Portland, OR.

————. 1982c. Myths and facts about the land use planning program. In *1000 Friends of Oregon Newsletter* (Fall):5–7.

————. 1982d. Report for the seventh year: 1975–1982. Portland, OR.

————. 1982e. Statewide land use planning and economic development: The benefits to date. Portland, OR.

————. 1986. Urban areas and areas zoned for residential, commercial, and industrial uses, Willamette Valley, Oregon. Portland, OR. Map.

————. 1991. Managing growth to promote affordable housing: Revisiting Oregon's goal 10. Portland, OR.

Oregon Department of Human Resources. 1989. *Business and employment outlook.* Salem, OR: Employment Division.

Oregon Department of Labor. 1986. *Oregon covered payrolls, 1979–1986.* Salem, OR: Department of Labor.

Oregon Department of Land Conservation and Development. 1991a. DLCD analysis and recommendations of the results and conclusions of the farm and forest research project. Salem, OR.

———. 1991b. Shaping Oregon's future: The biennial report for 1989–91. Salem, OR.

———. 1991c. Urban growth management study: Summary report. Salem, OR.

———. 1986. Oregon lands. Salem, OR.

Oregon Department of State. 1983. Oregon blue book, 1983–84. Salem, OR.

Oregon Economic Development Department. 1982. Problems with Oregon's land use planning program. Salem, OR.

———. 1985. Oregon: A statistical profile. Salem, OR.

———. 1986. Oregon economic trends project, vols. 1–7. Salem, OR.

———. 1988. Oregon: A statistical profile. Salem, OR.

———. 1989. *Oregon shines: An economic strategy for the Pacific century.* Salem, OR: State Printing Office.

———. 1991. Economic profile of Oregon. Salem, OR.

Oregon Executive Department. 1990. Oregon economic and revenue forecast, 10(2). Salem, OR.

Oregon Health Division. 1991. Safety on tap: A strategy for providing safe, dependable drinking water in the 1990s. Portland, OR.

Oregon Land Conservation and Development Commission. 1975. *Statewide planning goals and guidelines.* Salem, OR: Department of Land Conservation and Development.

———. 1984. The new state land use planning laws. In *Oregon planning news.* Salem, OR: Department of Land Conservation and Development.

———. 1989. *Report to the Oregon legislature.* Salem, OR: Department of Land Conservation and Development.

———. 1990. *Statewide planning goals and guidelines.* Salem, OR: Department of Land Conservation and Development.

Oregon Progress Board. 1990. Oregon benchmarks: Setting measurable standards for progress. Salem, OR.

Pacific Meridian Resources Associates. 1991. Task two: Analysis of the relationship of resource dwelling and partition approvals between 1985–

87 and resource management in 1990. Salem, OR: Department of Land Conservation and Development.

Pease, J. 1990. Land use designations in rural areas: An Oregon case study. *Journal of Soil and Water Conservation* 45(5): 524–28.

———. 1991. Farm size and land-use policy: An Oregon case study. *Environmental Management* 15(3): 337–48.

Peiser, R. B. 1981. Land development regulation: A case study of Dallas and Houston, Texas. *Journal of the American Real Estate and Urban Economics Association* 9(4): 397–417.

Penfold, G. 1988. Right-to-farm as a method of conflict resolution. Paper presented at the Conference on Resolving Rural Development Conflicts, Mount Allison University, New Brunswick.

Plotkin, S. 1987. *Keep out: The struggle for land use control.* Berkeley: Univ. of California Press.

Popper, F. 1981a. *The politics of land use reform.* Madison: Univ. of Wisconsin Press.

———. 1981b. Siting LULUs. *Planning* 47(4): 12–15.

———. 1988. Understanding American land use regulation since 1970: A revisionist interpretation. *Journal of the American Planning Association* 53(3): 291–301.

Porter, D. R., and R. B. Peiser. 1984. *Financing infrastructure to support community growth.* Washington, DC: Urban Land Institute.

Prestbo, J., ed. 1975. *This abundant land.* Princeton: Dow Jones Books.

Price Waterhouse. 1986. *Making the right turn: Protecting the public investment in Oregon's roads and bridges.* Portland, OR: League of Oregon Cities, Association of Oregon Counties, and Oregon Department of Transportation.

Reagan, M. 1987. *Regulation: The politics of policy.* Boston: Little, Brown & Co.

Richmond, H. R. 1984. Does Oregon's land use program provide enough desirable land to attract needed industry to Oregon? *Environmental Law* 14(4): 693–706.

Rohse, M. 1987. *Land-use planning in Oregon.* Corvallis, OR: Oregon State Univ. Press.

Rose, J. B. 1984. Farmland preservation policy and programs. *Natural Resources Journal* 24(3): 591–640.

Rosenbaum, N. 1976. *Land use and the legislatures: The politics of state innovation.* Washington, DC: The Urban Institute Press.

Ross, D., and R. Friedman. 1990. The emerging third wave: New economic development strategies in the '90s. *Entrepreneurial Economy Review* (Autumn):3–10.

Salisbury and Heintz. 1970. A theory of policy analysis and some preliminary application. In *Policy analysis in political science,* ed. I. Sharkansky, 39–60. Chicago: Markham Publishing Co.

Schaeffer, P. V., and L. D. Hopkins. 1987. Behavior of land developers: Planning and the economics of information. *Environment and Planning A* 19:1221–32.

Schallau, C. H. 1989. Oregon's forest resources. In *Oregon policy choices,* ed. L. McCann, 155–90. Eugene, OR: Bureau of Governmental Research and Service.

Schmisseur, W. E., D. Cleaves, and H. Berg. 1991. *Task three: Survey of farm and forest operators on conflicts and complaints.* Salem, OR: Department of Land Conservation and Development.

Scott, R. A., ed. 1975. *Management and control of growth.* Washington, DC: The Urban Institute.

Segal, D., and P. Srinivansan. 1985. Suburban growth and housing inflation. *Urban Geography* 6(1): 14–26.

Sharpe, E. 1990. Urban politics and administration. New York: Longmann.

Sidor, J. 1984a. *Affordable housing and land supply and development: The state role.* Washington, DC: Council of State Community Affairs Agencies.

———. 1984b. *Influencing land supply and land development for affordable housing: Massachusetts, California, and Oregon.* Washington, DC: Council of State Community Affairs Agencies.

Starnes, E. M. 1991. Concurrency: Linchpin or nemesis? Paper presented at the meeting of the Association of the American Collegiate Schools of Planning, Oxford, England.

Sullivan, A. M. 1990. *Urban economics.* Boston: Irwin.

Sullivan, E. J., N. Williams, Jr., and B. H. Siegan. 1984. The Oregon example: A prospect for the nation. *Environmental Law* 14(4): 843–62.

U.S. Department of Agriculture. 1981. National agricultural lands study. Washington, DC.

———. 1982. *Census of agriculture.* Washington, DC: U.S. GPO.

———. 1987. *Census of agriculture.* Washington, DC: U.S. GPO.

———. U.S. Department of Commerce, Bureau of the Census. 1971. *Housing units authorized by building permits.* Washington, DC: U.S. GPO.

———. 1972. *Census of governments, taxable property values and assessments.* Washington, DC: U.S. GPO.

———. 1982. *Census of governments* 4(5). Washington, DC: U.S. GPO.

———. 1983. *1980 census of population and housing, Oregon.* Washington, DC: U.S. GPO.

———. 1987. *Census of governments, taxable property values and assessments.* Washington, DC: U.S. GPO.

———. 1991. *Summary population and housing statistics, Oregon.* Washington, DC: U.S. GPO.

U.S. Department of Commerce, Bureau of Economic Analysis. 1991. Data from Regional Economic Measurement Division on CD-ROM.

University of Portland. 1992. *Metropolitan Portland real estate report.* Portland, OR: University of Portland School of Business.

Vaughn, R. J., and R. Pollard. 1986. Small business economic development. In *Financing economic development in the 1980s: Issues and trends,* ed. N. Walzer and D. L. Chicoine. New York: Praeger.

Wall Street Journal. 1982. *The Oregon trail.* 22(84) New York.

Weber, B. 1989. Oregon state government finance. In *Oregon policy choices,* ed. L. McCann. Eugene, OR: Bureau of Governmental Research and Service.

Whitelaw, W. E. 1980. Measuring the effects of public policies on the price of urban land. In *Urban land markets: Price indexes, supply measures, and public policy effects,* ed. J. T. Black and J. E. Hoben. Research Report #30. Washington, DC: Urban Land Institute.

Whitelaw, W. E., and E. Niemi. 1989. Oregon's strategic economic choices. In *Oregon policy choices,* ed. L. McCann. Eugene, OR: Bureau of Governmental Research and Service.

Windsor, D. 1979. Critique of the costs of sprawl. *Journal of the American Planning Association* 45(3): 279–92.

Zachary, K. J. 1978. Politics of land use: The lengthy saga of Senate Bill 100. Master's thesis, Portland State University.